A GAL
in a
PROUD PROFESSION

written by
CARI SOMMER

 www.trafford.com

North America & international
toll-free: 1 888 232 4444 (USA & Canada)
phone: 250 383 6864 ♦ fax: 812 355 4082

TABLE OF CONTENTS

PROLOGUE

*W*hen I first made a commitment to nursing it was simply a means to an end. While in the seventh grade, I had decided to enter the glamorous career of an airline stewardess. At that time all stewardesses were required to be RN's. So, like someone in a twelve-step program, becoming an RN became my first step.

Later, when I learned that I was too short and that my glasses were unacceptable, it didn't matter—I was already committed. Like the angel that moved Moses' hand to the hot coal, an unseen angel was pushing me in the direction of a career in nursing.

My parents, who had always ruled my life with an iron hand were dead set against it. They said they would be humiliated in front of their friends if I chose a life of servitude

(Although servitude to them was acceptable—even desirable. They wanted me to stay home and clean and cook for them.) I had never before defied them. Yet I quietly went about initiating a new step # 1— getting a job after high school graduation to earn the three hundred dollars for tuition and enough spending money to see me through that three years that I would be in school.

Most of my classmates had worked as aides and came shod in their white Girl Scout shoes with the flat heels and knew how to make square cornered beds. I had been in a hospital only once for a brief visit and arrived with my Cuban heeled nurse's oxfords that refused to wear out and caused horrible calluses on the balls of my feed. And I had to learn how to make square corners on the beds. Yet I persisted in my quest to become a nurse, never knowing that it would be the best thing I would ever do.

I had loved my job at the Union Pacific headquarters. With most of our young men at war I had been promoted three times in the year I worked there and was already earning, I would learn to my chagrin, twice as much as the head nurse. My co-workers were good friends and we had great times together both on and off the job. Still that angel kept pushing me in the direction of step # 2—entering a school of nursing.

And so, with my belongings packed in the khaki colored suitcase presented to me by the railroad employees for joining the war effort, I found myself somewhat reluctantly in the student nurses' residence commanded to attend a welcoming tea that first night. I just wanted to stay in my room and write thank-you notes to my friends, unwilling to let go of those precious relationships. But that command—the first in a three-year stream of them—was not negotiable. I went to the tea and, on an impulse, asked several of the student nurses to write in my autograph book.

Of course most of them wrote the usual schoolgirl ditties. But one senior—whose name was Hope—wrote a line that is still emblazoned in my memory fifty years later—"To a gal in a proud profession."

It was a lofty antidote to the shame that my parents had heaped on me. In the months ahead I would watch Hope at work. There was an air of class and dignity that Hope brought to her patients and her profession. I have always viewed the art of nursing through this vision of Hope. Carrying bedpans and cleaning up incontinent patients can have the same dignity as saving lives.

I was proud to be a part of this proud profession, but I always wondered if I really deserved the title. There are so many pans (no pun intended) and so few compliments. Then one day, when I had returned to my hometown after an absence of six years, I met one of my former OB patients. "You're back!" She shouted. "Good! Now I can have another baby." I knew then that I had made the right decision. I was, indeed, "a gal in a proud profession."

As I look over my fifty years nursing, I can see that it has been the best part of my life. I didn't mean for it to be. I meant for my home and my family to be my top priority and fulfillment. But sadly my personal life did not have the happy ending I hoped for. But nursing has given it the gratification and meaning lacking in other areas.

CHAPTER 1

SCHOOL DAYS

*A*fter four weeks of intensive classroom studies, clad in our newly sewn white uniforms, we were assigned to the floors passing fresh drinking water and caring for patients' flowers. When my first signal light went on, I trembled as I hurried to answer it. I was sure she would need something no less complicated than brain surgery.

"May I help you?" I asked in the most professional manner I could muster.

"Is there a nurse out there?" she asked.

"I'll see," I replied, relieved, as I dashed off to find the RN. The patient wanted to use the bedpan. After that I learned to probe further before going for the RN.

The private duty nurse, with their oodles of spare time, would tell us stories of the old days. They worked twelve hour shifts, six days a week. They had to stoke the furnace, mop the floors and wash the walls. It seemed only fair since they didn't do medical procedures like taking blood pressures, which only doctors did.

By the forties the RNs were working only eight hour days—but still six-day weeks. But the status of the students had not progressed much. We still worked many twelve hour days. Technically we were

CHAPTER 2

CENTRAL SUPPLY

*T*oday's modern hospitals have large departments stocked with a multitude of supplies—presumably everything that would ever be needed to practice medicine and provide quality nursing care. These departments are known by various names—, e.g., Central Supply (C.S.) Central Service (also C.S.) and, boldly foraging new horizons, Supply, Processing and Distribution (S.P.D.)

In the hospital where I took my training in the forties the equivalent of Central Supply was 'The Locked Closet on First Floor.' Behind the single door of the locked closet were four or five shelves which contained all the supplies that were available to us at the time. There were no disposables.

If we needed an inhalator or a catheterization tray, we would obtain the key from the director of the School of Nursing, remove the tray from the closet, return the key to the Director, take the tray to the utility room on the floor where we were working, open the wrapper being careful to maintain sterility, add solutions and lubricant and replace the wrapper. We would then take the prepared tray to the patient's room, perform the procedure, return to the utility room, discard the linens in the laundry hamper and wash the instruments and receptacles and send them the O.R. to be set up and resterilized.

At the end of each shift, because there will were no disposables and no supplies were sent home with the patients, all the glasses and glass drinking tubes had to be gathered up and boiled in a pot on the gas burner in the utility room. Rubber enema tubes were also washed and boiled after each use.

Hot packs and stupes were made by boiling bath towels and wringing them out in canvas hammocks with wooden dowels—with one student grasping a dowel on each end and twisting.

Cotton balls and applicators (Q-tips) were made in our 'spare time' from a huge bale of cotton and a box of toothpicks. Hypodermic needles were sharpened on a sandstone and boiled for two minutes—syringes for ten minutes—and placed in a 90% alcohol solution—to be used over and over again.

Used rubber gloves were washed and tested for pinholes. Those that were intact were dried, powdered and package and sent to the O.R. to be sterilized. When leaks were found, they were patched with small rubber patches and used for rectal examinations and for washing out dirty diapers before sending them to the laundry. Gloves that were too torn to be patched were used to make finger cots and patches.

Bloody sponges from surgery and the delivery room were washed and stretched on wooden frames studded with tiny nails. When dry they were sent to the sewing room. THE SEWING ROOM!—now there is a department you won't find in a modern hospital. The little old palsied woman who ran the sewing room single handedly would sew several sponges together and quilt them. They were then sterilized and used for procedures requiring sterile wash cloths.

Mrs. Wertz, the sewing room lady, performed enormous functions for the hospital. She single-handedly made all the students' uniforms until 1944. Since they were tailor-made, everyone had a perfect fit. In 1944 Uncle Sam created the Cadet Nurse Corps in an effort to recruit student nurses to replace the RNs who, like Lucky Strike green, had gone to war. After that, student uniforms were ordered from J.C. Penney.

There were still ample sewing chores for Mrs. Wertz. When bedspreads, which were all a generic white, became to raggedy to use for bedspreads Mrs. Wertz would cut them into squares, sew several layers together and quilt them for use as under-pads. She made all the wrappers for the sterile trays and instruments by sewing two pieces of material together. After each use the wrappers and all the towels and drapes used in sterile procedures were carefully inspected for pinholes which could allow microorganisms to enter the sterile packs. Each pinhole would be circled with a pencil and the article would be sent to the sewing room to be mended. Nothing with a shred of life was ever thrown away. The phrase "Reduce, reuse, recycle "would not be coined for another fifty years, and yet that was how we lived—in ways unheard of today. There was a war going on and a patriotic spirit prevailed that young people today could not perceive.

But we were people who had spent our senior year in high school going from house to house collecting newspapers and tin cans. We had to use a manual can opener to remove both ends from the cans, then place them inside the cans and stomp them flat. One of my friends was fortunate to own a "tin Lizzie." It had to be parked facing uphill to keep the oil from leaking out, but our town was all hills, so that wasn't a problem. With all of this frugality we didn't contribute much to the future garbage problem or damage the environment (except when we burned our leaves) and the average cost of a hospital bed was six dollars a day.

One piece of equipment that can be found in the modern hospital is the electric suction machine. In one of my favorite M*A*S*H episodes the 4077th loses its electrical power and they had no suction for their critical patients. While they were frantically attempting to obtain a generator, Colonel Potter had a brilliant flashback and endeavored to construct a Wangensteen. The Wangensteen is successfully assembled and the patient receives his critically needed treatment despite the power outage.

I'm not as old as Colonel Potter and we had adequate electricity in the forties, but electrical suction had not yet been invented. For any patient who needed the continuous suction or deeper suction than we could provide with a bulb syringe, we would set up a Wangensteen. Our supplies consisted of three one-gallon jugs, tubing and two rubber stoppers with holes for the tubes.

One jug was filled with water and hung on an IV standard. The water dripped slowly through one tube into the second jug. A second tube was attached to a catheter which was inserted through the patient's nose into his stomach. As the water dripped, the plug prevented air from entering to replace it and a vacuum was created, producing suction through the second tube. The third jar was placed on the floor to receive the drainage.

The assembly of the Wangensteen was fairly simple, but many times it just didn't work. The location of the problem was not readily apparent. So the only course of action available was to take it all apart and start over—sometimes again and again—till it finally 'took.'

Ironically, many years later, when I had been absent from nursing for several years to manage my husband's business office, someone asked me if I would do private duty for a weekend while the patient's regular 'special' was away. I agreed only on the condition that there would be no 'new fangled' equipment that I wouldn't feel qualified to operate. They assured me that there wasn't. So when I strolled into his hospital room in my outdated, too long uniform I was miffed to see a Gomco machine attached to the patient's N.G. tube. I had to confess to the nurse I was relieving that I was not familiar with this equipment and had been promised that I would not be confronted with this situation. The night nurse showed me the switch for ON-OFF and the one for HIGH (suction)-LOW (suction.) That was all I needed to know. I had to chuckle at myself for fearing this modern miracle which had replaced the really fearsome monstrosity, the Wangensteen.

Today glass thermometers have been replaced with electronic ones, IVs are administered through computerized devices that are programmed to do everything including talking to you, B.P's are obtained with the flip of the switch and . . . the list grows longer every year. And backup generators insure that never again need we construct another Wangensteen

CHAPTER 3

STUDENT LIFE

The babies all wore cloth diapers. At the end of each shift we took the soiled diapers to the bathroom and, wearing one of the patched rubber gloves, washed out all the stools before sending them to the laundry. Babies have been wearing disposable diapers in hospitals for many years but, for the ecology, many hospitals are returning to cloth ones. But they no longer have to be rinsed before going to the laundry. The diaper service takes complete care of them from the time they are removed from the babies. It's good for business.

All diaper changing is done wearing disposable gloves. Because of the AIDS epidemic universal precautions required the use of gloves whenever there is contact with any body fluids. Gloves are no longer washed and re-sterilize. They are discarded after each use. When a patient is being checked every 15 minutes or oftener an astounding number of gloves are gone through. In fact the number of disposable supplies discarded daily is mind-boggling. Our little sewing room lady would be amazed.

All baby formulas for the nursery and pediatrics were made in the milk lab by the students. Each student spent a two-week rotation in the milk lab. Formulas were mixed using sterile technique. All of the solutions and utensils were sterilized before mixing the formula. Then, for good measure, the completed bottles of formula were put into the autoclave and sterilized again. Newborn babies weren't given formula until they were twenty-four hours old. The first formula was week-three-parts water to one part of evaporated milk. The strength of the formula was gradually increased as the baby got older.

New mothers were instructed to have someone bring a quart jar the day before dismissal. We would sterilize the jar in the milk lab and fill it with a twenty-four-hour supply of formula for her to take home. At the end of each shift we scrubbed all the used formula bottles so they could be sterilized and reused. Formulas were kept refrigerated and warmed in an electric bottle warmer at feeding times.

Today hospitals use ready-made formulas, vacuum packed in individual disposable bottles and fed to the babies at room temperature. They are sterile but the mothers are no longer instructed to sterilize the formula or bottles at home. Full strength formula is usually fed to the babies as early as one or two hours after delivery. Small wonder that we see so many formula intolerances today. Weight losses, however, are small and quickly regained.

Even when we were off-duty our lives would be not our own. During the school year when we had classes our curfew was seven P.M.—the same time that we got off-duty. During the summer we could be out until nine o'clock. Curfew on Friday was ten P.M.—midnight on Saturday. Curfews were strictly enforced. The house mother would lock the door at the stroke of the hour of the curfew even when she could see us trudging up the steep hill that led to the residence. Then we would have to trek over to the hospital to get the key from the house supervisor. The next day we were severely reprimanded. The offense would not be repeated soon. Often we would spend the last hour of our Saturday night date sitting on the front steps so that nothing could delay our homecoming. A popular song of the day was 'Don't Get Around Much Anymore.

When we left the premises we were not allowed to wear slacks or anklets—it was not attire befitting to young ladies and would reflect poorly on the hospital. There was no nylon hose. All of the nylon was needed to make parachutes for the Air Corps. The rayon and lisle stockings that were available to us were thick and wrinkled on our legs.

If we were working 3-11 or 11-7, we got a whole day off rather than two half days. We still had to get up and go to class at one o'clock. If we weren't scheduled to be on duty at seven A. M., we could go home overnight if we first brought a note, to that effect, from our mother. In the summer we each got a two-week vacation on a rotating basis. We were required to go to breakfast and attend chapel every morning. Chapel services began at six A.M. The students took turns selecting two hymns and a Bible reading or a prayer. Any student who could play the piano had a permanent job as long as she was there.

In the dining room we had to line up behind all the RNs and upperclassmen. Breakfast consisted of cereal and toast or our choice of two strips of bacon or one egg and toast. We could have extra toast if we were hungry but usually we barely had time to rush to our floor and report for duty by six forty-five.

Food from home was one of the most prized things we could get and was always to be shared with our classmates. Those of us who lived in town could offer no greater kindness then to take friends home for a real meal. While working in the diet kitchen one day, I came across the dietitian's budget figures. Her calculated cost for an average meal was 17 cents. This figure included baby formulas, patient trays and meals in the dining room. Even allowing for the baby formulas and an occasional low-cost meal that took some doing. It was accomplished by making all meals low-cost, and using such strategies as pouring some white sauce over a soda cracker and calling it Welsh Rarebit.

The two weeks we spent working in the diet kitchen learning to prepare special diets was compensated by entering a world where food was bountiful. In the large refrigerated room where food and leftovers were kept we found huge vats of creamed chicken and other succulent morsels, gallon jugs of green and ripe olives and an array of tempting morsels. We never knew where they came from or where they were headed, but to starving students they looked like a banquet. Obedient though we generally were, we could easily figure a time when the dietitian was away to sample a tiny bit of this feast. Planning short, repeated trips into the refrigerated room could make for a satisfying day culinary-wise.

We didn't take laundry home to mother. Bed linens and uniforms were done by the hospital laundry. For personal things a laundry room was provided in the basement of the nurses' residence. Washers and dryers were not available—only a washtub. Since we didn't yet have Kleenex we had to wash our handkerchiefs by hand and spread them out on our mirrors wet so they would dry flat. When the patients were pleased with their care, they often gave us a pretty handkerchief when they were dismissed. We would wear one in our breast pocket, carefully arranged with the decorated corner showing. It was the only form of adornment we were allowed, plain, unadorned handkerchiefs were used for practical matters.

Occasionally I may confuse you by using the term 'nurses' when I am talking about student nurses—as in "the nurses' residence." That is because, other than the house supervisor and the head nurse and the assistant head nurse on each floor who were RNs, we were the only 'nurses' in the hospital.

We wore white uniforms (and caps after nine months probationary period) and didn't know how lucky we were not to have to contend with the stuffy starched collars and cuffs some of the other schools provided with white pinafores' and striped or colored shirts.

I was not pleased to learn that I had given up a cushy job paying $159.00 a month and could look forward, after three years of hard labor and intensive studying, to making $80.00 a month. As luck would have it, nurses' wages had risen to $160.00 a month by 1947; so I was actually making a dollar a month more than I had three years earlier. By that **time** my former colleagues at the railroad headquarters were making $100.00 a month more. But the Cadet Nurse Corps assuaged a lot of sacrifices. Uncle Sam provided our tuition, books and uniforms—including a summer and winter street uniform and hats. When we wore them, we could get into a movie or bowl a line for $.25. We even had our own song:

> "We're the cadets, we're in the corps
>
> Doing our bit to help the nation win the war
>
> Doing the job we're chosen for
>
> United States Cadet Nurse Corps."

That was the chorus. There were several verses.

We also received a monthly stipend—$15.00 a month the first nine months paid in a lump sum at the end of the probationary period, $20.00 a month from nine months to two and a half years, and $30.00 a month the last six months. The state hospital where I spent the last six months also paid us $30.00 a month. So with no board or room to pay we were quite affluent. I bought myself a mouton coat and went home in a blizzard to show it off.

Exposed to sick people from a wide variety of cultures and neighborhoods student nurses, before they have had time to build up immunities, are particularly vulnerable to illness. We never reported an illness unless we were too sick to go on duty because we would have had to be hospitalized. Only then would there be someone to keep an eye on us. Apparently it wasn't in our housemother's job description.

But during the mumps epidemic it was different. There was no mumps vaccine at that time. So we were urged to report even the most minor symptoms so we could be isolated to prevent any further spread of the disease.

Several of my classmates had already been diagnosed and placed in isolation. I began to experience vague symptoms—headache, dizziness and malaise. I had mumps on one side as a child but feared I could still get it on the other side. Not wanting to be the Typhoid Mary of mumps dom, I reported to our personal physician, kindly old Dr. Sarah. She asked me a series of questions:

"Have you had the mumps before?"

"On one side."

"Do you have a fever?"

"No."

"Pain behind your ears?"

"No."

And on and on. All my answers were 'no' I was feeling very embarrassed and thought Dr. Sarah must surely be wondering what I was doing there. I was convinced that I didn't have the mumps but I had suffered a spell of hypochondria. I was startled from my reverie hearing Dr. Sarah say, "I think she has it. Let's put her in isolation."

My classmates had been put in an empty storeroom in the basement of the hospital. There were no patients in that part of the hospital and a makeshift treatment room had been assembled there. I think the nurses were also dubious about my diagnosis because they didn't think that I should be in that room where I would be exposed to mumps if I didn't actually have it.

So I was placed in a room across the hall. This was the record room. In these times of microfilm and computer memory banks it's hard to picture a small room with a few filing cabinets containing all the records compiled since the opening of the hospital some fifty years earlier.

It was lonely in there by myself. I spent a lot of time in the doorway calling out to the students confined across the hall. Much of the rest of the time was spent reading those old records. My brother, my cousins and I had all been born in that hospital and all our birth records were there—even the one showing that one cousin had indeed weighed more than twelve pounds at birth. I found the record of my tonsillectomy at age seven and saw that the orderly who had carried that frightened little girl to the operating room in his arms was our very own 'Happy,' still with us in the same capacity after all those years.

Several years later I had a parallel experience—the reverse of the mumps one. In that instance I convinced the authorities that I didn't have a condition which I actually had. I had been hospitalized with ruptured membranes at thirty-five weeks gestation. Six days later I was convinced that I would be pregnant and on bed rest for the rest of my life. That night I was awakened by contractions. I put on my signal light and asked for something for the 'false labor pains' that kept waking me. While the nurse was out checking on it I turned on the lights and timed the contractions. They were five minutes apart. I blushed with embarrassment. Any OB nurse would know that when the BOW is ruptured the contractions are the real thing. "She must think that I'm really stupid," I thought.

Au contraire! Then the intern arrived to check me. I explained to him that I really was in labor. He timed a couple of contractions and pronounced that they were false. I guess he didn't have as good a script writer as Dr. Welby, who never missed on that subject. He gave me an emperin and codeine and a Seconal to help me sleep. That was nice in a way because that was all that I got to help me through that labor.

After a long night my 'false' contractions brought forth a tiny baby girl. Because of the extended period of ruptured membranes I developed an infection and spent a total of thirteen days in that hospital. My total bill, including penicillin, was three hundred dollars. Blue Cross paid seventy-five of it. That year was 1952.

In high school I had been an 'A' student. So I wasn't worried about passing my nursing courses. As it happened they were much harder for me because of the mountains of material that had to be memorized. It seemed that one day we would be required to learn all the bones of the body and the next, all the muscles. Every day there was a new load. Memorizing was difficult for me. Problem solving was my strong point.

In pharmacology we had to memorize all the drugs, their generic and brand names, classifications, indications, contraindications, desired effects, side effect's etc. All of this memorizing was painful and laborious for me.

Anatomy and physiology had some redeeming factors. For the optic nerve we had a little rhyme—On Old Olympia's Towering Top a Finn and German Viewed a Hop. The first letter of each word was the first letter of each nerve in the system. Today it is impossible for me to remember what these nerves were. But I still remember the ditty and it would be easier to relearn them now. Off-duty we made up our own learning devices. We would laughingly report to each other that someone had fallen on his OS innominatum or his acetabulum.

But pharmacology was just plain drudgery. I took my pharm notes on bits and scraps of paper—probably in an act of unconscious rebellion. When it was time to study for the final exam, I found it impossible to organize my notes for any kind of productive studying. So I petulantly tossed them aside and croaked "I can't do this!" Of course it never occurred to me that I could actually flunk the final. I didn't actually fail but I received a conditional grade—, i.e., I could retake the test and pass it or I would have to repeat the course. Repeating that course is a fate that makes me shudder even today, fifty years later. At that time it was like a death knoll. I borrowed a classmate's notes. They were neatly written and organized in a single notebook. (Why hadn't I thought of that?) I almost 'bought the pharm' but this time I passed the test with a solid 'B' and said goodbye to that boring course. But the joke was on me. Nurses have to study medicines all their lives. The pharmaceutical companies put new drugs on the market at a rapid rate. Each one has a barely pronounceable generic name as well as one or more brand names. Since many states permit substitution of one for the other, we must be familiar with all of them. Each has desirable effects and side effects. Sometimes a side effect will be a desirable effect for a different condition and the drug will be assigned a new use. E.g., a drug used to treat Parkinson's Disease is also used to prevent the production of milk in postpartum patients. Then there are contraindications and nursing implications and . . . but you get the picture.

How do nurses learn and remember all these things? Mostly by using them on a daily basis—the old 'use it or lose it' cliché. For drugs that are unfamiliar there are several reference tomes available on each nursing unit. If all else fails, we can go to the phone and called the hospital pharmacist, now available in most hospitals around the clock.

Nurses play an important role in monitoring the medicines of the patients in their care. Drug therapy has become a complicated matter because of the enormous numbers of medicines on the market. Not only does each one have its own characteristics but each interacts with other medicines in specific ways. Determining these things is time-consuming and doctors are generally grateful if an oversight is pointed out to them.

Some of my students, with only six months educational background have picked up discrepancies and reported them. I expect that many new mothers have been saved from unwanted pregnancies because an astute student noted that birth control pills must not be given with an anti-lactation medication or the birth control will not be affective.

CHAPTER 4

DISCIPLINE

I was in trouble only twice during my three years in nurses training. They happened to be just a week apart and only seven months before graduation. In the first incident I was working the 3-11 shift. Typically, a student working a split 7:00 A.M. to 7:00 P.M. Shift was in charge from three o'clock when the head nurse went off-duty until 7:00 P.M. I would then be in charge from 7:00 P.M. until 11:00 P.M. when the 11-7 student came on.

On that particular day a doctor's office nurse had left an order for a patient with the hospital's business office. That was unorthodox even in those ancient times. The business office called the order up to the floor and the day student transcribed it and made out a medicine ticket which she gave to me when she reported off.

The order itself was even more astounding than the manner in which it reached us. It called for eight ounces of magnesium sulfate (Epsom salts) to be given by mouth at 8:00 P.M. I attempted to contact the doctor to confirm the order. He had gone out of town. The nurse who called in the order was also unavailable. The intern and the house supervisor were tied up in emergency surgery. Eventually I did reach the assistant house supervisor who assured me that it was not uncommon to give large doses of mag sulfate to drug addicts and alcoholics. This patient was both.

I decided the patient would probably be unable to retain the medication anyway. We had only about 2 ounces of mag sulfate on the floor. By borrowing from the other floors I managed to accumulate a total of 5 ounces which I gave him deluded in water while holding an emesis basin under his chin to catch it on the rebound. The emesis basin was unnecessary. I charted the 8 ounces that had been given as ordered. I blush to report that was common practice at that time and was taught to us by the head nurses.

After a brief sleep I had to report back on duty at six forty-five A.M.—a popular form of student torture. When the 11-7 student gave night report, she repeated the order for the mag sulfate that I had given. The head nurse was indignant. She said she would never trust me again. (She left me in charge of the floor when she went off-duty at three o'clock the same day.) And she took away my day off for that week. Furthermore I was to be called anytime of the day or night to clean up any messes resulting from the medication. (Mag sulfate is a cathartic.) There were none.

Taking my day off away was a serious matter. It happened to be my 21st birthday and I had made special plans. I knew that I had been treated unfairly. I had done everything possible to check out that order, and had been given the go-ahead by my superior. At that time nurses were not allowed to refuse to follow an order. Most of the older doctors had only three years of education beyond high school and often hadn't kept abreast of the times. If a nurse felt that an order was unsafe she did what was safe for the patient and charted it the way it was ordered. Students couldn't refuse to do an RN's bidding or even an upperclassman's. And there were no channels available for students who felt they had been treated unfairly as there are today.

That extra day was a difficult one. One little old man, oblivious to the tear stealing down my cheek, had me constantly adjusting his various pillows and head and foot rests. There were no electric beds or even hand cranks. The head and foot rest had to be raised and lowered manually bearing the weight of the patient. When it was in the desired position, the crossbar had to be secured in the notches on both sides of the bed. Forty-seven years later I can still hear his whiny voice saying, "Move that pillow just a little more to the left—no, a little more to the right . . . ."

When the office nurse appeared the following week, she exclaimed, "why that order was for Mag Citrate. Anyone would know that! "Just as I had always suspected—I wasn't anyone.

A week after the mag sulfate incident I was running the water for a tub bath when the phone rang. It was the superintendent of nurses. "I was supposed to call you an hour ago, "she told me. Here are the orders you must have ready before he arrives." I thanked her and scurried about making the necessary preparations.

The next thing I knew lunch trays were piling up—so I began carrying them to the patients. As I was rushing past the bathroom, I noticed water running out the door. THE TUB! I ran in and turned off the faucets, bravely plunging my arm into the scalding water to pull out the plug. While the patients ate their lunch I mopped up the water and thought the incident was finished.

When I was called to the superintendent's office later in the day, I was naive enough to believe that they were going to tell me that my day off should not have been taken away and that they were going to give me another one to make up for it. What I didn't know was that at the exact time that the tub was running over the Board of Directors were touring the hospital. While they were in the bathroom of the floor below mine, they saw water trickling down the walls. My punishments would be that I would not be allowed to wear my cap for one month.

That was just too much! I had only forgotten the tub because the superintendent had forgotten to call me when she should have. I had worked for two and a half years to earn that cap and I didn't feel that one overflowed tub should cancel that out. I turned to the superintendent, a formidable looking woman with whom we students normally did not interact. Her position was the equivalent of the hospital administrator and had little to do with nursing. In a flash of courage I forgot my shyness and told her how I felt concluding with, "I'll quit before I go on duty without my cap."

She smiled a Mona Lisa smile and replied, "We'll miss you."

My classmates were sympathetic as they rallied around. Together they went to the superintendent and told her that if I couldn't wear my cap they wouldn't wear theirs either. She smiled her Mona Lisa smile and explained to them that would reflect poorly on the hospital. They understood and abandoned their stand. But it was a bold move for the times and I appreciated it.

One of my classmates—the one who had transcribed the order for the mag sulfate—came to my room and talked to me for a long time. Maybe she felt guilty for getting off Scott free in the mag sulfate incident. Maybe it was because she was a year or two older than the rest of us and had experienced some of life's hard knocks herself. Or maybe she was just a good friend. But she succeeded in convincing me that it wouldn't be wise to mess up my life by throwing away two and a half years of work.

"But I told Miss Elroy that it was just as much her fault as it was mine!" I gasped.

"Then you'll just have to apologize."

That was one of the hardest things I ever had to do. To add to the tension, the little old lady who was president of the board was there at the time. I apologized to Miss Elroy and asked her if I could stay and complete my training. She smiled sweetly—it no longer looked like the Mona Lisa—and said they would be glad to have me. The president of the board beamed. And so did I.

I will always be grateful to them and to the classmate who convinced me to go that extra mile and save a career that has been my primary focus of identification most of my life—a career that has been fulfilling and rewarding and has always provided me with a means of supporting myself and my family, allowing me a choice of hours to accommodate the changing needs of my family. Thanks, Smoky.

The next morning I went on duty on the all-male floor feeling naked without my cap. I didn't know that, as an L&D nurse, I would rarely wear a cap and that eventually most nurses wouldn't wear caps at all. After the first humiliating moments on duty barehanded I began to see the humor of the situation. As each patient demanded to know the reason for my plight, I became something of a celebrity telling and retelling the story of the overflowing bath tub in this humorous vein. The patients became my champions and I didn't care if I ever wore my cap again.

A week later one of my instructors from the School of Nursing slunk up to me and whispered in my ear, "you can wear your cap tomorrow," and skulked away. The Director of the School was due to return the next day after a two-week absence. I had always felt that she would have taken my part in both incidents—probably just wishful thinking, but they obviously didn't want that confrontation. I was tired of confrontations myself. So I reluctantly complied and wore my cap the next day.

Three weeks later I left with half of my class to spend the remaining six months of the course in the state psychiatric hospital one hundred and sixty miles away.

One strict admonition was against the use of first names. Such familiarity was both unprofessional and unacceptable—even in our own room in the students' dorm. So we gave each other nicknames or added a 'Y' or 'IE' to the end of our last names. Thus I became 'Brownie,' a name I still cherish nostalgically even though my name has not been Brown for forty-five years. Allowing a patient to know your first name was grounds for dismissal.

Why did we put up with all this nitpickery? Probably because that was the way we had been reared. Our parents had laid the groundwork by demanding strict obedience, and for a very good reason—because they said so. So, while we didn't like much of what was demanded of us, we went along with it with minimal complaining. Most of us were under twenty-one and looked forward to that golden day when we would graduate and be self governing. We didn't anticipate that we would get married and acquire a new master.

I was an especially timid probie and when one of the seniors told me I could call her Virginia I felt warm all over. One day in the dorm I tried it out. We were overheard by another senior who lost no time in threatening me with instant expulsion if such a thing ever happened again. I don't know what motivated Virginia. Perhaps she was so close to graduation that she had already begun to shed the rules.

After all of this conditioning I was understandably dubious when, many years later, nurses began introducing themselves by their first names. "Into whose hands would you rather place your life and welfare?" I would ask my students. "Cute Little Debbie, who seems to require reassurance that she is doing all right, or neat, trim Miss Oliver who apparently has everything under control?" So we called each other Miss and Mrs.(And occasionally a Mr.) for a little longer. By the time Ms came on the scene we were using first names.

As the years went by I would occasionally observe my students acting cutesy and immature with their patients. I thought that might make a hit with father figure male patients (reminiscent of my own student days when I went on the men's floor capless.) But our OB patients were all young women and I wanted to see a little more professionalism there.

Then one day I entered a postpartum room and overheard the students and the patient's 'rapping' about the Strawberry Alarm Clock. (It turned out to be a current rock group.) I felt very much 'out of it' never having heard of them. I began to understand that new mothers were young and had a special rapport with our students, who spoke their language.

This point was further brought home to me one day as I helped a patient fill out her birth certificate information. "I see you're from my hometown," I exclaimed.

"Oh, you probably know my mother," she shot back quick as a whip. As I was only forty-two and had teenagers at home it never occurred to me that I was a generation removed from our patients. Later, when it became fashionable for women to delay having families until their careers were well-established, I would encounter mothers who had even more gray hair than I did. But this patient actually was young enough to be my daughter. I began to recognize that some of my viewpoints were rigid and outdated and some of that rigidity began to crumble.

Today it is common for nurses' I.D. pins to show first names only—, e.g., 'Connie RN'—not because we've gotten carried away with youth and familiarity but for reasons of safety. With so much deviance in the world today it is better that unauthorized persons not have access to last names that can be used to procure telephone numbers and addresses.

CHAPTER 5

WORKING HOURS

*W*orking shifts was something we students looked forward to. To some extent it meant that we had 'arrived' or at least survived the probationary period and a lot of scrutiny. Because there were no RNs on the floors from 7:00 P.M. until 7:00 A.M. (LPN's had not yet entered the scene) we had to have proven that we were sufficiently experienced and capable to be in charge of the floor.

But the main advantage was that there was no 'Brass' around—no head nurses to nitpick and criticize and no doctors hovering around demanding service. Even as an RN that is a definite bonus. While it is true that we no longer jump to our feet and stand at attention when they enter the room nor wait on them hand and foot—they can now be observed hunting up their patients' charts and making rounds alone—they still have enough moxie to require mollifying. Nurses are the primary scapegoats when something goes wrong. E.g. if a patient develops an infection the doctor is likely to point his finger and growl, "you nurses must not be washing your hands." We call it the 'God complex.' Most doctors, we say, answer only to God but in the case of an especially arrogant doctor we say that he gives orders to God. One doctor was known among the nurses as "John Jesus."

Head nurses have also been known to have the 'God complex.'

Some of them seem to be constantly competing with the staff nurses to prove their superiority. Women's Lib has taken its toll. Ergo the atmosphere from three p.m. to seven a.m. is clearly more relaxed and easy-going.

Having the time-consuming baths and changing of bed linens out of the way was an additional bonus and gave us more time to ascertain and fulfill patients' needs. Working 'relief' is good if you don't mind giving up, or at least drastically altering, your social life. As students our social life was almost nonexistent. So that was not a serious problem. The relief shift is the 3-11 shift, so named because, before its inception, nurses worked twelve hour shifts from 7:00 A.M. until 7:00 P.M. and 7:00 P.M. to 7:00 A.M. The creation of a new shift resulting in three eight hour shifts must surely have been a distinct relief.

Today the twelve-hour shift has returned, along with a new ten hour shift—while still retaining the eight hour shifts. The difference is—the old twelve hour shift added up to seventy-two hours a week and the wages were barely minimal. The modern nurse rarely works more than forty hours a week and over time is well compensated. Some hospitals will pay a full week's wages for a twelve-hour/day, three day weeks-end. The ten-hour day was conceived to fill in the gap that occurs at the change of shifts when nurses are tied up giving and receiving report. So nurses are now coming and going at all hours.

The 3-11 shift has always been my personal favorite. When you have small children, it allows you to spend a large part of the day with them. And you have the comfort of knowing that the secondary care giver has put them to bed and they have slumbered through much of the time you were away from them.

An added advantage is that you're not required to get up at five a.m. as you must to work the day shift. This may backfire when your children reach school age and have to leave early in the morning. I occasionally overslept and sent them to school eating an egg sandwich on the way. When they are in school all day, you see less of them and by the time they are teenagers you are really needed at home in the evening. By that time they are capable of getting themselves ready for school without help. Then the day shift usually adapts best to their needs. The night shift is best when your children are young and in school all day. Then you can usually be home in time to ensure that they are properly attired and you are always there on those many days when there is no school. That of course requires that a responsible adult is there during the night while you are at work.

I always felt like a martyr when I worked evenings. I would work in the house all morning and cook the family dinner to be reheated that evening. My dinner was a sandwich and a banana in a brown bag. Then off to the hospital where I would put in another eight to ten hours of hard work (we often worked overtime without compensation) and return home at midnight to find the dirty dishes still on the table. Then I would crawl around the floor looking under the furniture for shoes and socks so the morning rush wouldn't be so hectic. Today most husbands contribute somewhat more to home management easing that burden a little.

As students working evenings or nights we finally got a whole day off every week instead of two half days. As a staff nurse you become very close to your coworkers and they are like a second family to you. Sometimes we would go out together at the end of our shift as our leisure hours didn't coincide with those of most of our friends and family.

When my six-year-old son was hit by a car and comatose, and I was staying with him around the clock, my coworkers would bring their sack lunches and share them with us. They took up a collection in the hospital where I worked and presented us with a check for twenty-five dollars, almost a day's pay at that time. Because I worked in L&D and wore scrubs on duty I owned only one uniform. The hospital where my son was a patient required me to wear a uniform or I would not have been allowed to stay with him. Parents were considered excess baggage at that time (1955.)

One of my co-workers was my size—at five feet one and a half inch there weren't many. She brought me her uniforms, freshly washed starched and ironed, and took the dirty ones back with her for the whole month I stayed with him. They were all far more supportive than my own family.

Working nights was another matter. As students we were required to sleep in the night room—a secluded room with enough beds for all of the students working 11-7. In that room we were sequestered from the bustle and activity of the day people. I marvel that neither the director of the school nor the house mother ever visited that room to see (and hear) what went on in there. At eight a.m. we would settle down to go to sleep. Dark green shades were pulled down to block out the sunlight. At nine a.m. the seniors began trekking down to the lobby to look for the mail. Many of them had boyfriends and fiancés in the service. They were looking forward to graduation, the end of the war, marriage and eternal happiness.

When the mail finally came they would zip up the shades and read the letters to each other across the room. By noon they were hungry and traipsed off to lunch. The rest of us would try to grab a few winks before they came thundering back again. Today we call this restlessness 'senioritis.' When my own final months in training came, I learned how little sleep you need when you're living on adrenaline.

Unfortunately this quest for sleep never improved when I became an RN working nights. The four cups of tepid coffee I downed at night lunch did nothing to stimulate me although I faithfully tried it every day. When I would finally arrive home in the morning, bone weary and mentally drained, I would have to fix breakfast for the family and get the children ready for school. By the time I was able to settle down in bed the room would spin me into unconsciousness.

In those pre-air conditioner days the window had to be open in the summer. The shade would flap in the breeze causing the sun to shine intermittently in my eyes. A pillow plopped over the telephone barely muffled the sharp ring. The dog barked at every leaf that blew by and a sign on the front door stating, "Please Do Not Ring Doorbell" resulted in loud knocking. Before I knew it, the children were home from school. And on many days they didn't go to school. I learned to hate teachers' conferences and other school holidays that seemed to be contrived just to sabotage my sleep. And there were always weekends and regular vacations.

You might think that a social life would be feasible on this shift. After all work didn't start until eleven o'clock. A movie was a possibility if you're willing to give up the after-dinner nap you always tried for because of constant exhaustion. Parties fared even worse. At ten o'clock when things were beginning to warm up and everyone was having a good time it was time to leave and get ready to go to work.

I've never understood the mind-set of the lifelong night nurse. These nurses are unable to adjust to any other schedule. On their nights off and vacations they stay up all night knitting and watching TV. They must lead solitary lives.

There is another shift that takes place after the nurse goes off-duty. She then begins her second shift—keeping the home fires burning. Often they stop in the grocery store on their way home from work. They may be in uniform but many will be wearing street clothes, having changed before they left the hospital. Or they have worn street cloths on duty which they do in areas like the psych wards.

One day I was in the grocery store rifling through the packages of meat when I heard a voice over the P.A. system—"Is there a doctor in the store?" Oh, oh I thought. Someone has a problem. A few minutes later the P.A. blared again—"Is there a nurse in the store?"

Now I had a dilemma. While I kept my first aid and CPR certificates updated I had never had an opportunity to practice them for real. Having worked in OB most of my professional life I didn't feel competent in my emergency abilities unless it was an emergency delivery. Still I felt I could probably do better than most lay people. So I headed for the designated checkout stand.

There, sitting on the floor, was a young woman in street clothes cradling an elderly woman's head in her lap. Probably her mother, I thought. The woman appeared to be unconscious. I stooped down and placed my fingertips over the pulse in her neck. The young woman began to describe her findings. "Her pulse is slow and strong. Respirations are deep and regular. Her color is good and her skin is cool and dry." Why, she was giving me report! I checked my watch. It was 3:45p.m. of course! The day nurses were off-duty and beginning their second shift on the home front. I left knowing the patient was in good hands until the ambulance arrived.

If you ever get sick in the grocery store, let it be between three-thirty and four-thirty in the afternoon. Some Angel of Mercy will probably watch over you.

CHAPTER 6

THE O.R.

*A*s the time approached to begin my three-month rotation in the operating room, I became increasingly apprehensive. I was certain that it would abort my career in nursing. Stories abounded about doctors yelling and throwing instruments at the nurses. Being a timid and sensitive young girl, (teenagers were called 'girls' in the forties, as a matter of fact we still call each other girls in our sixties. I was sure that I would not be able to cope.

The day I was scheduled to scrub for my first operation I had been sick all night, I was afraid I would be sick during the surgery and they would think I didn't have what it takes when, in fact, I had caught a 'bug.' My fears were groundless. I was so fascinated watching that thyroidectomy that I forgot all about being sick.

That first time was just for observation. I didn't have to be concerned with instruments, sutures or any of the other details scrub nurses are responsible for. It was the only operation I ever got to watch from start to finish. After that I would be too busy with my responsibilities to pay much attention. When I felt someone tugging on the back of my scrub gown I wondered what error, I could possibly have committed. It was the circulating nurse telling me it was time to go to class. The hours had slipped away unnoticed. My first confrontation was not with the doctor but with the OR supervisor. I was scrubbing for a D&C (dilation and curettage.) The patient's legs were elevated in stirrups and I was attempting to place sterile drapes over them.

Enter the O.R. supervisor, known un-affectionately behind her back as Hatchet Face. (The Title of Battle Axe had already been taken.) Every time I would raise the drape high enough to clear the legs she would scream, "Miss. Brown. You're going to contaminate yourself!" After each tirade I would back off and then try again—only to be blasted with, "will you listen to me, Miss Brown? You're going to contaminate yourself on the overhead light!"

Since I never touched the light, she had to be motivated by thinking that the light was too close. She could simply have moved it and resolved the problem. Seemingly it never occurred to her. It certainly didn't occur to me to talk back to her. I had never talked back to authority figures nor used profanity at that time. So Hatchet Face and I continued our farcical routine until the gynecologist came in from the scrub room. Middle-aged and maternal, she sized up the situation instantly, and probably heard it all from the scrub room which adjoined the operating room, and said, "You're doing fine, Miss Brown." I slipped the drapes on without further fanfare and without contaminating myself and the surgery proceeded without mishap.

One of my first major scrubs was for a particularly surly surgeon. I was already beginning to realize that the doctors' tantrums were not a personal reflection on us nurses. They were simply a way of 'acting out' their frustrations and the tremendous burden of responsibility they bore. Doctor Surly was in his usual form and grumbled throughout the operation. Several times he called me a dummy. I knew I had done all right. So I didn't have a problem with it. But apparently Hatchet Face didn't like it when anyone other than herself harassed her students.

After the surgery she put her arm around my shoulders and said, "Dr. Surly, I'll have you know that Miss Brown is one of our newer students and I think she did very well."

"Oh, yes," replied Dr. (No longer) Surly, startled out of his reverie. "You did fine, Miss Brown." Another of life's little surprises—and lessons.

Operations were scheduled between 7:00 A.M. and 3:00 P.M. So that was the only shift we were assigned in the O.R. But sometimes emergency surgeries were done during the off-hours. And people were needed to scrub and circulate. During our OR rotation we took turns being on call. Getting called in for surgery did not happen as frequently as, we would later find, it did when we were on call in L&D, but we all experienced our share. We learned to get up from a sound sleep and function with a clear head. And then to go back to bed and fall asleep quickly. Since we weren't, compensated for the time we spent on call, we learned to get up again at five-thirty the next morning and work all day.

We found that the Hollywood version of surgery was a fallacy. Doctors didn't call for instruments by name. They would hold out a hand while continuing an unrelated conversation and the scrub nurse would anticipate what was needed. Usually it was not difficult—first a scalpel to make the incision—then keep passing hemostats until all of the bleeders have been clamped off—suture to tie off the bleeders (later they began to cauterize them and it was much faster) then remove all the hemostats from the sterile field—all the while sponging the blood from the wound so that the doctor has good visualization and keeping an accurate count of all the sponges and sharps used.

Catgut was used to suture the layers of tissue beneath the skin, silk thread for the skin. The suture had to be threaded through the eye of the appropriate needle and secured with a hemostat. Years later this chore was simplified when the suture was manufactured already secured to the needle.

It is critical that no sponges or sharps (needles and scissors) are left in the patient's wound. If either count was not correct, it was necessary to impress this fact on the surgeon before he finished suturing the incision—information he was not interested in hearing. To say, "The sponge count is not correct, Doctor," would rarely get his attention. It was necessary to first get his attention with, "**DOCTOR**!" Followed by, "The sponge count . . . etc." It was not necessary to keep track of the exact number of sponges used. Sponges were put up in packages of ten. So, as the used sponges were discarded into the waste receptacle, the circulating nurse would put them into groups of ten with a hemostat. The scrub nurse had to make sure that all of the used ones as well as the ones on the sterile table and the ones that were still on the surgical field completed the groups of ten. Often the scrub nurse and the circulating nurse would count everything over and over looking for a shortage—while the doctor kept on suturing. The missing sponge was always found—sometimes in the surgeons hand.

We became familiar with all the instruments and experienced the various types of surgery that were done at that time until it became just one more routine. I decided that being scrubbed was the safest place to be. You couldn't leave the operative area because you would then be contaminated. So if you needed something that wasn't on the table you called for the circulating nurse to bring it to you. The circulating nurse had to know where everything was stored so that she could get her hands on it at a moments notice—before incurring the wrath of the doctor. Only RNs and students taking their senior cadet training were permitted to circulate. So we never had that problem.

Nursing education programs no longer have an O.R. rotation for their students. Surgical technicians do almost all of the scrubbing and few RNs go into the field. Those that do learn their functions through 'on-the-job' training. I think it was an unfortunate loss. There is a lot of transferable knowledge to be learned in the O.R., not the least of which is an internalization of sterile techniques that remain with the individual for a lifetime. Confusion over what can be touched with a gloved or un gloved hand is eliminated. That could have a direct effect on the number of nosocomial infections seen. Other benefits include an enhanced knowledge of anatomy and physiology and an empathy for the origin of postoperative pain, and a lot of neat memories.

CHAPTER 7

SEX IN THE HOSPITAL

*B*efore the sexual revolution many of us liked to think that sex took place only within the confines of marriage. The men I dated always told me that my friends were 'doing it.' But I refused to believe them. After all most men would use any method of persuasion, they can think of. Still, four of the girls in my small class of 14 were pregnant at graduation.

And there were times when it seemed that we had our own little Peyton Place going on in that small town, one hundred twenty bed hospital. My first peek into this world came when I was a student in charge of a medical floor on the 11-7 shift. One of my patients, a diabetic, was having an insulin reaction. I needed the approval of the House Supervisor to give her the orange juice with sugar she needed to bring her out of it. If my assessment had been incorrect and she was actually in a diabetic coma, the orange juice and sugar would have only made it worse

I dialed the operator and asked her to find the Supervisor for me. "Try the doctors' lounge on the first floor," she advised. I went down to the lounge and found no one there. As I returned to my floor, I ran into the student on the adjoining floor and told her my problem.

"She's in the doctors' lounge," she insisted.

"No, I just looked. It's dark and quiet in there."

"Did you call out her name really loud?"

"Well no—oh."

"Go back in there and call her name," she persisted.

I went back in this time I called out to her. And sure enough she answered. She was quite willing to accept my assessment of the problem and back me up on the treatment rather than go and check the patient herself. (Giving orange juice and sugar didn't require waking the doctor.)

I never actually knew whether she was in there with the doctor, someone else or just went in to get some sleep. Our entire conversation took place in the dark. Either way she was remiss in her responsibilities. And I suspect it was not an occasional thing. Fortunately the patient responded to the treatment.

One of the senior students had her eye on one of the staff doctors. I never understood why. She was tall, slender and attractive. He was old enough to be her father, more than a head shorter, stocky and not at all good-looking. In a Hollywood movie they would have been portrayed by Susan Anton and Robert Redford. In real life it was more like Mickey Rooney.

She stalked him for years. They always seemed to be in a vault somewhere—in a corner of whatever floor she was working on, in a stairwell or in the parking lot. After she graduated, he divorced his wife and married her.

Our interns were almost always a source of joy. They were even more overworked and harassed then we were, but they willingly answered our calls for help and catheterized our male patients for us. At that time it was taboo for women to catheterize male patients.

One of our friendliest interns came from Mexico. Apparently the only thing he inherited from his Irish father was his name of Hogan. His coal black hair, snapping brown eyes and deep tan skin were conferred on him by his mother along with his first name, which was José. The nurses all found him very attractive although he was shorter than most of them. Dr. Hogan made no secret of the fact that he had a wife and eight children in Mexico and that he would return to them when he had completed his internship. In defense of his many escapades he told us that his wife didn't expect fidelity from him. That was the Mexican way.

As the seniors graduated and began working on the staff most of them went out with him. Reports abounded on, who was the latest one to be seen coming out of a motel room with him. I'm sure that sexual harassment was the last thing on his mind when he would slip his fingers in a uniform's breast pocket with the name tag sewn on and crack, "Hmm, Miss Brown. What do you call the other one?" Such was his charisma that we would just giggle and our step would become a little lighter.

One of the graduates who had been seen going to a motel with him suddenly married a widower with four children. The date was promptly noted on a lot of calendars for future reference. Sure enough seven months after her wedding day she entered the hospital in 'premature' labor. The OB crew, eagerly, watched for a full term baby, with a crop of thick, black hair. There were a lot of red faces when a scrawny premie with light downy hair was delivered.

One of our obstetricians was always "up in his airplane" when we needed him. At least that was what his office nurse had apparently been instructed to say. He was an amateur pilot. But when it was emphasized that we needed him stat because his patient was crowning he always

One day one of our patient's breasts had engorged on the first postpartum day, much earlier than the usual third day we expect this to happen. Of course, that is what we charted. Apparently the nurse who followed us in caring for that patient was appalled. She scrawled on the chart in large letters, "**BREASTS ARE SOFT**," and underlined it twice. She obviously did not check. Oddly, no such aversion seems to exist to checking vaginal flow and the episiotomy-areas. I consider much more private. There should be some sage observation to make about a society that went from a Victorian attitude of believing it all right to touch the same-sex but not the opposite sex to a sexual revolutionary attitude of the reverse. Although I do remember one young RN, who was upset because she had to catheterize a man. Of course, some people get upset if they have to scrub a sink.

During the time I worked in a nursing home. I did have to do a few male catheterizations. The patients were quite elderly and accustomed to the procedure. So the deeds were accomplished with minimal trauma for all of us.

But I met my nemesis when I was assigned to a medical—surgical-floor with students. One morning, a student told me her patient's external catheter needed to be reapplied, and she wanted me to demonstrate it for her. I was reasonably certain that she had applied more external catheters then I had, which was none. But I was her instructor. Soooooooooooooooooo . . .

An external catheter is just a condom with a tube at the end to carry incontinent urine to a plastic bag. I had some very limited experience with condoms during my marriage, which had ended several years earlier. I figured I could just roll that little sucker right on and be done with it. I didn't even crank up the bed. It was an old County Hospital and didn't have electric beds.

The little black patient was ninety-three years old and weighed as many pounds. I leaned over and began to unroll the catheter. He had a foreskin and I wasn't sure what to do about that. But it had a mind of its own and slipped back. As I struggled to slip the catheter on, the glans began to swell. The more I struggled the more swollen it became, and the more elusive the achievement.

My back was aching from bending over for so long and my face was red and perspiring as I tried for what seemed to be an eternity. If he was any example, it must be true about black man, being well endowed. Fortunately, the patient was out of touch with reality and unaware of what was going on. Eventually I declared a time-out and allowed the swelling to subside. Soon after I got the job done without fanfare.

The student enjoyed herself immensely. For the rest of the year every time I saw her she would exclaim in her basso voice, "I'll never forget how gross you looked, trying to put that catheter on!"

Often you will hear it pointed out that the sense of hearing is the last sense to leave the body when death is imminent. That is why it is so important to be careful what we say within hearing range of an unconscious person. However, there is something else that also may hang onto the end—at least in one man. I know of—and that is the sex drive.

One of our elderly stroke patients had a dapper young /old look with his jaunty crewcut and bright blue eyes. He was paralyzed on one side and aphasic (unable to speak.)

Despite frequent turning and skincare. He had developed decubitus ulcers (bed sores.) I was holding him on his side, while the student cleansed and medicated them. Suddenly I felt a pinch on my breast. I looked around but there was no one there. I looked down at my patient. His good hand was still in midair and those penetrating blue eyes were staring up at me. I stroked his cheek and gently told him that he was a dirty old man. He died the next day.

CHAPTER 9

The E.R.

*T*oday modern hospitals have huge, bustling emergency departments with rows of rooms where emergency patients can receive prompt, efficient care using the latest technical life saving equipment and procedures. Some emergency departments are designated trauma centers. There, split second timing and the availability of the best equipment and personnel are crucial factors in saving lives.

Fifty years ago this department consisted of a single room—the emergency room or the E.R. As the time approached for me to begin this student rotation, I again became apprehensive. Did I have the ability to assess and react speedily and skillfully to all the emergencies I would encounter? While it was true that the O.R., which had once loomed ominously in prospect, had become, with knowledge and experience, simple routine, I didn't think the same would be true of the E.R.

Ultimately, I learned that all emergencies could be anticipated and classified. And that there were specific supplies and procedures for each one.

In those relatively quiet times. Most of the violence was taking place overseas. In that small town with a population of forty-five thousand, street drugs were unheard of, lay people didn't carry guns and street brawls were rare. There were fewer cars on the streets and far fewer motorcycles. So the majority of our emergencies were sore throats, ear aches and high fevers.

Students didn't work evenings or nights in the E.R. So maybe we did miss the more exciting incidents but, as it turned out, working in the E.R. also became routine once we learned the ropes.

The most distasteful E.R. task I had to perform was to write up the bill and escort the patient across the lobby to the cashier's office to pay it. The average bill for the use of the E.R. was six dollars. There was no extra charge for the use of the instruments or a Band-Aid. And no separate bill would be forthcoming from a doctor since there was usually no doctor in the E.R. Generally, a telephone consultation was sufficient to define the treatment and resolve the problem.

A quarter of a century later I had a student injure her leg and ruin her pantyhose on a defective bed. By then we had become acutely aware of the power of lawsuits. I could have disinfected her wound and she would have no doubt been fine. But I assumed the hospital would want to protect itself from future liability by examining the injury and documenting it. I even went so far as to expect them to spring for a new pair of pantyhose. Such a gesture tends to promote goodwill and deter legal action.

I sent her to the ER. and she returned a short time later with a Band-Aid and no hose. The incident was forgotten until the following month when she received a bill for eighty dollars. They were kind enough not to charge for the Band-Aid. I made several calls to the E. D. to try to resolve the matter without success. The bills kept coming. Finally I told her to have her husband call them. There seems to be a magical quality to a man's voice—with children, and apparently with

Emergency Departments. I don't know what he said to them, but she never received another bill.

From that experience I learned that hospitals no longer own their emergency departments. Kind of like in the department store, where the shoe department is a concession rather than being owned by the store in which it is located. By the same token, private doctors, own and operate the emergency department in the hospital. It makes for a high degree of efficiency and life saving potential, but has no interest in whether a student nurse is injured by a defective hospital bed and may initiate a lawsuit. I also learned not to send students to the E. R., unless they were covered by insurance. Unless, of course, it was a true emergency.

A few years later in a different hospital I walked into the nursery just in time to see the staff nurses sending one of my students "downstairs." The student had just cut her finger opening a bottle of baby formula.

"NO!" I almost shouted. "Don't send her to emergency!"

"We're not," they assured me. "We're sending her to the employees' Health Nurse"

"O.K., if you're sure she's not going to the E.D."

Unfortunately, the Health Nurse took her to the E. D. and it started all over again—the bills and the unrequited communications. Finally, several weeks later, the matter was resolved. Only then did the Health Nurse, who had remained conspicuously out of sight until then, approach me and say, "Well, I got that little matter straightened out, I was just about to pay the bill myself."

Sure she was.

CHAPTER 10

RELIGION

The hospital where I took my nurses' training was run by the Women's Christian Association. We were required to attend chapel every weekday morning at six A.M. before breakfast, which was also mandatory. Each morning a different student would select two hymns and a prayer to read. Normally the school accepted two classes of students a year, but the year I entered, because of the war, three classes were enrolled. During that time there were seven classes of students in attendance. So our time did not come up often.

I was the only student who wasn't a Christian and, as far as I knew, all but one other were Protestant. So none of them had a problem selecting their favorite hymns and prayers. After thirteen years in public school, I was used to being exposed to all this. But when it was my turn to lead the services I spent a great deal of time seeking out hymns and a prayer that were not antagonistic to my own beliefs. It would never have occurred to me at that time, but now I often wonder how the others would have reacted if I had called for, "Baruch Atau Adonai . . ." Possibly many would have just slept through it. But of course it wasn't in our prayer books.

split up when she told me, "My mother told me I shouldn't room with a Jew!" She quit the course the following year. But when I had my first baby a few years later she came to visit me, and acted like we were old friends. Go figure.

Many of the slights are more subtle, but they inevitably crop up from time to time. When people don't know your religious preference they generally accept you as being more or less like them selves. When they find out that you are Jewish, they may respond that they are shocked and can't believe it—or they may say that they could tell all along. But usually they are shocked because previously you had seemed so normal.

With a generic sounding name like Brown, I often got digs like, "What was your name before you change it?" These people would probably like us to wear a yellow arm band with a Star of David on it to avoid confusion for them. I often longed to marry a man with a name like Goldstein to offset these discussions and preclude hints that I was trying to conceal my identity. Instead I fell in love with someone named Sommer. Oddly, no one ever asked me what my name was before I changed it to Sommer. That would've been easy. It was Brown.

Although the pollsters would have us believe that educated people are less bigoted than uneducated ones, I have not found this to be true. I have heard slurs from people with bachelors and masters' degrees and even some with doctorates. One co-worker invited me to go to a bar with her after work. "I'll buy you a drink," she offered.

While I didn't intend to go, I didn't want to be rude. So to show recognition of her apparent generosity. I replied, "That's very nice of you."

"Isn't that just like a Jew?" She spat back.

After a lifetime of hearing such slurs I am still often caught off guard and without a snappy retort—especially with a room full of her fellow Christians snickering behind their hands. Ironically, she was married to and had three children by a minority person. But then it was just a joke, wasn't it?

I have noticed that those people who are themselves the cheapest are the ones who are the quickest to stereotype all Jews as cheap. They may make a big show of spending money on themselves, but when it comes to giving to charity or helping someone else. They are noticeably absent. This seems to be true of other traits as well, so the name-calling and stereotyping, are really just manifestations of the psychiatric defense mechanism—projection.

The reality is that my religious beliefs are eclectic—derived from a variety of sources over a lifetime. I believe that our true purpose in life is what Jesus taught—to love one another, non-judgmentally. I wish more Christians did. I also believe some of the Eastern precepts such as karma and reincarnation—, e.g., I believe that bigots will eventually be the recipients of the very discrimination they now show. But it will most likely occur in a later incarnation.

Not all incidents of a religious nature are negative. Some are humorous and some are even heartwarming. By the time I began teaching twenty years after I graduated, more Jewish women were entering this proud and noble field. At the community college where I taught practical nursing students, we had several Jewish students. Some were smart and dedicated while others were average and flighty. Some were pretty—others, plain; some were personable—others were introverted; some were nurturing while others were mechanical. In short, they were indistinguishable from their classmates. I was often unaware that they were Jewish until it was pointed out sometime later. Even though some Gentiles are sure we all recognize each other instinctively, and some are sure that we can always tell.

Hal was a senior student with blond, neatly trimmed hair and blue eyes. He was always neatly attired with a dapper blonde mustache. He would have looked right at home in a Hitler youth group. I had never been Hal's clinical instructor but he was in the community health class. I taught one day a week at the college. One day he came into my office and greeted me with, "So your Yiddish!" I had to giggle at this little used idiom. Then he told me his story.

Hal had been born in the United States and raised in the Lutheran Church. But both of his parents had been Jews in Nazi Germany. I don't know what specific atrocities they suffered, but they were eventually interred in one of the concentration camps. After the war they were liberated and immigrated to the United States. Here they started a new life and brought a baby boy into the world. Like all parents everywhere, they wanted their child to have the very best in life and be spared the miseries that they had endured. Because they could never be entirely sure that the same thing could not happen in this country that happened in their once beloved Germany, they joined and hid under the safety of the Lutheran Church.

What a story! I certainly did not feel critical or judgmental of their decision. We must all find our own ways of coping with life's difficult circumstances. As long as, these methods encompass kindness toward others and respect for their ways. I don't think it is anyone else's business. I found it very gratifying that they had raised a fine young man and had not deprived him of the knowledge of his roots.

Not all stereotyping is of a malicious intent. Often it is just the product of years of conditioning. One day I had a guest speaker for my Community Health class. The purpose was to make the students aware of various resources in the community, which were available to help their patients. The speaker was a member of the B'nai B'rith Women and helped administer one of their projects, known as Operation Stork. They obtained and assembled layettes for newborn babies. Whenever we had an indigent patient, a phone call would bring one or two members to the hospital with a complete layette and appropriate oohs and ahs over the beauty and obvious perfection of the very special, brand-new human being. I visited with Dorothy before the class started and learned that she had been born and raised a Christian but had converted to Judaism after her marriage—not an easy path, but one she appeared to have taken successfully.

After the class several students came to share their impressions with me. "She's Jewish, isn't she?" They asked. (Her last name was Goldman.)

"Yes," I replied without embellishment.

"We could tell," they said importantly. I then explained that she was a convert, but they didn't seem to grasp the significance of that. They just kept repeating, "We could tell."

In one of my clinical groups there were several young, naive teenagers. They were compliant and a joy to work with. One day, while waiting for the rest of the group to come off the floor for post-conference, they were discussing the popular TV show 'Welcome Back Kotter' and its star, Gabe Kaplan. "He looks just like my brother-in-law who's Jewish," commented one. "Did you ever notice that all Jewish people look alike?"

It was a benign, innocent remark, but I couldn't resist a little good-natured teasing.

"Yes," I replied. "Just like all black people look alike, and all Oriental and Hispanics."

They began to get a little uneasy. "What about white people?" they asked with their own touch of sarcasm.

"Oh, that's different," I told them. "White people are different because they're regular people." I think they got the point. And it probably got it again when they learned that I was Jewish and, unfortunately, didn't look anything like Gabe Kaplan.

Actually, I was stereotypical looking. I am short with a Roman nose and had black curly hair. Later I became blonde and blew my stereotypical image. But a visit to any synagogue will demonstrate that the percentage of the congregation with these features is about the same as society in general. My father was a handsome Irish looking man, but I inherited my genes with these characteristics from my mother's family, who were French.

One thing that makes me very nervous is when a student or any healthcare worker makes a comment like, "If he would just put himself in God's hands, God would take the illness away." This is usually said in reference to mental illnesses as if they are less legitimate than physical illnesses. If it were that easy to resolve illnesses our jobs would be unnecessary. And such an attitude can have a devastating effect on the patient, who is put in a position of having caused his own illness through lack of faith.

Another attitude I find unconscionable is when health professionals foist their own beliefs on patients. I have seen nurses put crosses on the cribs of non-Christian babies and even baptize them. And that was in a Jewish hospital. I don't personally feel that it hurts the baby but it is denigrating to the family and to the oldest, longest lasting religion in the world. Wouldn't it be a great beginning to peace on earth if we could all just show respect for each others' beliefs? Barring that concept it would be wise not to work in an institution where the beliefs are not compatible with your own or at least within your area of tolerance.

One of my classmates was Catholic. It didn't seem to make any difference during our training years, but after graduation, she married and swore at the altar that they would never use contraception. In time they had twenty-one children—a devastating idea for those of us who had problems raising two or three. She developed a chronically tired look and bad varicosities. But their marriage lasted nearly a half century and all their children grew into responsible adults, not bad for an orphan.

I had a young nursing student who was a nun. The traditional habits had already been given up in many orders and she wore street clothes, much like those of her classmates. She wore a wedding band but many of our students were married. While she was in my OB rotation. We had some opportunities to visit. I learned that after graduation, she would obtain a nursing position, live in her own apartment and budget her salary to her needs. I was still trying to adjust to the idea that nuns had shed their habits and wore street clothes. What would protect them from muggers and rapists I wondered? I was still naive enough to believe that these deviants would have some respect for a woman of God.

As the students and I chatted about her future. I learned that her life would be much like everyone else's except that she would never marry. I remembered a friend of mine who had a retarded child. His behavior was obstreperous and disruptive and it eventually became necessary to place him in an institution. She and her husband made an extensive search and finally placed him in a Catholic home where he would be enfolded in the bosoms of loving nuns who devoted their lives too caring for children like him. That, I felt, was a noble calling—lives truly devoted to God's work. But I couldn't equate this perception with the projected lifestyle of my student.

"How can you be a nun when you are living an ordinary lifestyle?" I persisted in my search for enlightenment.

"I pledged to devote my life to God."

"But what you do after you get off duty? In the evening when ordinary people watch TV?"

"Yes, we can watch TV."

It still remains a mystery to me. Even today it is an enigma. But as societal deviance continues to increase, I have concluded that anyone who can lead a pure and chaste life in these troubled times may, indeed, be pious.

Two of our students were elderly nuns from a cloistered order. They wore old-fashioned habits and I wondered, how they would handle their OB rotation where they would be required to wear 'scrubs.' They were not in any of my OB groups, but it was apparently no problem for them. They wore the scrub dresses and covered their heads with the scrub caps. They were probably more comfortable than they had been in years.

The sisters were not adept at learning theory, and it took them two or three years to complete the one-year program. But they more than made up for their lack of acumen with their cheerfulness, cooperative spirit and good humor. And their devotion to bringing the faculty home-baked rolls and other goodies made their graduation day a little sad

Their goal was to be able to care for the elderly nuns of their convent in their final years. One of them even shared my name—which is really 'Carita'—kind of neat bond between a Catholic nun and a Jewish woman. They were sixty-two and seventy-two years old when they graduated and began their new careers—ages at which I was looking forward to retirement.

I was a little apprehensive when I was assigned to teach OB students in a Catholic hospital. I didn't want to be in a situation where a mother's life might be sacrificed to save her baby. In the five years I worked there. The choice never arose and was probably less likely than being hit by a tornado. In fact the hospital actually was directly in the path of the worst tornado the city had ever had. The OB floor was one of the hardest hit. The nurses did a fantastic job of leading the patients to safety—especially in the self-care unit, which was demolished seconds after the last patient was evacuated.

My fears were reversed when I noted that, not only were the mothers not jeopardize in the interests of the babies, but the babies were put at risk to enhance the mothers' comfort as the mothers were administered excessive amounts of narcotics during labor. This will be elaborated more in a later chapter.

The Head Nurse in the L&D department was an ex-nun. She was a dignified, responsible young woman with a quiet, mature manner. I always treated her as if she were still a nun. Apparently that was unnecessary.

One day one of her staff nurses popped up with a comment, "My husband called me a dumb shit last night." I flinched and threw a sidelong glance at the ex-nun to see if she was in a state of shock. Her face was inscrutable for a long, frozen moment in time. And then she responded.

"That's what my husband calls me all the time—a dumb shit." So much for special treatment.

Although being black is not a religion. It has had an even more devastating effect on the treatment of some of my colleagues. In the fifties when we would all go out to dinner together for a special occasion, someone would have to call all of the restaurants under consideration in advance to find out which ones served 'coloreds.' It was heart wrenching. These women were our friends and, like us, were gals in a proud profession. It is a black mark on our great country that such practices ever existed. To our credit we have legislated them away. But like anti-Semitism, the more subtle discriminations cannot be legislated out of existence. A true professional will not use crude language like Nigger and Coon, but I have heard demeaning remarks referring to them as 'the minorities.'

Will it take a nuclear holocaust to erase the delineating boundaries of race, religion and color?

CHAPTER 11

ANTIBIOTICS

*L*ucky strike green and the RNs were not the only ones that had gone to war. Commodities like meat and sugar had to be rationed. None-essentials like silk and metals were non-existent at home. They were needed to make parachutes and airplanes. We didn't mind. We loved our country and strongly supported our 'boys' on the front. They were fighting the war to end all wars. When it was over, we would all live happily ever after.

They say you can't miss what you never had. Not true. We had never had penicillin but we sure did miss it. We did have sulfonamides, but some infections were beyond the scope of sulfa. People died every day from infections like peritonitis, mastoiditis and osteomyelitis. When we watched our patients die and knew that penicillin could have saved them, we truly mourned the loss of something we never had.

Brownie was a patient with chronic, recurring osteomyelitis. The senior nursing students knew Brownie well. He had been coming to the hospital for treatment during all the years that they had been there. They cried every time that he was admitted. "If only we had penicillin we could save Brownie," they would weep. But we needed all the penicillin that could be manufactured on the battlefields for our boys. We at home would have to wait until the war ended for the wonder drug.

But alas poor Brownie couldn't wait any longer. He succumbed during an acute episode, leaving a pall on the student body. I hardly knew Brownie, even though we shared the same name. But I will always remember the sorrow of the seniors who lost him for want of a few doses of penicillin.

Today penicillin is so commonplace that it's almost boring. People think that it's a panacea and demand it for everything even though it is completely ineffective against viruses. Sometimes it can be a killer. People who develop an allergy to it may die of a single dose. One woman insisted that her doctor give it to her for a cold. He knew it wouldn't help, but he was tired of arguing and complied. The result was an anaphylactic reaction, and death.

But we should not regard penicillin as a villain. It is still a hero. Our old enemies—syphilis and gonorrhea—curled up and almost died in the face of the new wonder drug, just in time for the sexual revolution.

When I was teaching Community Health the only teaching films, I had access to were old and outdated. The subject matter was still current but the students didn't take them seriously because the dress lengths and hairstyles were so passé. One day at a Health Fair I saw a newly released V.D. film, narrated by James Brolin, who was a hot T.V. idol at the time. "How can I borrow that film?" I asked the nurse in the booth.

"Just ask me to be your guest speaker and I'll bring it with me," she replied agreeably. That sounded great and that is just what I did.

On the day of her presentation she came in five minutes late, strolled to the front of the classroom and lit a cigarette. The students were appalled and later told me they didn't like her because her fingernails were dirty. I was reasonably certain they couldn't see her fingernails from where she was sitting but rather were shocked by her lack of professionalism.

She told them how to recognize a chancre and even mentioned the second stage of syphilis, which is characterized by a rash. Then she added, "There used to be a third stage, but with penicillin, nobody gets to that stage anymore." Then she showed the video. It seemed the James Brolin film was out on loan. So she brought, instead, one of the old relics that I had been trying to get away from.

Now I was the one that was shocked. The whole point was that too many people fail to get treatment after the rash abates spontaneously. And then the third stage is inevitable with all its horrible lifelong complications. After the first and second stages disappear without treatment, it is all too easy for the victim to deny the whole thing. Seeking treatment is absolutely essential. Even now in the middle of the AIDS epidemic, syphilis and gonorrhea are still with us, along with several other sexually transmitted diseases.

In time the spirochete and the gonococcus did become resistant to penicillin, but stronger doses took care of the problem. And there are dozens of new antibiotics for organisms that have become resistant to penicillin.

Because of the new miracle drugs, people became complacent about the war against germs. Some didn't bother washing their hands as often or as well. Hot packs and stupes became almost nonexistent.

In the beginning penicillin had to be given intramuscularly every four hours around the clock. By the time I reached my pediatric rotation in training the war was over and we had penicillin at last. The first day I had to give medicines in Peds was a nightmare. Almost all the children were getting penicillin. Trying to talk to each child into turning over for his shot took so long that, by the time I finished one round, it

The seven of us shared an apartment which consisted of two bedrooms with a bath between them. Sharing a bathroom became very touchy at times—like Saturday nights when everybody was getting ready for dates. While we had shared bathrooms in our home school, they were large dormitory baths with multiple booths and everyone went in at the same time. This was a small, private bathroom where one went in alone and locked the door. It was unfortunate that I chose a Saturday night to try my first tampon and, finding it more troublesome than I had anticipated, spent forty-five minutes and there were six classmates pounding angrily on both doors.

Our meals were taken in a large, community dining room, which served several shifts of employees and students. Since we were on duty from five forty-five a.m. until seven p.m. with four hours off during the day, our mealtimes varied with our work schedule. Breakfast was first served at seven thirty a.m. after we had been on duty for some time and were ravenous. We were not disappointed with breakfast. Bacon and eggs were no longer strangers to each other. There was more food than we could ever dream of the eating.

Because this was a state hospital and most of the patients did not pay for their care (and, of course, to enhance their treatment) many were given regular jobs. One of these jobs was providing a service to the students' apartments. Our maid never spoke to us although she carried on a running conversation with her hallucinations. She always had a very short cigarette butt between her lips. We never saw her with a fresh cigarette or even a half-smoked one. That Christmas we presented her with a carton of cigarettes. But still we never saw her with anything but the familiar butt. We had no idea where she got them or what she did with the carton we gave her.

In the dining room the patients did all the cooking and serving. I had never before seen such an abundance of food. Huge platters heaped high. Steaks and potatoes and vegetables were brought to each table. When the platters were half empty, they were removed to the kitchen to be refilled and returned to the tables. Like the bacon and eggs, pie and ice cream, and other familiar food combinations were once again united. No more of the either/or we were used too in our home hospital.

Most of the food came from the state-owned farm located on the property adjoining the hospital complex—with labor, of course, provided by the patients. The result was an abundance of food and service that was very satisfying. Until then, we had provided all the nurturing and received little in return.

In addition to all this luxury, the house mother at the residence went home at eight P.M. and we were on our own. No more locked doors, if we were thirty seconds late for curfew. Many times we would stay out all night, coming home just in time to shower, don our uniforms and report on duty. We were young, often in love, and could handle missing a night's sleep. And there was time off in the middle of the day (which we could now count on) to catch a nap.

The nearest town was just a few miles away with a movie theater, bowling alley, stores and a bus station—if perchance we wished to leave this paradise for a visit home. While it was a long walk, the townspeople were used to the ever-changing variety of nursing students and offered us rides before we had walked very far. In those simple times it was safe to accept a ride in the rural Midwest. In this way, my girlfriend and I met brothers fell in love with them. While we were getting acquainted, I kept thinking, "I want Dale. What if she likes him too?" Later she told me she was thinking the same thing, only about Walt. The brothers reached a similar conclusion and we were paired off in mutual harmony. For the next several months, we struggled with, and were eventually defeated by, the vast differences in all our religions. But I will always remember Dale, my first love, with the deepest affection. He made that period of my life a very special time—unencumbered by any sense of shame or regret. So pure was his love that it was never necessary to defend my honor. We maintain a loving relationship without any compromise of virtue—something I thought was important at the time, and still do, even though the other guys told me all my friends were 'doing it.' I never believed them even though four of my classmates were pregnant at graduation.

My girlfriend and I both married other men but from that time on, we always called each other 'sister-in-law'—something our husbands never understood.

One of my first patients at the State Hospital was a motherly, middle-aged woman. Much of our time was spent just sitting and talking with the patients. This lady was always weepy as she told me how she and her husband owned and operated a motel and how much he needed her to help him. It was too hard for him by himself. She couldn't understand why she was not allowed to go home and help him.

I was indignant all over again that evening as I told my roommates about the poor woman's dilemma. Most of these 'crazy' people didn't seem crazy at all. Each day we played pinochle and cribbage (which they taught us) with them it became increasingly more difficult to understand why they were being kept locked up.

Then, as the moon waxed, the 'natives' began to get restless. Our motel lady stopped weeping and began singing. She sang the same song over and over. At first it sounded like "By the Shade of the Old Apple Tree," but careful listening revealed that she was providing original lyrics:

> "By the shade of the old Apple tree
> When he turned his ass up to me . . ."

The words got dirtier as the song continued, and she became increasingly restless.

By the time the moon was full we had learned to deposit her dinner tray on the table, leave the room and close the door behind us very quickly. That way, the tray and its contents would hit the door rather than our head when she hurled it back at us.

As the moon waned she began to quiet down and was soon ensconced in the day-room lamenting her incarceration.

I was startled one day when a patient, looking askance, told me, "I know what you girls are. You're fairies."

"Really," I retorted. "How do you know that?"

"I saw what you do."

"What do we do?"

"I saw you open the window and fly away."

Elizabeth was a shapeless, drab looking woman with leathery skin and dull, sandy colored hair. Even dullar then her hair were her blank, staring eyes. Elizabeth never spoke and rarely moved. She stood or sat where-ever we put her and appeared to live in a world apart.

Her sole purpose in life seemed to be waiting for the twice daily calls of "Rosalie" from a fellow patient. At that Elizabeth would get up and take the other patient to the bathroom. It remained a mystery how they had arrived at this understanding, as both of them were profoundly withdrawn, or why Elizabeth would respond to the name Rosalie.

One day, when the patients were napping and the chores had been completed, I sat down to read Elizabeth's chart and case history. By so doing, my sensitivities were awakened to the worth and dignity to which these people were entitled. Elizabeth had a long history of psychiatric problems and had consulted several psychiatrists over a period of years.

When Elizabeth was young, she had fallen in love with a married man. It was the era of World War I and Elizabeth had internalized a strict moral code. She had tried to break off her adulterous affair many times and eventually succeeded. But she apparently could not reconcile her conscience to what she had done. Over the years, Elizabeth had retreated deeper and deeper within herself.

What was most amazing about Elizabeth's history was her psychiatrists' reactions to her. The chart contained documents of five different psychiatrists. Each of these presumably wise and austere men, who must have seen and heard everything in their professional capacities, felt compelled to describe the stunning beauty of the young patient, detailing her flaming red hair, flawless complexion and gorgeous figure.

It was difficult to picture our drab Elizabeth as that exceedingly attractive young woman. She could surely have and any man she chose. Poor Elizabeth had been born fifty years too soon—before the sexual revolution—and had chosen unwisely. As a penance for her choice she had relinquished her life and her beauty for this nonexistence. No court of law could have meted out so severe a punishment. Elizabeth had chosen her own form of self-imprisonment.

Often the schizophrenics were adept at 'word salad' and nonsense rhymes. One memorable one became incorporated into our family mores when we were trying to rush each other along:

'SKO

S—K—O

Fifty fo 'and Baltimo'

B—A—L—T—I—M—O.

Few were that clean.

The underground tunnel system was a confusing maze, poorly lit, and crossing and crisscrossing to connect a dozen or so buildings.

Because it was spooky and scary, we only used it when necessary. So it was some time before I learned where to turn off for each building. One day I had to transfer a patient via a stretcher to another building. I was sure that I remembered the way. They sent along two male patients to push the cart. All I had to do was carry the chart.

As we made our way along the dark tunnel, I was unable to engage the men in conversation. Nor did they talk to each other. They just lumbered along with a single-minded purpose—getting that Gurney to its specified destination.

I reviewed the itinerary in my mind and, as we approach what I thought was the correct turn-off, I cheerfully called out, "Here we are, fellows. This is where we turn." And turn I did. The men didn't respond. Looking neither right nor left, they just kept plodding along in the direction they had been going. Suddenly I realized I was going the wrong way. I ran back and caught up with them and meekly followed them, the rest of the way to our rightful destination.

There was more going on in those minds than anyone realized.

One of the buildings on the campus was a general store. The town was too far away to run out for a tube of toothpaste or a package of gum. So to break the monotony or satisfy our need to shop we would drop in and visit with Blackie, the mild-mannered, genial manager. In time, we learned that twenty years earlier Blackie had killed his wife and cut her up into little pieces.

All the patients who received electroconvulsive therapy knew that when Dr. Cans entered the ward. It was 'shock day.' Shock day came twice a week and they feared it like the black plague. They would follow the doctor's long stride down the hall, hanging on his coattails and sleeves and throwing their arms around his legs, crying, "No, Dr. Cans," and "Please, Dr. Cans."

language in their former, sane life. These tip of the iceberg expletives denoted tremendous repressed stress. But, young as we were, we just thought it was funny.

In the entire complex of twelve hundred patients, there were only a handful of RN's. There were numerous students from hospitals in the state and bordering states on their three-month psych rotations who were there to work with and learn about the patients. But the attendants ran the wards.

Then came the Senior Cadet Students. For the first time ever they were grooming us to be in charge of the wards. What would the attendants think of that? How would they react when they would be answerable to the student nurses? Whatever they thought they didn't let on. In fact, they continued to run the wards as usual. A bunch of green students, we weren't likely to challenge them, especially when we saw how successfully they reigned.

Military order prevailed on the wards. The patients lined up to go to meals and receive medications. Sometimes they would store the medicine in the back of the cheek and spit it out later. But it was done very unobtrusively and, on the surface, discipline reigned supreme. When psychiatrists proclaimed that punishment is not an effective deterrent to unacceptable behavior, they only proved that they did not spend any time observing what went on those wards.

Case in point: One totally withdrawn little man was not shuffling along fast enough in the dinner line one day to suit the attendant, who doubled up his fist and hit the little fellow in the eye. A hemorrhagic spot appeared on the sclera of his eye—proof that an injury had occurred. To cover himself, the attendant wrote up an accident report, which stated, "The patient was lying in bed, staring up at the ceiling when a piece of plaster fell into his eye." Since the patient never spoke, the attendant was never confronted and that ridiculous excuse, went unchallenged. One of the women's attendants used to wear a garden hose draped around her neck. If a patient wasn't eating, she would threaten to "ram this down your throat" if she didn't eat. As if it were a mammoth feeding tube. Sometimes she would cram a whole tomato or hard-boiled egg into a patient's mouth and stand over her menacingly until the poor lady somehow managed to dispose of the mouthful. What was this all about—this attendant's concern for her patients' nutrition? It was about power. These people craved power.

In a more carefree moment this attendant would grab a patient and screech, "Tell me you love me, God damn it, and give me a big old kiss." You can't tell the patients from the care-givers without a program, (or a uniform) folks.

It was a pleasure to be one of the ones carrying the keys (all of the wards were locked) and, I must confess, gave us a taste of that sweet sense of power. But we students were always kind to the patients. We became like parents to them, settling their minor disputes and helping them resolve major problems like, "How can I go to dinner when I have to stay here and worry about my problems?" For that particular problem I had convinced the patient that I would worry about them for her while she ate. But at the last minute she decided that I wouldn't do it. Meals were not an incentive. In contrast to our excellent cuisine, their meals were all an overcooked, mushy stew.

But the order that was maintained on the wards was directly attributable to the attendants. The only problem was—the patients didn't get well.

One of the buildings in the complex was a hospital. After all, a psychosis doesn't protect the patient from physical illness. There was even an operating room in the hospital where minor surgery could be done.

Our patient, Ella Mae, was a respectable married woman with a husband and four children at home. She was psychotic but she was also pregnant. And on this particular day, she was in labor.

By that time I was the charge nurse on the ward. At that point I didn't know that in the near future, I would become a reasonably competent labor and delivery nurse. I only knew that I didn't feel at all qualified to oversee this delivery.

In fact the RN supervisor was to take over during the delivery itself. All I had to do was to get her there at the right time. Ella Mae's contractions were increasing in frequency and duration. When the supervisor stopped by to tell me she was going to dinner. I told her that the patient would be ready to deliver very soon. I wasn't qualified to do a rectal exam to determine how fast her cervix was dilating. The RN didn't check her either and made a nasty comment about how I was unnecessarily nervous.

By the time she returned from dinner nearly an hour later Ella Mae had been bearing down so hard that her face was blue. I told the RN to get her up to the OR, where the delivery was planned to take place, right away.

The RN was really disgusted with me now. "She's not ready," she spat at me. "But I'll take her just to shut you up." We moved her onto a Gurney and the supervisor pushed her through the door and out of the ward, much to my relief. But before I had finished changing the linens on her bed. The supervisor was back wheeling Ella Mae into her room. "Do you mean she wasn't ready?" I asked incredulously.

"She delivered in the elevator," Was the disgusted reply. Sure enough, Ella Mae was cradling a baby in her arms. Whew! A close call for me.

Having a new baby on the ward was an absolute blessing. Ella Mae was still withdrawn and didn't participate much in her care. But the other patients and personnel alike loved taking care of her. In that dolorous atmosphere, she brought us a message of new beginnings and bright tomorrows.

Ella Mae was one of the few patients at the State Hospital that I saw recover and be released to go home. She lived in the same city where I have now lived for more than thirty years. I often think of her and wonder if I have ever passed her on the street—or her baby, who would now be a woman in her forties. I hope with all my heart that Ella Mae was able to conquer her demons completely and permanently. For what could be more befitting for a new beginning then a happy ending?

Our youngest patient was a little thirteen-year-old girl. One of the patients on her ward took her under her wing and acted as a mother image, fixing her hair in Shirley Temple curls so she would look like the little girl she was. Several times she was caught in the underground tunnels 'consorting' with men. By the time we left, our little thirteen-year-old girl was pregnant.

The names of the wards didn't necessarily seem appropriate for the patients that inhabited them. I never saw anyone convalesce in the Women's Convalescence Ward. Nor did I ever see anyone violent on the Violent Ward. However, one patient did give me some bad moments on that ward. While I was in her room, she grabbed my fountain pen out of my pocket, ran out of the room and positioned herself against the door so I couldn't get out.

The patients' rooms didn't have locks but she was stronger and huskier than I was and I couldn't budge it. I felt helpless knowing she had a dangerous weapon in her possession (my fountain pen.) But a few minutes later she released me and returned my fountain pen, laughing heartily. She had only been kidding around.

Our six months ended all too quickly. I understood psychoses so much better than when we had just read about in a textbook. We have made some good friends with some of the other students and had some wonderful times. We had lived in an adult world and functioned as adults. We had made it! And now we were going to go home, pass the state boards and become RN's

Twenty-five years later when I read of state institutions releasing hundreds of patients, I was incredulous. While it was true, the psychotropic drugs were an innovation in the field they weren't a panacea.

I remembered our psychiatric patients of the forties and I couldn't see how they could have been cured. And the patients that we had worked with had been the good ones. We had toured the back wards where the patients received only custodial care. Hundreds of patients sat on padded chairs in fetal positions, wearing only a camisole. Two aides wove up and down the aisles. One would lift each patient while the other one changed the soiled pad. When they had gone through the whole room, it was time to start over. This pattern continued until nighttime, when the patients were put back in the beds.

How could 700 of these patients have been released from a state hospital, which now boasted a population of fewer than 500 patients.

In time there were answers to some of these questions. Many of the patients were merely transferred to nursing homes where their custodial care continued and their mental status remained unchanged. Most of the rest of them are living on the streets, grossly swelling our vast army of homeless people—with no one to see that they take their medications or see their doctors, much less have food and shelter. Someone has finally seen to it that the psychotics have their rights.

Case in point: in 1992 the college football hero was riding around in a car with two teammates. Suddenly he began to beat one of them up. The other one left to get help. Then, the first man got away and went to help his friend look for assistance.

When they return to the scene, the hero had removed his clothes and was beating up a young woman who had been out walking her dog. He was pounding her head against the sidewalk. She would be in a coma for a long time and would never completely recover from the assault.

In court the football hero was found not guilty by reason of insanity. He was hospitalized, released and advised to take his medication and see his counselor once a week. Soon he was feeling better and didn't think he needed any more medication. So he stopped taking the medication and canceled two appointments with his counselor.

In a short time another incident occurred. The football hero tried to hurl his naked body through a plate glass window. The police arrived and attempted to stop him. He grabbed for one of the officer's gun and was shot in the scuffle. The bullets damaged his spinal cord and he is permanently paralyzed. He will never play football again. He will be in a wheelchair for the rest of his life.

Many people were very angry about the treatment of their hero. The police officers were both women. They think they should have sent men. They think they should have spoken to him softly. They should be given a course in how to handle psychotics. (They were.) They shouldn't have shot their hero.

The woman he battered recovered somewhat, and married her fiancé, who had stuck by her throughout her ordeal. She later accused him of embezzling her money and they eventually divorced. There were no winners.

Shakespeare was wrong. "All the world is not a stage." All the world is a psych ward. And the people are not actors. They are psych patients—or attendants. But you can't tell the difference without a program, folks—or a uniform.

Nurses are not immune to the problems suffered by other psychiatric patients. Statistics show that the two groups of people at highest risk for developing a psychosis are nurses and teachers. Since I was a nursing instructor for twenty years, I figure I was in double jeopardy. I feel fortunate to have avoided it. (I did, didn't I?). Maybe that unscheduled electro-shock treatment helped.

One of our patients at the state hospital used to stand in the middle of the day room all day, every day screaming, "Stop that! Stop that awful stuff!" She had been a public school teacher. Imagine if she were teaching today!

The learned scientists are now removing some of the blame for Psychoses from the environment and placing it where it rightfully belongs—on the individual's body chemistry. This is especially true of schizophrenia and manic depression (also called bipolar disease.) But studies done on identical twins showed that, in some situations, one twin living in a sheltered, protective environment may escape a psychosis while the twin living in a stressful existence may succumb to it. Thus Nature, in her infinite wisdom, insists upon a delicate balance between nature and nurture.

The choice of a career in nursing fosters an environment which is fertile for triggering a response in those who are addiction prone. I have known several nurses who were narcotic addicts—not the type that steals and sell their bodies for street drugs, but kind of addicts that will steel a narcotic from a patient and substitute a placebo. Sometimes they become addicted in the same way that many lay people do—by well-meaning or careless doctors who prescribe a narcotic for pain and continue to allow the prescription to be renewed long after the initial need is over. Sometimes the patient will become addicted in the first week following surgery just as an alcoholic will sometimes become addicted with his first alcoholic drink. Nurses also become alcoholics, at the same rate as the general population—one out of every ten.

One of our OB nurses who worked the evening shift would listen to report and then keep visiting with us, obviously reluctant to let us leave. Perspiration would drip from her face and her whole body would tremble, but her eyes would beg us to stay a while longer. We knew that she was addicted and we presumed that she wanted to put off that first 'fix' of the day as long as possible. And of course she couldn't take it while anyone was with her.

Jan was a personable, complacent woman who would do anything for her patients and friends. Who would want to blow the whistle on someone like that, nobody—except maybe the patient who got the placebo instead of the analgesic she needed for pain? But the authorities already knew about her and were gathering evidence. Eventually, she faced a decision—to enter a treatment center or lose her nursing license. We never saw her again. Because she was an intelligent, well-meaning person we were hopeful that she had made the right choice and did not come back to her old job because of embarrassment. And that she continues to recover and lead a healthy, productive life.

No matter how nice the nurse is, the patient always suffers when the nurse is addicted. In that same era and the same small hospital, I was alone on the floor with one student at lunchtime one day. Trays were waiting to be passed and doctors were making rounds. At that time nurses always made rounds with the doctors so they could assist them with changing dressings, removing sutures and other procedures. It was also useful to witness what the patient told the doctor and what he had promised her so that when the patient told her version later you knew exactly what had transpired. In later years, nurses stoped making rounds with doctors as part of the process of losing the 'hand maiden' image. Even what is more important, nurses have ever increasing duties and responsibilities as well as mountains of paperwork. Making rounds with doctors would be a severe imposition on their limited time.

But at that time we still had to work rounds into our busy schedules. So when the recovery room called and said that they were bringing our surgical patient back to the floor at that inopportune time, I asked them to hold her for a while longer. They agreed to do so, but five minutes later her Gurney was being pushed through the door and she was yelling at the top of their lungs. In frustration, I snapped at the orderly, "You were supposed to keep her up there for a few more minutes!"

"We would have." He replied amiably. "But she needs something for pain and the nurse with the narcotic key is at lunch." It sounded like a lame excuse, but I didn't have time to argue. I hastily flipped the chart open to the doctor's order sheet, read the order and hurriedly prepared a shot of Demerol and administered it to our noisy patient.

In a few minutes, the patient was resting quietly, when I went to chart the medication I saw that one had been charted just forty-five minutes earlier, the order clearly stated that the Demerol should not be repeated oftener than every three hours. I was furious—with the orderly for lying to me—but mostly with myself for taking his word and not checking for myself. That was the last time I ever made that mistake.

That was a lot of Demerol for patient to receive within such a short period of time and, while she did not appear to be having any side effects, I needed to notify a doctor of the medication error. I called the doctor in surgery and told him what had happened. "I wouldn't worry about it," was his uncharacteristically mild response. "Just watch her respirations and let me know if you have any problems." I was puzzled that everyone was being so nonchalant. At the very least I had expected a stern rebuke.

The patient never had any problems and made a normal recovery. Two months later we learned through the hospital grapevine that a nurse in the Recovery Room had been fired for stealing narcotics from patients and substituting placebos. No one can hide this horrible affliction for long. Everyone around her knew what was going on. Perhaps our unfortunate incident had furnished the proof they had needed to bring the matter to a climax.

Manic depressives are generally friendly, extroverted people who, with proper treatment, can make a good adjustment to life. Because they are not inhibited, several of our nursing students revealed to us that they were manic depressive. Controlled with lithium carbonate, they are indistinguishable from their classmates. Without medication they often exhibit erratic behavior. One student told me that when she wanted to buy a lot of new clothes she would go off her medication. She knew she could then count on herself to go on a spending spree and buy lots of new things.

Connie, another student, was bright and attractive with a cheerful, outgoing personality. One of the theory classes I taught was Psychiatric Aspects of Nursing. Many of our students found this class personally threatening and had a difficult time with it. So I always offered them options for getting extra credit—a book report, a field trip, a research paper or an oral report to the class.

Connie asked me if she could give a report to the class on her own condition—she was a manic depressive. I told her I thought that should be very interesting for the students.

On the day that Connie was to give a report, she came to my office at 8:00 A.M. she wanted to give me an idea of what she was going to say. She talked nonstop until ten o'clock when the class started.

In the classroom she began again and delivered a well-thought out dissertation, stressing that she now realized that her father was also a manic depressive, and that she had inherited the condition from him. She added that lithium carbonate was the key to treatment. It was a simple matter of determining the lithium level in the body, and then administering the amount needed to normalize that level. She continued at a frantic pace for about an hour and a half, citing anecdotes and analyzing them. One of the students raised her hand and asked pleadingly, "Connie, could we have a break?" We were required by the State Board of Nursing, to give our students a ten minute break every hour and they had become accustomed to it. Sometimes, like Connie, we would have liked to have continued talking, but we always pause for the break. But Connie wasn't bound by our rules and regulations. And besides, she was on a roll.

"Sure, sure, just let me say one more thing," Connie countered and continued on. At noon the class filed out en masse to lunch and Connie was forced to stop.

Unfortunately, Connie remained 'wound up' and soon had to be hospitalized. Her hospitalization period was a stormy one. At one time she escaped and was found wandering down a main thoroughfare in her hospital nightgown. Ironically, she was released soon after that and eventually returned to her classes.

Connie's allegation that a simple adjustment of the lithium level was all that she needed to normalize behavior did not hold true in this case. Never again did she appear to come down to earth. She would stop me in the hall for "just a minute "and talk right through lunch period. She would relate tales of incidents that occurred with her husband that displayed a total lack of insight into her erratic behavior.

Once I asked her if she thought that telling her story to the class had anything to do with precipitating her psychotic episode. She said that it had definitely set her off. She told me that she had never before looked within herself or analyzed her experiences or behavior. Manic Depressives are usually extroverted and not prone to introspection. The experience had been a tremendous jolt, which had a profound effect which she couldn't seem to shake.

Finally Connie's desperate husband divorced her and was given custody of their young son. I hope it made him as sad as it made me. Connie had finished her nursing course by then and obtained her license. Soon after that she left town. It was like the extinguishing of a bright flame. I can only hope that Connie was eventually able to conquer her inner demons and put her life together again.

The onset of a postpartum psychosis can occur any time from one to twenty-eight days following delivery. It is rarely seen in the hospital, especially in these times of early dismissal, when the euphoric hormones of pregnancy have not yet been eliminated from the body of the new mother. But two memorable cases do come to mind.

The first patient was a classical case with clear-cut etiology and symptoms. Mrs. Shemp was a Catholic woman, married, and the mother of six children. She was Rh negative and Rho Gam was not yet on the market. Her last four children had all received exchange transfusions after delivery to treat erythroblastosis Fetalis. (See chapters on OB) Her doctor had admitted her to the hospital to do an early Cesarean Section (more recently referred to as Cesarean Birth) to prevent further damage to the fetus.

The first few days of her hospitalization were to be for rest, which any mother of six can verify is a necessity—not a luxury. During this time, the father of the baby was a faithful visitor. Then we learned that this man was not her husband, nor the father of her other six children.

This information brought the potential for good news. If this man should happen to be Rh negative, the baby would also be Rh negative and would have no problems. Even if he were positive there was still the possibility of a negative baby. We requested permission from Dr. Krum to send him to the lab to be tested.

As usual, Dr. Krum knew better than "we girls." He said that the last four babies had to be transfused and therefore, this one would too. He insisted that he would proceed with the surgery as planned. The hapless Mrs. Schemp was just a few years ahead of the modern miracle that has all but resolved the Rh incompatibility problem. A few years later she would have been able to have an amniocentesis which would have determined whether or not the fetus was in trouble. But at least she had been able to have the advantage of the exchange transfusions, which undoubtedly saved her children's lives.

On the morning of surgery, we went to the OR with a pint of Rh negative, type O blood and the equipment necessary to administer the exchange transfusion stat. To our delight, but not our complete surprise, the baby was pink and healthy with a lusty cry. Her only problem was her below average size because she had been delivered four weeks prematurely. As a post Cesarean patient Mrs. Shemp would remain in the hospital for seven days—longer than the three-day stay we see now, but less than the ten-day average stay of a few years earlier. By the third post partum day she began displaying classical symptoms of schizophrenia. Her eyes darted back and forth when we spoke to her and she picked at the bedcovers. She had no memory of having had the baby and was suspicious of everyone who came into her room. When the baby's father came to visit, she refused to talk to or to even look at him.

For maximum safety we decided that she should never be left alone with the baby. We thought that, since she had already delivered six babies and was familiar with hospital routine, that she surely would find it strange when someone stayed in the room the entire time she had the baby with her. Instead, she seemed to welcome our presence as though she also feared that she might harm her.

We reported her symptoms to Dr. Krumb and requested a psychiatric consultation. Dr. Krum proclaimed that Mrs. Shemp was fine and didn't need a consultation. On the day of her dismissal, we did manage to persuade the doctor to let us keep the baby on the basis of her premie status.

Baby girl Shemp was too healthy to keep for long and soon her dismissal day also arrived. The baby's father came in his truck, and a few minutes later Mrs. Shemp arrived by cab. She sat on the other side of the room from him while we relayed the doctor's instructions, refusing to look at him or answer when he spoke to her. They left the hospital in separate vehicles.

We had no idea where Mrs. Shemp's husband was or who had charge of the six older children, but it seemed clear that she was having a rough time with her conscience. Her Catholic upbringing did not prepare her for the transition from being a faithful wife and mother of long-standing to having an adulterous affair and the baby out of wedlock. With the added trauma of surgery and concern for the baby's well-being it was just more than her psyche could deal with.

We wondered if we would ever learn the outcome of this real-life soap opera since Dr. Krum was not likely to share this information with us. Eventually we saw Mr. And Mrs. Shemp's names listed in the divorce column of the local newspaper. Sometime later it was noted that Mrs. Shemp and the baby's father had obtained a marriage license.

These people were not young, movie star—like sex symbols. Rather, they were middle-aged, plain, lower middle class, ordinary people. But they have needs and feelings universal to all of us. We could only hope

CHAPTER 13

GRADUATION

*G*raduation day arrived at last, after three long, difficult years. It was a crisp January day—too cold to have the ceremony on the lawn as was the tradition. It was still impressive with each of us carrying a Florence Nightingale lamp. We each received a diploma—no degree and no license to practice nursing. We were graduate—not registered—nurses. To become registered and licensed to practice nursing in our state, we had to first pass state boards.

State boards were administered in the state capital. There were three grueling eight-hour days of written tests to look forward to. It was terrifying to contemplate. On a bitter cold day in February the fifteen girls in our graduation class boarded a train for the capital city, where we would join graduate nurses from all over the state to write boards. I was becoming more nervous with each passing hour. There were no state board review books to study from at that time. So I brought along several textbooks from the most difficult courses and studied during the entire three-hour train ride. Who could remember everything they have learned during three very intensive years?

After we checked into the hotel room, my classmates hid my textbooks and told me I had studied enough. If I didn't know it by now I never would. Strangely, I felt more relaxed after that. Now it was out of my hands and left to destiny.

With nothing more to do that night, someone decided that it would be fun to go out for a malt. We were already in our pajamas, but we rolled up the legs under our coats and trekked out to the drugstore. Most drug stores had a soda fountain in those days. It was the most daring thing I had ever done. Caught up in a situation that was fraught with danger and excitement, I became exhilarated and found my confidence building. When we returned to the hotel, I was in a mellow mood and ready for a good night's sleep.

At eight o'clock the next morning we began the first long day of tests. Basically it was just a matter of regurgitating back all those volumes of memorized information. It was impossible to determine how well (or how poorly) we had done.

At the end of the third day we again boarded the train—this time going back to our homes and jobs. The war was over, but there was still a nursing shortage and fewer students were entering the school of nursing. So the hospital had 'generously' offered us full RN wages until our state board results came, one-hundred-sixty-five dollars a month—hardly a fortune, even in those post depression times.

Waiting for the test results was agonizing. My mother had instructions to open the envelope as soon as it arrived and call me at work. Finally the day arrived and the call came:

"Your test scores are here."

"Did I pass?"

"I don't know. Is 70 passing?"

"What did I get 70 in?"

"Everything"

Only then did I expel the air pounding in my lungs. I knew I couldn't have gotten 70 in everything. **I WAS AN RN!**

That afternoon I learned that I had average in the ninety-seventh percentile. That was how they scored State Board exams at that time. It was well worth all the frantic studying. A minimum passing grade would have served just as well. No employer has ever been interested in what grades were obtained—only that they were passing and that the license has been kept current. By passing state boards, I've been able to keep my license valid without retesting for forty-seven years. When I moved from one state to another, reciprocity has allowed me to become licensed in the new state based on the validity of the original license. In later years, license renewal became contingent on working the required number of hours and obtaining a specified number of continuing education units (CEU's) but the benefits of those original scores have endured through the years.

After graduation I was ready to lie back and rest on my laurels. I estimated that I had spent at least nine thousand hours working on the floors and in the classroom during the past three years. I was mentally and physically exhausted. Today we call it burnout. In the forties we didn't think in those terms. A more apropos term for those times would have been 'work till you drop.' Most of us didn't have the means to shop to that point.

I had no idea where I would work. In spite of having been in charge of the floors, much of the time I didn't feel ready to be a head nurse or supervisor. And I couldn't see being a private duty nurse and spending all day with one patient. Besides staff nurses didn't have a very good opinion of 'specials.' So I just lolled around for a couple of weeks thinking it over and enjoying my first real vacation in three years. I hadn't spent any of the money I had saved to pay for the course or even all of the stipends from the government. So I had plenty of time.

Then once again fate, or my guardian angel, stepped in. I received a telephone call from the Director of Nursing at the hospital. "Miss

Brown, you're needed on OB. *Now you git oveh theh, ya heah?"* Although she was from rural Iowa, she had a definite southern accent. It didn't occur to me that I no longer had to obey her—that I was as much my own boss as I ever would be.

"Yes, Miss Wilding," I blurted back. "I'll be right there." Thus, was my destiny determined. Most of the rest of my life has been spent as an OB nurse. That first job was by command—but all the rest had been by choice—a choice that has been infinitely fulfilling and brimming with the joy and the wonder of birth. Never, in all those years has the miracle of the creation of a new life ever diminished. And it requires nursing skills, hard work, compassion and a lot of sensitive teaching to new parents and students. All of this leaves the OB nurse with a complete sense of worth and accomplishment.

At that time, the nursing staff rotated through all the OB departments—L&D (labor and delivery). PP (Post Partum) the newborn nursery and NICU (Newborn Intensive Care Unit) when the hospital had one. This made for an interesting variety for the nurses and highly efficient use of personnel for the hospital. It may even have helped delay the introduction of the term 'burnout.'

Later, when hospitals acquired expensive equipment and grew much larger to justify and absorb the additional expenses, the nurses began working in only one of the departments and lost the qualifications to even be of much assistance in other areas. By that time I had become an OB clinical instructor and needed to be able to teach my students in all the areas. My earlier orientation Made me feel very comfortable in this familiar concept.

Working in OB was a continuing joy. Happiness prevailed everywhere. Patients were rarely cranky or demanding. Yet they had a genuine need for skilled and empathetic nursing care. Few things are more frightening than facing labor. And the need for education was enormous. The naïveté of the forties and fifties was astounding. Many young women thought their 'belly buttons' would open up for the baby to come out. Child care and related topics like sibling jealousy needed to be addressed.

Although most children at the time had stay-at-home mothers, having a mother who was a nurse provided a number of benefits. My children practically learn to read on my OB textbook. They were fascinated with the process of birth and became better instructed on the facts of life than any of their classmates. They never complained when I went to work and always greeted my homecoming with, "How many babies did you have today, Mom? "They had a mother who knew how to maintain family health and not push the panic button in an emergency—one who had learned self-reliance, assumption of responsibility and how to accomplish a lot in a limited amount of time. And I tried to make up for the time I had to be away from them by spending all of my off-duty time with them. That was before they began telling us that we had to meet our own needs. At that time there was only guilt if we failed to provide for our families needs.

I have made many wrong decisions in my life. But the decision to have a career in nursing was made during one of my most shining hours.

For one hundred sixty-five dollars a month, we worked six days a week—usually twelve days in a row so we could have a weekend off. We worked most holidays, but were compensated with a week day off. There was no time and a half or double time. Most overtime was not compensated at all. When I was working nights in L&D I stayed an extra hour every morning while they took reports and passed trays on post-partum waiting for someone to come back to L&D to relieve me. Punching a time clock would have been a blessing.

If we worked an extra day, we were paid an additional one seventh of our weekly salary. They explained that they generously paid us for seven days. Even though we worked only six. On the other hand, if we failed to work one day, we would be docked two sevenths of a week's salary. The reason: They weren't going to pay us for a day off unless we had worked the other six. It seemed that they had us coming and going. Joining a union would have been unethical at the time. Going on strike would not only have been unethical but would not have been in the best interests of our patients, who were always our first concern.

They weren't just picking on us. Frugality prevailed everywhere. The business office, was staffed by only one woman. There was only one woman operating the switchboard. She was relieved at lunch time by the office manager.

With fewer students and more staff nurses to be paid, room rates went up from a modest six dollars a day to a whopping eight dollars a day.

CHAPTER 14

OBSTETRICS

*O*ne day I was waiting for an elevator with a family practice physician who had stopped delivering babies several years earlier. He glanced at my L&D scrubs and quipped, "Tell me, do babies still come out the same way?"

Yes, babies still come out the same way, but almost everything else has changed, one considerable change has been the length of the hospital stay. In the forties mother and baby stayed in the hospital for ten days. We didn't get our new mothers out of bed until the ninth day. The following day, they were dismissed in wheelchairs—too weak to walk. Where did those stories originate, we wondered, about women, who worked in the fields, stopped to deliver their babies, and went right back to work? Today, if you substitute the word 'office' for 'fields' we have almost the same situation universally. Although he didn't realize it at the time, the women were weak from being in bed for such an extended period, not from childbirth. Nor did we recognize that the occasional patient that died of an embolism was also a victim of the inactivity of bed rest. We had literally killed her with kindness.

When we began getting our mothers up earlier—on the fifth day—we were afraid that they would hemorrhage. And they were afraid that they weren't getting their money's worth. They were now paying eight dollars a day—so they would think up ways to justify that—like asking for a bedpan because "it hurt the stitches to go to the bathroom." But they were still moving around more and that was a step in the right direction.

Binders were used in abundance, held in place with dozens of safety pins. One binder was placed around the abdomen, pinned from the waist down, "to hold the fundus in place"—topped by an ice bag for good measure. Another binder was pinned from the waist up to support the breasts—tight for non nursing moms to help 'dry up' the milk, and supportively for nursing moms to support the increasing weight and prevent sagging later. Another pin on each shoulder strap adjusted the generic sized binder for a perfect fit. Velcro had not yet been invented, and it was many years before anyone realized that an ordinary bra could do the job just as well.

Peri pads were held in place—more or less—by a T-binder. A big safety pin held the three ends of the binder together. Often the pad would fall out, leaving only the T-binder in place. Again, it was many years before the transference of the ordinary, sanitary belt was effected. That breakthrough has been replaced by another breakthrough—many of our modern patients had never before worn a sanitary belt—nor had many of our young student nurses, who didn't know how to apply them or instruct the patients. So that 'archaic' practice was succeeded by sani-pants. The abdominal binder was replaced by—nothing. In time, we learned that the fundus will stay in place without a binder, and it was eliminated.

Babies also wore binders—wrapped around their mid-sections to prevent hernias and to hold an alcohol sponge around the umbilical cord to help it dry up. And, yes, we also learned that umbilical hernias are not deterred by binders, and cords dry up much faster when exposed to the air than when covered by a binder.

New mothers now get up as soon as they are vertigo free—often within the first hour after delivery. They frequently go home in twenty-four hours. Those who stay longer will almost certainly be dismissed on the second post-partum day. With hospital costs reaching astronomical heights most new mothers pretty much take care of themselves. They even transport their babies to and from the nursery. Most of the care is instructional, supportive and checking for complications. Most insurance companies won't pay beyond a two-day stay unless there is a complication—and the trend is moving toward only one day. If a major complication occurs after dismissal, the mother returns to the emergency room.

Minor complications are not necessarily a deterrent to dismissal. Only to the nurse does the hospital seem like the best place for a sick person. Most patients just want to be home. They think that all their problems will resolve once they get there. They will go home eagerly with a catheter in place, without having had a bowel movement (a milestone after delivery) weak parenting skills, and poor or an absent support system. Babies go home underweight, jaundiced, nursing poorly and spitting up. Bilirubin lights are now available for rental to treat jaundice at home. Presumably the babies' problems will also resolve themselves in the relaxing atmosphere of the home and family circle. Often they do. If not, again, they have the option of returning to the hospital.

As a nurse from a bygone era, I have been repeatedly dumbfounded as well as genuinely concerned for patients going home with these weighty problems. I have heard horror stories about women suffering through days of mastitis before receiving help. And babies having to be bottle fed because the mother just didn't know how to get her to breast-feed. But because the vast majority of problems do get resolved satisfactorily, it is not considered prudent to retain everyone. Nurses, like mothers, had to learn to let go.

One thing that has not changed significantly over the years is the fundus check. Every woman who has delivered a baby will probably remember this painful procedure. After the contents of the uterus have been expelled, the only thing that prevents hemorrhage from occurring is the uterus contracting into a firm ball and clamping off all the blood vessels that previously carried blood to the placenta. Should the uterus relax even slightly excessive bleeding can occur. Massaging the fundus frequently after delivery is necessary to ensure that this does not happen. Unfortunately, it is most painful during this period. One evening I had taken my six clinical students to Lamaze class. One of the pregnant women in the class held up her hand and commented that someone had told her that there was a nurse there that "really pushed down hard on your stomach." All six of my students stood up and pointed at me. It is difficult to convince students, whose empathy is rightfully with the patients, that firmly massaging the funduses is a necessary, life saving measure and I wouldn't have them any other way. I'm always suspicious of the rare student who is able to inflict that much pain before she has become seasoned.

Ever since Eve ate the 'apple' labor has been associated with pain. Throughout the centuries man has endeavored to find ways of controlling this pain. One of these methods we studied about in nurses' training was twilight sleep—a combination of morphine sulfate and scopolamine—morphine for pain relief and scopolamine to induce amnesia of the entire experience. Why should amnesia be desired if the morphine relieved the pain? Morphine is a powerful narcotic, but labor pains are even stronger. The morphine can dull the pain for a short time but then the pain breaks through the barrier.

Scopolamine does more than cause amnesia. The side effects of scopolamine are best forgotten. We used to say that it made the patients "climb the walls"—literally. The patients became wild and unimaginable. Any nurse who has ever cared for a patient who has received 'scope'—especially multiple doses—will usually refuse to receive it herself when she is the patient.

Of course we never gave twilight sleep in that hospital. We were taught that it was from a bygone era and was not used anymore. We gave Demerol, a synthetic narcotic, which came with the claim that it did not cause respiratory depression in the baby as true narcotics do. All new synthetic narcotics make that claim but time usually proves it to be invalid.

We were careful to adjust the Demerol dosage so that it took the edge off the pain without altering the patient's consciousness. With the pain reduced to a manageable level and the support of the L&D nurse, the patient could remain conscious and in control. Although sometimes fear, a powerful factor, interfered with this optimal result.

Very few of our newborns failed to breathe spontaneously. The cord was not cut until it had stopped pulsating, a sign that the placenta was continuing to provide the baby with oxygen. So there was not a rush for that first cry. Today, most doctors cut the umbilical cord as soon as the baby is delivered. The theory behind this is that, by eliminating that last flow of blood from the placenta, (called the placental transfusion) there is less chance for jaundice as the additional red blood cells break down and die.

In the past, if a baby failed to breathe after the initial slap on the buttocks, we would squirt some air or cold alcohol from the bulb syringe on his chest and abdomen or dribble a little cold ether from the ether can, which would usually cause the baby to gasp and begin breathing. When stronger measures were called for in those pre-CPR times we got out two small tubs retained for that purpose and filled one with very warm water and the other with cold water. The doctor would immerse the baby alternately, from one to the other until the baby was stimulated to start breathing. It was rare, but devastating to lose a baby.

It wasn't until many years later, when Lamaze entered the scene that I realized that, even though we had been very cautious about the use of narcotics in labor and had few depressed babies, the ones that we did have were none-the-less caused by the drugs. Every person (and babies are people) has his own level of tolerance for narcotics. Because the baby is so small, this tolerance level is reached long before his mother's. While not the entire drug the mother receives is delivered to the baby, unfortunately, enough of it is to be traumatic. Since the baby doesn't need to breathe until he is separated from his mother, the trick is to have the last dose administered at least an hour and a half before delivery so that most of it has already been metabolized.

As I moved to different states and sought employment in other hospitals, I found myself working in two hospitals that actually use twilight sleep. In the first one, when I was being oriented to L&D, the head nurse told me, "We give all of our new babies oxygen for fifteen minutes."

I found that to be a startling statement. "But what if they don't need it?" I blurted out.

"We give all our new babies oxygen for fifteen minutes," She repeated, her face a mask, void of expression.

I would soon learn that they all needed it. The first patient I admitted in labor giggled nervously and confided, "I hope it will be like the last time. They gave me a shot and I went to sleep. And when I woke up the baby was here." I found that very unusual. She was a lucky lady. But this time she had a difficult labor. She was given Demerol and scopolamine alternately with Pitocin—one or the other every hour. Pitocin makes the contractions stronger and more painful. Before long she was out of control and unmanageable throughout the long labor, quite different from her memory of the last labor.

I began to notice that many of the multi paras came in with the same story of having slept through the previous labors and yet proceeded to have difficult, painful out of control labors while being heavily sedated.

One day I was sitting with a patient whose cervix was completely dilated trying, unsuccessfully, to get her to bear down when her doctor came in. "How's she doing?" He asked.

"She's complete but I can't get her to cooperate." I replied.

"Cooperate?" He looked genuinely puzzled. "Oh! You mean pushing! We don't do that anymore."

As it turned out he was right. Most of the patients were given spinals to keep them from pushing until the doctor had time to deliver them. It was a large, busy hospital and the L&D had the atmosphere of an assembly line. The spinal anesthetic prolonged the labor, but it was a blessing in disguise—the patient could no longer feel the pain and was at last quiet and at peace.

It finally dawned on me. Although we had learned in the forties that twilight sleep was passé, here in the fifties it was alive and well—only the medication had been changed from morphine to Demerol. The mothers clamored for it because they had no memory of what they had endured. And the fathers were at the other end of the hall drinking strong coffee. I put in a request for a transfer and spent the rest of my stint at the hospital working in post partum.

It was 900 miles from there and in the seventies when I again found myself in a hospital that used twilight sleep. Again the drugs were different, but the results were the same. By that time I was teaching and not on the staff. Behind closed doors I could express to my students exactly how I viewed such practices.

That hospital had a coffee urn and a logbook in the fathers' waiting room. To help pass the seemingly endless hours of waiting many of the fathers wrote their feelings down in the logbook. Most of the entries would bring a lump to the throat and tears to the eyes of the staunchest observer.

One entry said, "I don't know how much more of this battery acid (sic). I can take. If God will only let my wife be all right, I'll never complain again." And several entries later in the same handwriting, "I am a father! I have a seven pound, eleven ounce baby girl. My wife is fine. Thank you, God."

Then—da-da-da-dum—Lamaze to the rescue! And none too soon, the 'Natural' era was officially here. Everyone wanted to deliver the natural way. One day I was at the spa when a pregnant woman came in. The attendant was visiting with her about her impending labor.

"You are going to go natural, aren't you?" She gushed.

"Well, I don't know," replied the mother hesitantly. "I have talked to my doctor. He might give me a spinal."

But the attendant wouldn't give up. "Oh, you have to go natural," she persisted.

Normally I don't interfere into other people's conversations. But this time I couldn't help myself. After all, she was infringing on my field of expertise, "Please don't tell her that," I admonished. "Her doctor may have other plans for her. How would you feel then?" I could tell that she wanted to retaliate, but couldn't because I was a customer. I hadn't meant to have an unfair advantage over her, but she needed to learn to let people make their own decisions.

Lamaze came to the Midwest like everything else—long after it had infiltrated both coasts and slowly worked its way inward. In 1971,

I wrote an article for American Baby Magazine about methods of managing labor. I had included nothing about natural childbirth. The editor asked me to add information about it. Without even a modicum of enthusiasm I added a short paragraph. It didn't appear very workable to me.

Then came Lamaze—like a steamroller rolling over everyone that got into its path. Most of the doctors resisted it. They were used to having their patients anesthetized when they delivered. Sleeping patients don't ask questions or refuse to cooperate. And having the husbands underfoot during the labor and delivery did not appeal to them.

But the women were determined to have this. If a woman's doctor refused to deliver her using this technique, she would simply find one who would comply. The doctors didn't want to lose their patients, and eventually they all had to go along with it. Their days of saying, "Do it my way or find another doctor," were over. And when they saw how well Lamaze worked they even began to take credit for it.

Nurses and lay persons began getting certified to teach classes on the use of Lamaze techniques. Mothers-to-be and their husbands or significant others—or even their mothers or girlfriends—took the classes. The husbands et al learned how to coach the patient in practice and in labor.

The classes taught breathing and relaxation techniques and the use of a focal point to divert the pain message from reaching the brain. They also taught practical things, like when to go to the hospital and what to take with them. And they taught the anatomy and physiology of labor. Never again would a patient need to ask if her baby was going to come out through her belly button.

We nurses had to learn a new language. We were never to use the word 'pain' because of the power of suggestion, but were to say

'contraction' instead, or at most referred to it as 'some discomfort.'
L&D nurses had to learn the Lamaze techniques so they could help
coach. We would also teach some of the techniques to women who
hadn't taken the classes. When they learned that we would do this many
of them opted to save the cost of the class. But they did themselves
a disservice. There was too much background information and too
many techniques to be learned at the last minute. The key phrase was
Prepared Childbirth. That preparation needed to begin early.

At first the men were reluctant to participate. Most of them would
sit stiffly, in a chair far from the bed, not timing contractions or
contributing anything. The women were frantic. They loved having
their men with them and didn't care if they did nothing more than just
sit there. They made excuses for them like: "Oh, he's tired. He's been
up with me since 2:00 this morning." They were now well informed.
We could tell them, "You're dilated 4cm and 50% effaced." And they
knew what we were talking about. The labor room changed from a
noisy bedlam to a place of quiet dignity. The word was out that labor
did not equate to pain. Ergo if anyone felt any pain they wouldn't
admit it—even to themselves. Conversations over the backyard fences
and bridge tables had a lot of influence in the labor room. Now, when
I toured my students through the L&D suite I told them that if they
heard any hollering it would be coming from the OR Recovery Room
adjacent to L&D.

Other things were changing as well. We no longer were doing
painful rectal exams to determine the dilation of the cervix. We now
did vaginals—not exactly comfortable but much more so than the
old way. Monitors had begun to appear in the labor rooms, which
permitted the patients to lie on their sides—a much safer position for
the baby and usually more comfortable for the mother—and still have

continuous monitoring of FHT (fetal heart tones) and contractions rather than intermittent checks.

The word 'husband' practically disappeared from our vocabularies. The man in the room might be a boyfriend, a neighbor, a brother or the patient's father. The gray-haired, fatherly looking man might actually be the husband, as might the youngish looking teenager. Or there might not be a man involved at all. It became more prudent to ask, "Who will be your significant other?" The S.O. would be the only one to be granted the privilege of being with the patient throughout the labor and delivery as well is being in the postpartum room while the baby was in the room. The patient could designate anyone she wanted to be the S.O., but the privilege couldn't be shared or alternated.

Another area we learned to be careful about was past pregnancies. The chart might note that the patient is a gravida II, para I (meaning that it is her second pregnancy and has had one previous viable delivery.) It is best not to ask about the child at home unless they bring up the subject first. The first baby may have been adopted out or may have died.

After Lamaze had been around for several years, the pendulum began to swing slowly back. One day the L&D supervisor showed me a presentation she was preparing for an in-service program and asked for my input. I pointed out that she had said 'pain' instead of 'contraction.'

"Oh, we're saying pain now," she responded. "They come in expecting a pain—free labor and they're not prepared for the reality."

Once again, women began to get medication for the pain of labor—only now they were calling it, "Something to relax me." Epidurals became very popular. Does all this mean that Lamaze was a failure? Not at all, Lamaze classes continue to thrive. The mothers experience an informed, relatively comfortable labor which they share with their significant others. Being awake and in control during the entire experience makes for a poignant bonding between mother and baby, mother and father, and Daddy and child. When complications occur they are less terrified, more cooperative and better prepared to cope. Observing the activities of the doctors and nurses helps them recognize that everything possible was done.

Lamaze—long may it reign!

What is so ironic about the dedication with which women brought about the Lamaze movement—which originated in France—was that they ignored another delivery technique, which also came from France—the Leboyer method (pronounced La Boy yay.) The thing that is so interesting about it is that Lamaze is for the mother's comfort while Leboyer is for the baby's.

Dr. Leboyer discovered that the birth process, as it had been practiced, was very traumatic for the baby. The baby is removed from an environment that is warm and dark with noises muffled into an atmosphere that is cold and bright and noisy. He may have been pulled out with a pair of hard steel forceps clamped around his face and head. A Bulb syringe is stuck down his throat to suction out the mucus, and he is prodded to cry immediately and fill his lungs with oxygen. Independently of all this, he is feeling the pull of gravity for the first time after the buoyancy of floating in the amniotic fluid for the past nine months.

Dr. Leboyer, a French obstetrician, had delivered more than a thousand babies using a new technique when it was brought to the United States. In the Leboyer method the room lights are turned off. A single spot light enables the doctor to see. All personnel speak softly. No forceps are used unless absolutely necessary.

After his birth, the baby is placed face down on his mother's abdomen with his head slightly lower than his body to allow the mucus to drain out. No bulb syringe is usually needed. The cord is not cut until it stops pulsating, which may take up to twenty minutes. So there is no hurry for the baby to begin breathing. Usually he is having quiet, regular respirations by the time the placenta has stopped delivering oxygen to him. It is not necessary to stimulate him to cry. He may or may not be crying anyway. After the cord has been cut by the father, he places the baby in a tub of warm water. Relieved of the cold and gravitational pull, the baby stops crying. When he is removed from the water, he may begin crying again. He may then be placed back in the water. Now he is receiving the message that, even though life may not be as good as it was, it does get better again. At the same time, father and baby are undergoing a powerful bonding process.

We used to think that a baby couldn't smile before it was two months old. If a baby appeared to smile earlier then that, we rationalized that he was having a gas pain. But Leboyer babies smile while in the delivery room—not from gas but from pure joy.

I have never known an expectant mother to ask for a Leboyer delivery. Occasionally, a doctor will suggest a modified Leboyer delivery, which falls far short of the real thing. The lights are dimmed and the baby is bathed in an inch of water—by the circulating nurse, 'because sterile water is expensive,' and 'the father might drop the slippery baby.'

Is this an idea whose time has passed, or will we someday see it widely used in this country? People have been hypnotized and regressed back to the time of their birth. They generally reported feeling cold and overwhelmed by the bright lights and noise. They also report feeling fearful of being dropped by the gloved personnel, because of the slipperiness of the amniotic fluid on their bodies.

If more people believed in reincarnation—that they might be undergoing the birth process again—I think they would be more interested in making that process more pleasant for the baby.

Monitoring the FHT's used to be very time-consuming. They were often difficult to obtain and not always accurate. And the labor patient was required to turn on her back each time a check was done. An ordinary stethoscope with its long tubing is not the best way to hear this elusive sound. So long ago, an ancient sage invented the fetoscope. The fetoscope has a deep bell to pick up the sound and short tubing to conduct it more efficiently. A rounded metal strip fits over the head of the care giver, enabling the cranial bone to enhance conduction. It also permits both hands to be three for palpitation or hand holding, and eliminates all of the static and interference caused by fingers touching the bell.

Every time the nurse put the fetoscope on her head she had to remove her cap. Soon it became such a nuisance that L&D nurses just stopped wearing their caps altogether. That may have been the beginning of the movement for nurses in all the services to stop wearing their caps.

Using the fetoscope necessitated coaxing the patient onto her back and remaining still while the nurse located and counted the FHT. Sometimes this is difficult because of the fetal position, excessive amniotic fluid or layers of maternal fat and muscle. It was very time-consuming getting around to all the labor patients and performing all the necessary duties. Sometimes the nurse was not able to monitor the FHT as often as today's standards dictate. The possibility of picking up fetal distress early was less than desirable.

Then came the electronic age. It brought with it more than video games. It also brought us electronic monitoring. With the aid of a little conductive gel we could now hear the sound of the FHT magnified several times without having to press a cold metal object deep into the patient's abdomen to get as close to the fetus as necessary.

The first devices were portable but bulky and cumbersome. Today the portable one fits in the palm of your hand and can pick up the FHT at a gestational age of four weeks. Compare that to the fetoscope which can't pick up the FHT until at least four months. Modern monitors found in today's modern L&D departments are highly sophisticated computers, which provide a continuous reading of both fetal well-being and maternal contractions. These readings are given in the patient's room, as well as at the nurses' station. The patient can assume and remain in any position she wishes. But if she needs to get up she must be disconnected from the monitor.

The purist would explain that it is not the actual sound of the FHT that you are hearing, but the echo of the sound waves bouncing off the heartbeat. I personally find that about as interesting as the inner workings of my car, but I'm grateful to the scientific minds that brought it about.

With electronic monitoring the nurse is no longer tied down to hours sitting at the bedside with her hand on the patient's fundus timing contractions. She now has continuous access to the frequency and duration of the contractions and the rate of the FHT and, what is most important, the reaction of the FHT to the contractions—a significant development in detecting fetal distress.

The fetal monitor is often blamed for the increased number of cesarean deliveries that are done. While it is true, the monitor may indicate the possibility of fetal distress when there actually is none, there is no way of being absolutely certain. Who would be willing to take that chance with their babies life? To illustrate my point, let me recount two incidents which happened within a week of each other in a hospital where I was teaching. Monitors were just beginning to enter the scene and only an occasional patient was being monitored.

Our first patient was not attached to a monitor, but the nurses were monitoring her closely—every five minutes at times. When I came on duty at 7:00 A.M., I read her chart to determine if she would be a good learning experience for a student. I saw that she had decelerations of the FHT all night. Periodically the heart rate would recover and then drop again. On two occasions the fetal heart stopped beating but then resumed the third time the little heart stopped beating. It did not start again.

The night nurses periodically recorded that these findings were reported to the doctor. Of course the chart did not document his response. By morning the fetus was dead and the patient later delivered a stillborn baby—one of those rare heartbreaks in OB.

A few days later we had another patient exhibiting the same pattern of fetal decelerations. Glumly I wondered if we would have to watch another baby die, then her doctor swaggered in—a cigar clenched between his teeth. When the staff nurse explained the situation He removed the cigar and drawled, "Wal, let's get her into the C. Section room!" Minutes later, the baby was delivered through an abdominal incision. I will remember that sight for the rest of my life! The cord was wrapped around the baby's neck once and crossed over her chest. Because it was a short cord, the circulation to the baby was being compromised each time a contraction pushed the baby lower in the birth canal. The doctor cut the cord and the baby immediately cried and turned pink. That babies life was saved by timely intervention. Just as the other babies could have been.

Today all labor patients in major hospitals are monitored electronically. The belts may be slightly uncomfortable, but it is a small price to pay for your baby's life and well-being. If the BOW has ruptured, an internal electrode can be applied directly to the fetal scalp. It may leave a small, temporary sore but it is more accurate and eliminates the necessity of one belt. An internal contraction monitor precludes the need of the other belt. Patients can assume any position that is comfortable. We have learned that the safest position, for both mother and baby is for the mother to lie on her side because it takes the weight of the uterus off the main artery that carries oxygen to the fetus and the kidneys.

For patients with elevated blood pressures there is a BP monitor that delivers the BP with the touch of a button or it can be set for continuous monitoring or to take a reading at specified intervals.

Ultrasound or sonogram is another modern day diagnostic tool which has aroused some controversy. It has never been shown to be harmful but many people feel that it should be used only when there is a definite indication rather than routinely as many doctors do. One thing is certain—the high cost of the sonogram is a contributing factor to the skyrocketing cost of having a baby. But it does pinpoint a number of complications that can be corrected before birth as well as the sex of the baby. And that is a thrill for some expectant parents.

Statistics on cesarean deliveries show the national averages, to be 25% of all deliveries. Several times I have sat down with the delivery book in our Midwestern metropolitan hospital and figured up the percent of cesareans that we were doing. Invariably it came to between ten and 12% of the total number of deliveries. And that is much higher than it was thirty years ago. So 25% does seem excessive. Cesarean deliveries do save lives, but there is also a risk with major surgery. It is also expensive and the recovery period is longer and more painful.

One fairly recent measure to reduce the number of cesarean deliveries performed has been the VBAC (pronounced vee back) standing for "Vaginal Birth After Cesarean." We had always followed the adage "Once a C. Section always a C. Section" because of the possibility of uterine rupture. Scar tissue does not stretch as normal uterine tissue does and the tension of the contraction may cause it to tear. Making the incision across the lower segment of the uterus rather than vertically, where it extends into the fundus, reduces this risk since the fundus is the part of the uterus that contracts the hardest. Women anxious to have their babies the "natural" way have clamored for VBAC. Of course, if the original indication for the Caesarean still exists—, e.g. a small pelvis—VBAC would not be possible.

How can you be sure that you won't have an unnecessary cesarean? Talk with your doctor early in your pregnancy. Let him know how you feel about details that are important to you and insist on answers. In the heat of labor is no time to make a rational decision. You must have selected a doctor in whom you have confidence and permit him to make emergency decisions for you. And you can have your baby in the Midwest, where the odds are in your favor.

Having babies in hospitals delivered by medical doctors has been common practice since before I was born but prior to that, most of our ancestors had their babies at home, attended by midwives. These midwives were lay women who learned their trade serving an apprenticeship, with an older *granny* midwife. Newborn survival rates were poor and maternal survival was not a great deal better.

Most OB nurses believed it is both a privilege and a blessing for women to be able to deliver their babies in hospitals where instruments and other materials used are meticulously sterilized, trained personnel provide support and comfort measures as well as skilled observation and care, doctors are trained to handle all kinds of complications as well as normal deliveries, and the finest equipment is readily available for any emergency. And of course there are monitors to let us know those emergencies are imminent.

Unfortunately, the Lamaze movement brought with it the desire for everything to be 'natural.' To the lay public home is natural. A hospital is unnatural. Women who have had their babies at home and suffered no trauma (some of them are even doctors) have written articles describing to the public how safe and fulfilling home deliveries are. Having one's baby at home in one's own bed with one's family gathered around—able to get up and walk around and sip a cup of tea—what a contrast to the cold stainless steel of the hospital equipment, strapped down by the monitor, family members restricted, an IV inserted in the arm, being taken care of by formidable strangers, and having to move onto a Gurney and be transported to the delivery room at a most painful time.

The hospitals responded with the Birthing Room. The Birthing Room was fixed up to look like an attractive bedroom. The bed was made of attractive wood but had all the utilitarian features of a labor bed and a delivery table. All of the instruments and even the bassinets that would receive the baby were camouflaged behind a handsome chiffonier. The labor room converted into a delivery room; so there was no need to transfer the patient.

In the beginning only one significant other was allowed to remain throughout the labor and delivery. Later this was expanded to include other family members. In some areas of the country the patient's children are permitted to watch the delivery. The prospective parents were encouraged to submit a letter telling us what their expectations were, which we would do our best to fulfill. Yet, to most people, a hospital is still a hospital.

On the coattails of this new move came the new lay midwives. While most states have legislation permitting the practice of Registered Nurse Midwives, lay midwives are not legal anywhere. Nurse midwives are RN's who have a BSN (Bachelor of Science in Nursing Degree) who have graduated from an approved school of midwifery. They work primarily in hospitals under the supervision of MDs.

Lay midwives are of uncertain origin and practice in secrecy, away from the watchful eyes of professionals. But they can offer their clients one thing we can't—a home delivery. But even they may feel the lack of quick access to modern facilities. We had a couple of these women in our city who would panic periodically and bring their patients to the hospital where I was teaching. They were usually in advanced labor and the midwives were unable to hear FHT. Generally, the outcome was satisfactory and no serious problems occurred.

I had not yet met either of these women when I read a four page typed incident report written by the night nurses about an incident with one of them. As I read the report, I had the feeling that the midwife had shown her good intent by bringing the patient to the hospital. It also sounded as though the staff was most incensed because the midwife had come to the hospital barefooted, although she was compliant when they refused to allow her into the delivery room.

Soon after that, I learned that the same midwife was conducting a workshop at a community college in a neighboring city. I decided to attend it and form my own opinion about her. Several of my students wanted to go along. Two of them were former 'flower children' who had worked with her at one time and were very protective of her.

The midwife entered the room where the workshop was taking place wearing a floor length, see-through organdy dress reminiscent of the depression era prom dress obtainable through mail order catalogs. It was most inappropriate for the occasion. I began to understand how the night nurses had felt about her bare feet, although on this night, she was wearing sandals—without hose. Two students who championed her told me later that wearing the party dress was not a matter of defying convention, but it was just her favorite dress.

Her presentation did not improve matters. It was not geared to the professionals who were there, but was presented as if she were teaching a natural childbirth class to pregnant women. Her knowledge of the anatomy and physiology of labor was sketchy and her pronunciations were incorrect—signifying that she was probably self-taught from a book.

She repeatedly made derogatory remarks about hospitals and said 'we' should not accept what 'they' told us but that we should tell them what to do—, e.g., we were to tell the labor nurse to massage the perineum throughout the labor so that an episiotomy would not be necessary.

She admitted that she was illegal—in fact she was under arrest at that moment and was out of jail only because she had agreed to leave the state. She said she was going to California that night, but that she would return soon.

And return she did. We continued to get her patients in the hospital. Many of them had severe lacerations that would probably cause them serious problems in later years

She found a doctor who signed the birth certificates of her home deliveries and covers her in emergencies. He was an honorable man but young and probably sympathetic to the young couples who wanted home deliveries. One day he was out of town when an emergency occurred and his patients were being covered by his middle-aged, middle class father. So Dr. Dad got stuck picking up the pieces. He delivered the patient in the hospital delivery room. Her husband stood behind him dictating every step over his shoulder. He wouldn't permit the doctor to do an episiotomy. Then, after she had torn through both the urethra and the rectum, the refused to allow the doctor to suture the lacerations. Two hours later when the couple insisted on taking their new baby home, Dr. Dad perked up considerably.

The woman's movement has worked long and hard against the concept of keeping wives 'barefoot and pregnant.' I would like to see them work to eliminate the barefoot midwife.

It's odd to see women wanting to be delivered by midwives when, for so many years, all they ever wanted was their doctor. Despite the fact that the nurse was always providing almost all of the comfort measures, emotional support, monitoring and checking—if the labor seemed too long or too difficult. The patient would always wail, "where's my doctor?" To a large extent Lamaze has corrected this. She still wants her doctor to deliver the baby, but she recognizes that she and her husband and the L&D nurses are in partnership to handle the labor.

During forties when we couldn't call the doctor until the patient was REALLY READY TO DELIVER, getting him there on time was often hair-raising. One doctor couldn't come early in the morning until he had made the coffee and taken a cup to his wife in bed. The astonishing thing about this was that his wife was a nurse. While we secretly congratulated her for taming one of the elite, we still thought she should have been more understanding of the urgency of the situation.

A woman doctor who didn't marry until her late thirties (she was considered a confirmed old maid in those times) went on to have seven children. Whenever we would call her for a delivery, she would always counter with, "I'll see if I can find a babysitter." She always did.

One of our obstetricians was an amateur pilot and owned his own airplane. His office nurse always had the same stock phrase when we called him for a delivery, "Doctor is up in his airplane." How she always managed to get him down and to the hospital within a half-hour remains somewhat of a mystery.

One of the G.P.s left his car at home every morning after he had made hospital rounds. When he was needed to come and deliver a baby he would stand in the middle of the town's main street and flag a motorist down to drive him to the hospital. It was only about a mile and a half. After the delivery he would need a ride back to the office.

If it was around the change of shifts he would try to bum a ride from one of the nurses. Often the would coerce the new father into leaving his wife's side (she was usually still asleep from the anesthetic) to drive him back. I used to tease him that I was going to take up a collection to buy him a second car so he would always have a ride. "Oh, we have two cars, dear," he replied. "There's just no place to park near the office."

All too often the phone at the doctors' homes would be answered by a toddler. Like typical toddlers they rarely said more than "Huh-uh, and uh-huh." We often wondered if a responsible adult was ever going to come to the phone. According to the children there was never anyone there with them. And the doctors' wives never seemed to grasp the urgency of the situation. Despite all these problems our precipitation rate was very low. This will be explained a little later.

Ironically, there was one doctor we could call and always count on his phone being answered very professionally by his wife with, "Dr. Crandall's residence." But his services were rarely needed outside of his regular nine to five hours. He was the hospital pathologist.

Third-year medical students and interns have always been the most pleasant of all doctors. Like nursing students of the forties they don't have clinical instructors. We were their instructors in the hospital. They would show up in the department at the beginning of the rotation, and we would show them what to do and how to do it. We taught them how to do rectal exams (and later, vaginal exams) find the FHT, time contractions etc. In return, they were cheerful and cooperative and quick learners. They treated us like equals (as we did them), and it wasn't uncommon for them to help transfer a patient to the delivery room, or even bring us a cup of coffee.

One thing that was very difficult for them was the long hours they had to be on duty. While I was working the 11-7 shift in one hospital, one of our obstetricians wanted an intern to scrub for all his deliveries no matter what hour of the day or night they happened. In that hospital there were sleeping rooms for the interns right outside the L&D suite. One night when Dr. Farrell's patient was taken to the delivery room I knocked on his door and told him to come and scrub. He promised he would be right out. He still hadn't come when Dr. Farrell got there, and Dr. F. had to do all the setting up and draping. He was furious. So I went back to the night room and banged on the door for a long time before I finally heard a feeble, "Yeah?"

"Are you going to come and scrub for this delivery or not?" I asked, exasperation creeping into my voice.

There was a long pause and then, from the other side of the door, "Didn't I already do that?" The poor guy—in his extreme exhaustion his subconscious had taken over and caused him to dream that he had done the delivery so that he could continue to sleep.

The medical students' schedule has remained virtually unchanged to this day. Internships are no longer required. They can now go directly from medical school into residency or even into private practice if they choose, although most doctors who opt for a family practice take a residency in that field.

Most doctors' offices are now located near the hospital where they can pop over to the hospital at a moments notice. That is one reason they want you to go to the hospital of their choice. Most doctors have one or more partners or someone else who can cover for them when they are not readily available. Today they are more willing to come early and wait around for the patient to be 'ready.'

Thank you, Dr. Lamaze.

Among the sisterhood of nurses many doctors are known as prima Donnas who take orders only from God. The exceptionally high and mighty ones, we say, give orders to God. One smug Doctor was nicknamed, "John Jesus."

When they pick on us, we know the reason behind it—it's not usually the thing that we are being called down for but because of the tremendous responsibilities that are theirs. While they are doing their best there are all kinds of extenuating circumstances getting in the way of the ideal outcome that they're looking for. We might say, "Can't you pick on someone else for a change?" But we really don't want that. We respect a doctor more when he treats his patients and their families with kindness and dignity.

So over the years nurses have had to learn various methods of coping with doctors'

'Put-downs'. For the most part we cope in the same honored manner that nurses have used through the ages—, i.e., we bite our tongues and take it. You say that's not really coping? You're right. And it accounts for a good deal of burnout and migration to other fields.

The American Nurses Association (ANA) has tried to offset this dilemma for many years by upgrading nursing to a true profession through higher education. To be considered a real profession a college degree must be a requirement. The ANA has long endeavored to make a BSN (Bachelor of Science in Nursing) an entry-level requirement for all nurses. They want anyone with less than a BSN to be considered the same as an aide. Ergo doctors would respect nurses as colleagues and stop viewing them as handmaidens.

Many RN's now go on to obtain masters degrees and some continue on to a PhD. When you attend a health-related workshop and the speakers are introduced as Dr. this and Dr. that, you can always pick out which ones are the nurses because the shoes are a little shabbier and their clothes are not as expensive. Nurses are underpaid at all levels. So the M.D.'s are not fooled by the higher level of education. As long as we are in positions which require carrying out doctors' orders. We will be treated as hired help by some, and put in our places from time to time. We can determine a nursing diagnosis, plan our objectives and evaluate the outcome. But the doctors will still call the shots, and when it is a standoff, the hospital will always stand behind the doctor because they can always hire another nurse, but it is the doctor who brings the patient to the hospital.

So if we want to continue to be nurses we must learn coping and survival methods. One way is to 'tell the doctors off'. This is a difficult one for me because I was indoctrinated, at an early age, to respect authority. It is only a viable method when a doctor repeatedly picks on someone just because he knows he can get away with it. One well-known tyrant was famous for having good days and bad days. If he was in a good mood, things generally went quite smoothly. But if it was a bad day you could be sure that nothing you did would be right. The hospital L&D suite had a long hallway that led past all the labor rooms and terminated at the nurses' station. As soon as he came in the door and began shuffling down the hall we could clearly see what kind of mood he was in. Sometimes it's in like the long walk to the electric chair waiting for him to complete the journey and erupt.

One night he had a labor patient in who was dilated 3cm, but was screaming and thrashing about with every contraction. I checked his routine orders which stated, "call for sedation when 5 cm." Because I was young and easily intimidated, I waited for her to reach a dilation of 5 cm.

That night when he opened the door and began and especially dragged out shuffle down the hall to the accompaniment of his patient's screams, I could see that his mood was the worst. I used those nerve-racking minutes to pull his card from the file box and compose myself, crossing my arms over my chest. As he began to berate me and shout that I was not to ever let his patients suffer like that again, I slapped his order card down in front of him and snapped, "Then you'd better change this!" He quieted right down and never got on my case again.

And yet, ironically, he had been right and I had been wrong. No matter what that card said, I knew that the patient needed sedation and I should have called him. It only proves that you can fight unreasonable behavior with unreasonable means and conquer. But it was a hollow victory. Still, I learned a valuable lesson from that experience. From that time on I never hesitated to call a doctor when I felt it was indicated. I knew you could be 'damned if you do and damned if you don't'. And I prefer to be damned for doing. I also learned that as long as I was doing what I knew to be right I could let the tantrums roll right off my back.

I have told doctors that a patient's FHT were 108 (the should be between 120 and 160) and got that special look reserved for morons, with a tittering, "So? Let me know if they go below 100."

I just say, "fine," and note it on the chart that he was informed. Then when they drop to 90 and he asks why he wasn't told they were dropping I have recourse.

When I went to nurses training, most of the younger doctors were in the armed forces. The doctors and the hospital were mostly octogenarians. They had probably come out of retirement as their contribution to the war effort. Those elderly doctors had a very scanty educational background—only three years beyond high school—and hadn't kept up with modern advancements. When the war ended and the younger doctors returned home from the battlefields it was a grand era. We were all in a mode of love of country and fellow man that preceded John Kennedy in wanting to give of ourselves. The doctors were happy to be home and in one piece. They had learned to be calm and cool in emergencies and didn't find it necessary or even desirable to rant, rave, and scapegoat. We all had coffee together in L&D and they told us slightly off-colored jokes and called it "the intellectual hour."

I only wish that our OB Chief of Staff could have lived to be a role model for all the generations that came after him. I never heard him raise his voice or reprimand anyone. And in return we gave him 200% in effort and loyalty.

I remember his having a difficult breech delivery. The head was large and wouldn't budge. Skillfully and patiently he delivered that head, seemingly unaware of the clock ticking away. (The head of a breech baby must be delivered within about five minutes after the body was delivered or brain damage may occur.) After the head was delivered, he glanced at the clock and whispered, "whew! That was a close one." With doctors like that guiding our early years it was hard to excuse the tantrums of the less mature ones.

Eddie was a doctor we had known almost from adolescence (his and ours.) His father and older sister were both doctors on our staff. He had served his internship with us and he had married one of our nurses. She was the wife who had to have her coffee in bed before he could leave the house in the morning. We decided that she must also have had a fit if he came home with blood on his clothes—an occupational hazard for doctors in those times of last-minute appearances in the delivery room.

One day Eddie didn't have time to change into scrubs before the delivery and the inevitable happened—the blood had soaked through his sterile gown onto his shirt. He was very upset. After the delivery he stomped through the department leaving a trail of his cap, mask, gloves and gown as he took each one off and slam-dunked it to the floor. Then he astonished us all by retracing his steps and picking everything up. Mrs. Eddy had trained him well.

Whenever Eddy called us about a patient, he always identified himself as Dr. Eddie, but we never called him anything but plain 'Eddie.' It was not very kind of us—perhaps it was the ultimate revenge against doctors in general. But it wasn't to get back at Eddie. Eddie was harmless and never upset us. We were merely amused by his antics. He brought out our maternal instincts and taught us not to let such incidents get under our skin.

When I became a nursing instructor, I no longer had the close working relationship with the doctors that I had as a staff nurse—and consequently lost some of the rapport. Students were even lower on the totem pole than the staff nurses and were often targeted for displaced anger.

One day, just as I was taking two students into the delivery room to observe a delivery, a staff nurse was telling the attending physician that there was no one to scrub with him—no nurse or medical student. Without a moment's hesitation he turned to the students and began to rail at them. "Do you have permission to be in here? You shouldn't be in here unless you have." And to the patient, "do you mind if these students watch your delivery?"

The poor woman had enough on her mind for the moment, but valiantly responded, "Oh, no. Everyone has to learn." After the delivery, the doctor made a new ruling—only one student could be in the delivery room at a time and permission must be obtained from the patient and the doctor. Another doctor had a difficult time doing amniocentesis on a toxemia patient. We heard later that he had stuck her five times before he found a suitable location. Ultrasound has now eliminated this problem but at that time it was just beginning to be used for that purpose. He countered by barring students from taking care of his toxemia patients—he said THEY were too stimulating for them.

Because of these and numerous other similar incidents, I was always cautioning the students to stay out of the doctors' way and not bother them with questions etc. Young students reared in our modern culture where freedom of expression is considered desirable for children can never quite understand old-fashioned fear and respect for authority held by earlier generations. One student saw nothing wrong with interrupting a conversation between a pediatrician and a postpartum patient to ask if the patient needed her stool softener. I was in the nursery when the doctor stormed in to recount the incident and tell us, "My stool was considerably softened."

So I winced when a middle-aged male student came to clinical conference one day after watching a delivery and told me, "I told Dr. Lomax, 'You sure done a nice delivery.'"

Predictably, doctors have more respect for male students than females. For one thing, they have always worn white uniforms while the women have been saddled with gray, pink, yellow, brown or blue ones. Male students were indistinguishable from interns and medical students. And of course they are men. Even women doctors respect that—as do women nurses. One day a guest speaker, in my Community Health class, pointed to the single male student in the class and announced, "Come see me when you graduate. We have the job for you."

But Joe was a bit 'hayseedy' and I wondered how Dr. Lomax felt about Joe's presumptuousness in judging his delivery, no matter how complementary he had been. "What did he say?" I ventured cautiously.

"Oh, he just beamed and said, 'why, thank you very much.'" I don't know which was greater—my surprise or my relief. It would appear that flattery will get you anywhere. Another coping mechanism.

Joe may have had a rural manner but he was sharp and on the ball. One day he was quite late to clinical conference on a day when we had a lot of material to cover. He had noticed that the ID band on the baby's arm did not match the one on its leg. One of them matched his mother's ID band and the other matched that of another mother. I had to delay our conference and check out the situation. I found that several of the babies had the same phenomenon.

ID bands, come on a large role, in sets of three—two for the baby and one for the mother. Each set of three has identical numbers stamped on them. Other pertinent information is added after the delivery. Apparently someone in the delivery room had ruined one band and, instead of discarding the entire set, had just taken the next one, breaking up the set. No one had noticed the error and everyone just kept taking the next three bands with mismatched numbers.

Because the nursery was small and generally had a population of only six or eight babies the nurses all knew which baby belonged with each mother. And the mothers all knew their own babies from the moment they watched them deliver. (No, newborns do not all look alike.) So the chance of sending a baby home with the wrong mother was minimal, but to ensure that there was absolutely no chance at all of a mix-up the babies had to be foot-printed again and issued new ID bands.

The nurses were furious with Joe for bringing this to their attention and causing them all that extra work and didn't let him forget it. Now doesn't that sound just like a doctor?

One evening I heard a riddle on a TV program that caught me embarrassingly off guard. I was miffed with myself for not getting the answer. The riddle:

> A father and his son in an automobile accident.
> The father was killed. The son was taken to the
> emergency room, and a surgeon was called in. The
> surgeon arrived and said, "I can't operate on this
> boy. He's my son." How could that be?

At the time we had a very youthful looking medical student who wore her hair in a Dutch boy style. It made her look like a little girl. And she had a little girl personality to match. She would frequently complain that people were always assuming that she was a nurse. She thought that in these enlightened times people should be more cognizant of women in medicine.

I told her the riddle expecting her to get the answer immediately. Instead, she tried all the usual guesses—he was adopted and the surgeon was his real father; the surgeon was his stepfather; his father didn't really die. The answer, of course, is—the surgeon was his MOTHER. When I told her the answer I expected her to react as I had—with embarrassment. Instead, she replied, "Well, how many women are surgeons?" So much for logic.

While the number of women in medicine is increasing, they are still in the minority. Despite the women's movement, changes come slowly. In one hospital we shared a classroom with the medical students. One day I heard the doctor through the partition asking the med students if working on Saturday would be a problem for anyone. A feminine voice spoke up—

"I don't think my husband would let me work on Saturday."

Women doctors have been around all my life. Remember, the kindly woman doctor who did the D&C during my student OR rotation? Her daughter also became a doctor and I went to her for my pre-entrance physical. I chose a woman doctor for reasons of modesty. But my own biases went into effect. Although I weighed only 114 pounds, my family had succeeded endowing me with low self-esteem and I felt that she was looking at my body critically. Since then I've always gone to male doctors. But that is not because I think that men are more competent. But that is typical of the kind of biases that women in medicine must face—as must a man in nursing.

During our training years we had our own personal physician—an elderly woman. We called Dr. Libby. She was gentle and motherly and always had a kind word for us. But she had her own private practice also and it was exasperating to be on OB call and get called in the middle of the night for one of her deliveries. She believed babies should be delivered v-e-e-e.-e-r-y slowly to prevent trauma to the head. To accomplish this, she would hold the head back with her arthritic fingers for an interminable period of time until nature finally won out. We were anxious to finish the delivery, clean up the room, wash the instruments, wash the blood out of the linens before throwing them into the laundry, set up the room for the next delivery and go back to the dorm to catch a few more winks before being called back again. The urge to yank those gnarled fingers away and scream, "Let that baby out already!" was strong. Of course, we never did, and we all survived the ordeal.

When I became an L&D nurse, I expected to have a special rapport with the women doctors. I couldn't have been more wrong. In those early years when women were still trying to blaze a trail in medicine they seemed rigid and all business. By far their most common and most aggravating quality was that no matter what you told them their patients dilation was they would always examine her and find something different. Like the old song, "You say potaytoes and I say potahtoes . . . ." only it was, "you say. 6cm and I say 4cm, and you say 80% effaced and I say, 50% effaced . . . ."

These woman learned to be 'as tough as nails' as they struggled their way through medical school with the men putting obstacles in their path and betting against them. This toughness endured after graduation and they were ready to prove to one and all that nothing could stop them. Nurses were an easy conquest. Today, it is not as difficult. Women do not need to constantly prove themselves and can retain more of their feminine qualities.

Sometimes (only sometimes, mind you) nurses can be unfairly judgmental of doctors. We had one Hispanic Doctor who impressed me as being crude and unprofessional. He had a large practice of Hispanic women and addressed them all as "missus," eliminating the need to learn their names.

One evening I had one of his patients in labor—a gravida XII. She screamed and thrashed about all night but her dilatation remained at 3 cm. I was startled when the intern called and asked if I had a passion for Dr. Fuentes. I was about to reply, "Certainly not!" when I realized that he also had a Spanish accent and was merely inquiring about a patient.

Dr. Fuentes eventually sauntered in and did a rectal exam on his patient. He agreed that she was 3 cm. She got a contraction during the exam and he instructed her to, "Bear, missus." I mentally rolled my eyes and thought, "The dummy doesn't even know they're not supposed to bear down until they're completely dilated."

Fortunately he couldn't read my mind but looked at me and said, "you ought to feel that cervix dilate! Let's get her into the delivery room."

"Now", I thought. "We'll be tied up in the delivery room all night." But, like a good soldier, I was trained to do as I was told and I did. I put her on the delivery table and scrubbed and draped her. And she immediately delivered a healthy, squalling baby. Could it be that the 'dummy' had learned something from experience that the 'learned' writers of the textbooks hadn't?

I was to learn that a uterus that has been stretched out throughout twelve pregnancies, and subjected to contractions during eleven hours, loses its tone like a stretched out rubber band. It no longer has the strength to push the fetal head against the cervix hard enough to dilated it. Having her push during a contraction compensated for this and accomplished the deed.

So it turned out that I was a real dummy. But I had learned more than one thing that day—not the least of which was not to judge a doctor for doing things differently from the way I had been taught. As I got older and gained my own experience I developed a genuine respect for experience as a teacher. And I also learned that the printed word is not always correct. I would sometimes research topics from several books and find that they all had identical passages. They had copied from each other! I came to the conclusion that people who write books are too busy writing books to know what is going on in the field. I would later be twitted by students for thinking I knew better than the textbooks about certain things. But I knew when I was right I have learned from experience.

The term 'multiple births' refers to more than one baby resulting from a single pregnancy. They can be some of nature's finest spectaculars. I have always been fascinated by the birth of the Dionne quintuplets in 1934—five beautiful, perfect, identical tiny little girls born to a poor Canadian family—delivered at home and kept warm in the oven.

Today quintuplets and even sextuplets are fairly common due to the advent of fertility drugs. We had even reached the advanced plateau of 'harvesting' the embryos—i.e. removing the least hardy appearing ones to give the survivors a better chance. These spectacular deliveries are done by the fertility specialists in the large medical centers—not your friendly neighborhood hospital.

Far less sensational is the birth of twins. Because they are not rare, all OB nurses of any vintage have seen several of them. To the involved family they are anything but mundane. One baby is a miracle—two babies add up to far more than double the miracle. They are double the work and double the expense. Sometimes it is overwhelming.

Years ago I had a neighbor who had twin sons. She told me that when the doctor told her to expect twins she walked out of his office and sat down on the curb and cried. Then she called her husband and cried some more. Eventually they became adjusted to the idea. They made it through the sleepless nights and mountains of dirty diapers that were always waiting to be washed. And the gallons on formula that had to be made. As all new parents do. And they found that they also had amassed double the love and double the joy.

Multiple births usually deliver early as the uterus can bear only so much weight and stretch only so far. So it is no great surprise when twins are born four weeks prematurely. It is a process. It is a persistent old wives' tale that an eight-month baby has no chance for survival while a seven month baby has a much better chance. To try to dispel this myth, I even had one of my own children at eight month's gestation. But the skeptics remained unconvinced. "It must have been a day more or a day less than eight months," they would respond to my tale of my healthy, five pound, six ounce baby girl. Today a baby of only six month's gestation has a fifty percent chance of survival. So perhaps we are less hung up on the fragility of the eight-month baby today. Not so forty years ago.

One day we were awaiting the delivery of twins whose gestational age was eight months. To be on the safe side the obstetrician had called in a pediatrician to be present at the delivery in the event of any immediate problems.

The delivery was uneventful. Both babies breathed spontaneously, had good color and weighed slightly over five pounds each. While weight is not, in itself, a reliable indicator of a newborn's condition, it is still a positive sign when the birth weight exceeds five pounds.

Typical of the times the mother was anesthetized and the father was in the waiting room. So neither parent saw the babies at birth. We took them to the nursery where they required only custodial care. No oxygen or incubators were used and they were put on ordinary formula.

Later, when I took the babies to post partum to meet their parents, the pediatrician accompanied me. His first words to the parents were, "I think we can save them." I was stunned. He had examined them himself and pronounce them normal newborns. Where on earth had that statement come from?

During the next five days he reported remarkable progress of the babies to the parents. All three of them (mom and twins) were dismissed on schedule.

I can only assume that the histrionics had served a dual function. They had probably justified a larger than average bill and, even more importantly, they had brought forth adulation from very grateful parents. Doctors, like actors, seem to have a deep-seated need for appreciation.

Applause! Applause!

Another twin delivery was not as upbeat. The mother had come in at seven month's gestation in advanced labor. The first baby delivered a short time later weighing in at a little more than a pound. After the placenta was delivered the cervix closed up again. We hope that the doctor would put the patient on bed rest and let the pregnancy continue as long as possible. Instead he manually dilated the cervix and delivered the second twin—also a one pounder. Tragically, neither baby survived. That was the seventies.

Twenty years later someone sent me an article from the Canadian newspaper. I read that triplets had been delivered there five weeks apart. A short time later I read of twins born three weeks apart in New Jersey. They were touted as being the first twins in the world to have been born so far apart since 1953 (sic.) That is no doubt why it seemed so logical to me. The forties and fifties were, for me, the logical years.

The most babies that I have seen delivered from a single pregnancy have been triplets. I have had the awesome privilege of seeing two sets of triplets delivered vaginally in the 50s—something that would probably never happen in modern times. I also had some involvement with two sets of triplets delivered by cesarean section in the eighties.

Our first triplet mother was a primigravida and she actually carried the babies to full term. At birth their combined weight was eighteen pounds. A tall, big boned woman, she had not lain down at all during the last trimester. She sat up throughout the entire first stage of labor as well. She had to be anesthetized before we could lay her down on the delivery table to deliver the babies. Than, in hushed silence, we watched the miracle of three babies, following each other in close succession, wending their way through the birth canal to make their entry into the world. There was no fanfare as three lusty cries gave proof to the absence of complications and health of these three perfect individuals.

Mr. And Mrs. Triplet Maker have learned about their impending triple blessed event from an x-ray taken late in the pregnancy. They had spent the rest of the time making elaborate plans for their care. In those post-depression days hiring help was pretty much out of the question for the middle class couple. Husbands rarely got involved in child care—especially infants—at that time, but in this case it was the only viable solution.

Mrs. T. M. stayed in the hospital the usual length of time—seven days. I'm sure she needed every minute of it to prepare herself for the enormous task that lay ahead.

A few months later she paid us a visit, leaving the babies at home with a sympathetic relative. Of course the first thing we wanted to know was how they had been getting along. Taking care of the babies was only part of the tremendous load they shared. Ready-made formula and disposable diapers were still far in the future. So they adopted an assembly line approach. They took turns getting up very early in the morning to prepare and sterilize three batches of formula, for the day. As the babies awoke the other parent would start changing them and getting them ready for feeding. When the formula was ready both parents begin feeding them the first of the day's seven feedings. The 'late' sleeper got to stay up late doing the mountains of laundry that had accumulated during the day. Only selflessness and complete cooperation had gotten them through the first year.

A few months after the Triplet Maker babies were born we had a second set of triplets—a very different scenario altogether. Like the Dionnes this couple was noticeably poor and already had six children—all boys. These babies were only two and half weeks early and made their entrance into the world through a well blazed trail without difficulty and no harrahs. Three more boys! They were somewhat disappointed but this family did not appear to be accustomed to experiencing much in the way of gratification.

Because the odor of their kerosene stove clung to the baby clothes they had brought for the little guys to wear home, we scraped up some extra diapers, shirts and receiving blankets so that the boys would at least begin their a journey through life in clean clothes.

A year later Mrs. T.M. number two came in and delivered her tenth baby boy. And the year after that we delivered to her a dainty baby girl. If at first you don't succeed . . . . we never saw her again. We hope that their family had been completed and that that one measure of success have been the start of many more in all phases of their lives.

It was twenty-five years later and another hospital in a different city when I again experienced the birth of triplets. Medical attitudes about multiple births had changed a great deal by that time. Three babies in a womb have more than likely assumed three different positions. Rather than all three be in the ideal position with the head down facing the mother's back, it is likely that one may be transverse (lying horizontally) and cannot be delivered in that position. If one is in breech position (buttocks or feet first) there is some danger that the delivery of the head may be delayed after the delivery of the body, resulting in brain damage or death. So it has become customary to deliver these babies by Cesarean section.

Mrs. Triplet, Mom of the Seventies, was admitted to the hospital at thirty-six weeks gestation with early contractions. She was placed on bed rest and remained hospitalized. Because she could have gone into active labor at any time, and the hospital had never had triplets before, the OB staff and the OR staff combined forces to plan ahead and stage rehearsals so that, whatever time of the day or night the action began, the same people would be available. And each member of the team would be thoroughly acquainted with his/her role and responsibilities. At least two unexpected drills were called and everyone went through the motions. It appeared that everything would go like clockwork when the actual time came.

Mrs. Seventies T.M. waited more or less patiently but nothing was happening. Then, out of the blue, another mother came in—in labor with triplets. The well-prepared team came in for the delivery, functioning at peak efficiency to deliver three healthy babies by Cesarean Section. This family lived in a small, upstate community and no one had any advance notice of her condition. But she had reaped the benefits of all the planning that had taken place.

The spotlight had been stolen from the discouraged Mrs. S.T.M., but she eventually did deliver and the special team continued to operate at maximum efficiency. Both moms and all six babies went home on schedule in good condition.

The spotlight stealer wrote to us at least once or twice a year for several years, enclosing pictures and news of the babies. Fortune seemed to smile warmly on this family. Everyone thrived. The babies had swimming lessons while they were still infants. Later they added dancing, music and riding lessons.

But the other triplet family continued to take a backseat in the luck department. We heard that one of the babies had died from SIDS (Sudden Infant Death Syndrome) and we soon lost track of them.

After the birth of the second set of triplets in the seventies, one of the medical students remarked that we would probably have one more set. "Triplets come in threes," he said, giggling at the double entendre.

"No," I replied looking back over my 'vast' experience with triplets. "Triplets come in twos."

And indeed that was the end of the triplet deliveries. Perhaps twins come in threes. I've never kept track of that.

A precipitate delivery is one which:

1) Is rapid
2) takes place on an unsterile field and / or
3) no doctor is present

In the forties allowing a patient to precipitate was about the worst offense that an L&D nurse could commit. Primarily, a 'precip' meant that we didn't get the doctor there in time. Precip trays were available for those unfortunate events so that the essentials could be taken care of. At various times we would run these packs down to the admitting office, the ER and even to cars that hadn't arrived at the hospital in time. Rarely is there a complication when a woman delivers that easily. So our main concern was the doctors' wrath.

Today Lamaze training allows the prospective mother to remain in control. If she suddenly attains complete dilation and feels the urge to push, she has been trained to 'blow' through the contractions until the doctor makes a hasty entrance. Since no patient wants her baby to deliver without her doctor present to guide the newborn into the world, she usually cooperates fully.

Prior to the introduction of Lamaze training, most patients did not maintain control. The faster the labor progressed the more out-of-control the average patient became. Often the medications they were given to ease the pain stripped away the level of consciousness that governed control. Then she was unable to rationalize that painful stimuli and chaos resulted. The fathers, waiting in their own room down the hall, were unaware of the furor. And they liked it that way. At least it was better than the alternative—which was the frightening unknown.

Since gaining the patients' cooperation was not usually possible we used anesthetic to accomplish the same result. The doctors wanted the patients to be ready to deliver the moment they arrived so that they could return to their offices at the earliest possible moment. So we would encourage the patient to push until the baby was crowning. Then one nurse would hold her legs together while another 'snowed her down' with ether.

Yes, that does sound cruel in the light of the nineties. But in the forties we accepted it as the status quo. In those militaristic times we obeyed our commands without question; we had little choice. If the patient didn't deliver as soon as the doctor arrived he would leave and head back to his office. Many times I would stick my head out of the window overlooking the parking lot and shout, "come back. She's ready now." I don't remember a single time when the doctor heard me and came back. We would have to wait until he reached the office, received the message, and returned to the hospital.

Ether was quicker, but I was happy that they had begun using nitrous oxide (gas) administered by a registered nurse anesthetists by the time my own children were born. Looking back I marvel that I could have actually administered ether without any training and very little knowledge of anesthetics. Thank goodness there were no adverse consequences. In today's enlightened times we can now refuse to do procedures which we are not qualified or educationally prepared to do. I figured I had balanced the scales when an anesthesiologist asked me to inject additional anesthetic into a patient's epidural tubing which had been taped in place. He was disappointed when I refused but took it in stride.

Back in the fifties one of the women's magazines ran a series of articles entitled

"Cruelty in the Delivery Room." Women across the country related horrifying experiences that occurred in labor and delivery rooms. We were accused of impossible and contradictory things like, "they held my legs together for four hours and then left me alone all night with my legs up in stirrups." Of course everything was grossly exaggerated but there was a grain of truth throughout, and slowly things began to change.

As a labor and delivery nurse I was proud of my record of rarely ever having a precip. Initially I worked alone in L&D no matter how many patients I had in labor. I could call for someone to help only if I needed someone to scrub for a delivery or to help me anesthetize a patient.

My first experience with a precipitate delivery and the first baby I ever delivered

(caught, actually) came while I was still a student. I had scrubbed for my first twin delivery. The patient was scrubbed and draped and the doctor was right there in the room. In that postwar period the scrub sink was in the delivery room and kindly, laid back Dr. Hawkins was standing there, with his back to the delivery table, scrubbing.

After she was draped the patient resumed pushing and a big bubble, which was the Bow, bulged out—with the fetal head inside. "Dr. Hawkins," I called. "You'd better hurry. The babies coming."

"Now, now," he twitted without turning around. "Don't get excited." He continued to slowly and carefully scrub each finger.

At that moment the BOW? ruptured, and the baby popped out all at once. It actually flew through the air. I opened up my hands and the baby landed neatly in them. On the football field there would've been loud cheering.

"Dr. Hawkins," I said, keeping any hint of excitement out of my voice. "The first baby is here." Dr. Hawkins then lost no time getting into his sterile gown and gloves. The second twin was delivered fair and square by his doctor.

As an RN in my first precip was unavoidable. It was provoking, but it was also the beginning of one of those rare times in life when one experiences poetic justice. That made the blot of my record almost worthwhile. I had admitted a multipara in active labor. She and her doctor were from a neighboring town which was about thirty minute drive away. I examined her and found her to be in early labor—dilated 4 cm and not too uncomfortable. I called her doctor to report on her condition. "Do you want me to come in?" he asked.

Foolishly I told him I could call him when she was 7 cm if he liked. Actually it was all rhetorical, because as I was hanging up the phone the patient began to scream, "The babies coming!!! The statement no L & D nurse worth her salt ever ignores. I ran into the labor room just in time to 'catch' the baby.

When her doctor came he was irate. "Where the hell were you?" he fumed.

"I'm sorry," I replied. "She went from four to complete just like that."

"They don't do that," he snapped as he stormed out.

A few days later I admitted another labor patient for the same doctor. Since he no longer trusted me he came in with her. He examined her and informed me that she was 4 cm and he was going to take a nap. At that moment—I know. I can hardly believe it myself and I was there—the patient had hollered, "The babies coming!!!" The doctor ran into the labor room just in time to catch the baby.

I took the precip tray into the room and carried the baby to the nursery. The doctor came out of that room with a sincere look of astonishment on his face. "I can't believe it," he said. "She went from four to complete just like that!" He had even echoed my very words. I just smiled sweetly at this fifty something doctor who had learned what all L & D nurses knew well and kept my silence.

I never received an apology per se, but the next time he came to town he brought me a bag of lemon drops. It was kind of a bittersweet victory.

There is an old adage that says that with each succeeding pregnancy the labor gets easier and shorter and the after-pains get harder and more painful. This generally proves to be true. Doctors breathe easier when the patient is a multi-para because she has already proven that she can deliver vaginally and is less likely to have problems. Nurses feel just the opposite because a multi-para is more likely to precipitate.

The following incident occurred in the hospital where I was teaching and was considered newsworthy enough to be published in the daily newspaper of the city with a half million population.:

A gravida XIII was admitted to the hospital in labor. An L&D, RN met her in the admitting office and took her on the elevator to L&D which was only one floor up. But the mother couldn't hold out for the short ride and, much to her dismay, delivered her baby in the elevator.

"Don't feel bad," the nurse said soothingly. "Last year we had a patient deliver on the hospital lawn."

"I know," sobbed the patient. "That was me!"

Only Dr. Welby can tell when a patient is in true labor merely by placing his hand on her fundus. In real life the only way to tell is if the cervix is dilating. Since all labors are different, sometimes the cervix doesn't begin to dilate until the end of the first stage. True contractions and false ones feel the same to the patient. Many seasoned veterans come to the hospital in false labor several times during the same pregnancy and are sent home still pregnant each time. It becomes embarrassing as well as frustrating.

One such hapless lady had just come in for the third or fourth time with strong contractions. The L&D nurse checked her and found no dilation. Once again she was sent home. But this time was different. This time she never got home but had to stop at the fire station on the way and have the firemen deliver her baby. I didn't work at that hospital at that time but learned about it when it was featured in the newspaper. Later I did go to that hospital with nursing students and it became my favorite hospital. When I felt I knew the staff well enough to tease them, I brought up the incident as there was a fire station located only a few blocks from the hospital. They dryly informed me that she had not delivered at that fire station, but at one on the other side of the city.

As Frank Burns once said so magnanimously to Hawkeye, "anyone could have missed that."

The humane way to deliver babies in the forties and fifties and most of the sixties was to put the mother to sleep for the delivery and keep her anesthetized for the repair of the episiotomy. During this time the baby was usually whisked off to the nursery and kept warm in a heated crib with his head lowered to promote the drainage of mucus. If the baby or the mother had any problems she might not see and hold him for twenty-four hours or longer.

As with most things we accepted this as status quo and never viewed this policy as a problem. Every woman has known to come equipped with the maternal instinct which would kick in whenever that glorious moment came when she first looked at her new baby. Since we nurses felt maternal toward all our patients and especially toward those adorable newborns, we never doubted that the entity existed in every woman.

No one knew that there were women who didn't experience these feelings—those women hid their real feelings from the world, and probably from themselves as well. It was considered O.K. for the father to say, "You take care of him now, and I'll step in when he is old enough to play baseball." But for mother to have felt that way would have been regarded as unnatural.

It was many years before the illustrious scholars, who gave us operant conditioning, figured out that maternal love often needed to be kindled and nurtured through an intricate process. Thus, on the coattails of the Lamaze movement, was born a new concept that would be known as "bonding." Bonding filled in the gap that existed when a new mother looked at her little stranger and felt—nothing.

In truth, bonding is just another name for love. It begins when the mother participates in and really experiences the birth of her baby. Seeing the baby leave her body and enter the world with the umbilical cord still joining them has a tremendous impact. No one will ever need to tell her that this is her baby; she knows it.

As an added bonus the baby's father is at her side experiencing many of the same feelings as he too bonds with their baby. The benefits are legion. Today's fathers change diapers and feed, cuddle and kiss their babies. And having the father share in the entire experience creates a powerful bond between the two parents that is heartwarming and lasting.

Why should we need bonding when we have gotten along fine the old-fashioned way for so many years? Actually it is that old-fashioned way that we are going back to—to the time before the era of anesthetics. But there are some elements of those days that will probably never return—primarily that woman's role is that of sole caregiver of children—husband and home.

Studies have shown that the children who have suffered the most parental abuse were those who were born prematurely. It is ironic that the very ones that require the most nurturing should, instead, receive the least—and, to top it off, experience abuse. Traditionally premies were placed in an incubator or isolette in the nursery and left there for weeks and sometimes months. Until recently the nursery was considered a medically aseptic area where only medical personnel, after thoroughly scrubbing and gowning, were permitted. Parents did not see or touch their babies for extended periods of time—unless you count standing outside the nursery window and peering across the crowded room, past the glass chamber with its sleeve encased armholes and all the tubes and wires.

By the time the parents actually saw and touched their preemie they had more or less put their lives together around his absence. On top of that he was scrawny and ugly compared to the other chunky little newborns. And they were probably struggling under a mountain of bills—caused by the birth of this baby. As dismissal time neared it was necessary for the mother to practice bathing and feeding him. Her fear of hurting the tiny stranger was magnified under the piercing scrutiny of the nursery nurse, who had already bonded beautifully with the baby. It was small wonder they didn't feel the same bond with this baby that they had with their other children. So this child, through the process of displaced anger, was destined to receive the brunt of all his parents annoyances, often to the point of neglect or abuse.

Today it is common to see parents everywhere in the newborn nursery and the N.I.C.U. (Newborn Intensive Care Unit) sitting in rocking chairs holding and feeding their babies. If the baby must remain in the Isolette, the parents may touch their baby by putting their scrubbed arms through the portholes. Touch is a very important factor in the bonding process. Just as kittens and puppies curl up next to each other and their mother, so also do human beings need skin-to-skin contact.

This skin to skin concept was first introduced at about the same time as birthing rooms made their entrance to the delivery room suites, offering a homelike environment while still providing the safety of the hospital facilities. In the beginning, when there was only one birthing room in the department, the prospective parents were required to furnish written approval from the doctor and letters documenting their willingness to follow hospital policy and outlines of their own expectations.

I will never forget one young primigravida who wrote a three-page letter of explicit requirements. One was that she must have skin to skin contact with the baby immediately after it was born. If a Caesarean was necessary, and she was asleep, her husband, Jack, was to be allowed this immediate skin contact. I always get a mental image of Jack ripping his shirt open so that the baby can be placed against his skin. These were parents who would bond with their baby under any circumstances because they were so dedicated. Their concern was that the baby needed to be bonded to them. They need not have worried. Babies will bond with anyone who meets their needs. (And often to parents who fail over and over to provide.) It is the bonding of the care-givers that we are concerned about.

So now we are in the bonding business. We bond the parents so they will love and provide for their babies' needs. We do this by letting them have their babies as often and as long as they wish during the hospitalization period, and by teaching them and allowing them to participate in their babies' cares (e.g. giving the baby a bath) while we are there to guide and assist them.

We assist in grandparental bonding so that the grandparents will offer that special kind of unconditional love and so they will babysit and lend other assistance to the parents so they don't become overburdened and damage their bond. We bond grandparents by letting them hold the baby right after the delivery and in postpartum.

And we bond the siblings to reduce sibling jealousy and to increase the feelings of security. In by-gone times when mom was whisked off to the hospital, perhaps in the middle of the night, and not seen again for many days, the children suffered separation anxiety. They may have thought that Mommy didn't love them anymore and was never coming back. To relieve their anxiety the temporary caregiver may have promised them that mommy was bringing home a surprise when she came home. When she finally came and the "surprise" turned out to be a noisy, wriggley blob that everyone made a fuss over, they found a previously inviolate position as baby of the family abruptly terminated. Suddenly they were "too old to sit on laps, whine, want milk from a bottle or any other 'cute' things they used to do. Now they were "big brother" or "big sister" and nothing they did was cute anymore.

So we initiated sibling classes. They are still placed in the big brother—big sister category, but with it come rewards—status and self-esteem. Their pictures are taken wearing their new "I'm a Big Sister" (or Brother) T-shirt. And when the baby is born the picture is taped to its crib. In the beginning they were allowed one visitation when they could scrub and gown and hold the new baby. Their gowns were cute little gowns from the pediatric department with Mickey Mouse pictures. But that was so traumatic for the ones who had been pediatric patients that they were replaced with plain white ones.

Over the years visitation surveillance relaxed and now the postpartum department seems always to be overrun with visitors of all ages—rarely bothering to scrub or gown when the baby is in the room. Rather distressing to an old timer like myself who remembers outbreaks of impetigo and staph which closed up nurseries for extended periods of time. But the young staff nurses take it in stride and, because the mother and baby are almost always dismissed by the second day, the incubation period is usually longer than the hospital stay, forestalling infections from being transmitted from baby to baby.

Now that we are aware of the importance of bonding, we observe for signs of its presence (or absence) and chart our observations. We note whether the mother holds the baby close to her body (skin to skin contact) or plops it down on her legs or the bed—whether she looks into the baby's eyes (eye to eye contact) or watches TV or gabs on the phone while the baby struggles to nurse, and we note whether she talks to the baby in a high-pitched voice. Most of us automatically raise the pitch of our voice when talking to babies. Now research has shown that babies hear high pitched sounds better. So some pediatricians are counseling their new moms to do this. I was a little concerned about one patient who was bathing her baby, and wanted to wash the side of his face he was lying on. "You're doing that on purpose!" She said in a tone normally used on older children.

By noting these things on the chart we are not attempting to pass judgment on our patients. Hopefully we are calling attention to symptoms of future problems which can be averted. And if this child is admitted to the hospital sometime in the future with suspicious bruises and fractures, the birth record can be consulted to help determine if the child is being abused. It could also act in the parents' behalf and help exonerate them in a case where the baby has an impairment like osteogenesis imperfecta, or brittle bone disease, which causes spontaneous fractures.

In the meantime we do all we can to contribute to the bonding process. The family and friends can use some of the same techniques—like telling the new parents what a good job they are doing—to increase their self confidence and feelings of well-being. Parents who lack self-confidence or feel that things aren't going well often resent the baby and blame him for the way things are.

The hospital's social service department is called for all single mothers and cases of physical, financial, mental and emotional problems. After dismissal many hospitals offer follow-up calls and visits and a baby 'hotline' where every question is answered or referred to a doctor. This line is available twenty four hours a day so that those middle of the night emergencies need not be postponed until morning. Parents are encouraged to consider no question too trivial or 'dumb.'

One of our most memorable patients was in the ICU for her entire hospitalization. Barbara was a gravida X paraVIII (it was her tenth pregnancy and she had previously delivered eight viable aged babies.) She was admitted with asthma, bronchitis, hypertension, pneumonia and cardiac complications. It was the late sixties and we were proud of our modern Intensive Care Unit, equipped to cope with every serious illness—but not pregnancy. Ergo-an OB nurse stayed with Barbara in the ICU around-the-clock.

Barbara had a tracheotomy, was receiving oxygen and was attached to a heart monitor. The ICU nurse took care of her suctioning and monitoring; an inhalation therapist provided IPPB (intermittent positive pressure) to expand her lungs and used a nebulizer to dissolve the mucus; and the OB nurse monitored her FHT and her obstetrical status. Or, as the ICU supervisor put it, we took care of the lower half and they took care of the upper half. During her last three pregnancies Barbara had developed psychosomatic asthma. Small wonder as her seven living children were all under ten years of age and her religion forbade contraception.

Since Barbara's baby was due on her day of admission we hoped she would begin labor spontaneously and that her grand multi-parity would effect a brief, easy labor. Nevertheless we tried to anticipate and be prepared for every eventuality that might possibly occur. Every day we would carry some additional equipment to the ICU—OB drugs, resuscitation equipment, a heated crib for the baby, a precip tray in case she took us by surprise and a major surgical pack in the event that a posthumous Cesarean section became a brutal but swift necessity.

Barbara was given morphine sulfate to curb her restlessness and apprehension and digitalis to strengthen her heart beat. As a result the fetal heart rate slowed from 142 to 128. At times it was difficult to distinguish the FHT from Barbara's rapid pulse. She was maintained in Fowler's position (her head was elevated) and often could not tolerate being lowered for a few minutes for more accurate assessment of the FHT. We didn't yet have access to electronic monitoring equipment.

Because of her tracheotomy Barbara couldn't talk unless the trach was covered, and she found it difficult to communicate with us—especially when she was the most fearful. By the second day her respirations had improved somewhat and we were hopeful of having a live mother and baby.

At that time she began to have mild contractions. A vaginal exam revealed a dilation of 2-3 cm—inconclusive of whether or not she was in true labor. To the growing supply of OB equipment in the ICU we now added packs and instruments for a normal delivery. However the contractions stopped and the next two days passed uneventfully.

On the fourth day the doctor decided to induce labor. He manually ruptured the BOW, and ordered an I V with oxytocin (a contraction stimulator.) Within a few minutes she was having strong, regular contractions.

The ICU nurse continued to monitor and administer to Barbara's medical problems while two students and I monitored her labor and fetal status. I was unsure of my FHT assessment as the rate was identical with Barbara's pulse and they could be heard concurrently. In her agitated state she would not permit us to lower the bed for a more accurate assessment. Fortunately her contractions were not causing her much discomfort but her BP remained elevated and unstable.

During the early part of her labor we thought Barbara's needs could be met best in the ICU but as her labor progressed we began to consider moving her to the delivery room where it would be more convenient, especially if she would need an episiotomy. And the baby would be considered 'clean' for admission to the nursery if born in the OB suite.

We were dubious about the length of time she would have to be on a gurney while we transported her through several corridors and two floors with only portable equipment. And she could precipitate en route. We had no precedent to which to refer. So we kept both units in readiness.

When her dilation reached 5 cm we called an anesthesiologist—standard procedure at that time. He advised that no anesthetic is given. Suddenly I yearned to be 'home' and we began to prepare to transfer Barbara to the delivery room. We procured a stretcher that converted to Fowler's position. Portable oxygen was administered along the way and we arrived in the delivery room without incident.

An anesthesiologist was waiting for us to administer oxygen and suction the trach. The delivery table was tilted to facilitate Barbara's breathing. By the time she was settled on the delivery table her doctor had arrived. Barbara was still 5 cm and when he tried to speed things up she became extremely agitated, thrashing about and acting paranoid and suspicious of all of us. We had all taken turns spending the day with her but the ICU supervisor had been with her every day. Hoping that her familiar face would calm Barbara, we called the ICU supervisor who arrived minutes later, breathless from running up two flights of stairs rather than waiting for the elevator.

Eventually our reassurances reached her or else she had exhausted herself and she quieted down. In a moment of hushed silence the fetal head began to emerge. Our silent tears greeted a healthy baby girl who breathed and cried spontaneously.

Barbara remained in the ICU for sixteen additional days. Her heart condition was diagnosed as pericarditis. We kept the baby in the nursery and bonded lovingly with her. On the fourteenth postpartum day Barbara made her first trip to OB to visit her daughter.

Now highly protective of the baby we decided that, since Barbara was coming from an area considered contaminated by OB standards, she should view the baby from her wheelchair on the other side of the glass door that led into the department. She seemed quite satisfied with that arrangement, but now our perspective returned and we brought her into the department and place the baby daughter in her arms. We all stood around them beaming like proud nannies.

"What are you naming the baby?" Someone asked.

"I dunno, it was supposed to be a boy," was the dull response, shattering our lofty illusions of this double miracle of life.

In a Hollywood version Barbara would be beaming even more than the nurses. But this was real life.

Although the maternity floor is generally the happiest place in the hospital, losing a baby is one of the most tragic experiences parents can have. If the baby is lost before birth—i.e. any time during the pregnancy—it is usually perceived as equally tragic by the prospective parents.

The reasons for spontaneous abortions (miscarriages) are not always apparent. It is believed that fifty percent of these are the result of nature recognizing that she has produced a defective embryo and wiping the slate clean.

One of the most distressing situations is when a woman is a habitual aborter—especially when the pregnancy has progressed to a gestation of four or five months. Happily, a cause and treatment for this syndrome has been found in recent years and women who were formerly unable to achieve motherhood after repeated disastrous attempts are now able to bear normal, healthy babies.

The condition largely responsible for this series of tragedies is called incompetent cervix. Normally the cervix remains essentially closed, with only enough dilation to allow the menstrual flow and the entrance of semen. Ideally the cervix remains closed throughout the pregnancy until shortly before labor begins when the Braxton Hicks contractions cause it to soften and efface and dilate a little.

Some cervices lack this degree of competency and, when the weight of the uterus reaches its level of tolerance—usually between four and five months gestation—the cervix dilates and the fetus literally falls out.

Once the cause was recognized, the solution was simple. A suture is run through the cervix like a purse string and pulled tight. Miraculously, the pregnancy is maintained resulting in the birth of a viable baby.

At term the pregnancy can be terminated in one of two ways. The suture can be left in place and the baby delivered by Cesarean section, leaving the suture intact for any subsequent pregnancies the mother may have. Or the suture can be snipped and removed—without the necessity of an anesthetic—at the onset of labor. Labor then proceeds at a normal pace. But in the event of future pregnancies the suture will have to be replaced.

Usually, with either method, everything proceeds so normally that the casual observer would not be able to discern that the patient had had a purse string suture. I have seen only one instance that deviated from the norm and it was actually rather bizarre. The patient had been admitted to L&D in active labor. The obstetrician removed the cervical suture and the contractions increased in intensity and frequency, but vaginal exams determined that the cervix was not dilating. Normal bleeding of labor increased and became excessive. Two units of blood were ordered stat. But still no dilation.

Then suddenly the baby's head appeared on the perineum and an angry cry announced his birth. I was just outside of the delivery room when I heard that cry. I knew that she had just been checked and had not dilated. How, I wondered, could that baby have delivered through a closed cervix?

The doctor's examination revealed that the cervix had lacerated at the portion where scar tissue had formed over the suture line. Scar tissue doesn't have the elasticity of normal tissue and wouldn't stretch to allow the cervix to dilate. But the pressure of the contraction pushing the fetal head against it caused it to rupture, allowing an exit for the baby. This tear was sutured up and mother and baby were as good as new.

Another interesting phenomenon came to light when we admitted a woman who had become pregnant even though her right ovary and her left fallopian tube had been removed. The mystery was how the ovum could have got from the ovary to the tube on the opposite side to become fertilized.

The students who went to the OR to watch her Cesarean section came back with this fascinating explanation. Nature, in her eternal campaign to perpetuate the species, had caused the tube to wind around the back of the uterus until it reached the ovary on the other side. Just as a flower reaches out towards the sun.

One of the most dreaded but common complications of pregnancy is toxemia. It occurs all too frequently and is one of the primary reasons that prenatal care is so necessary.

Recently renamed P I H (Pregnancy Induced Hypertension) because elevated blood pressure is a classical symptom, it can have its onset any time from beginning of the last trimester to a month after the delivery. It may begin and progress slowly or have a sudden onset and progress rapidly.

The three classical symptoms are elevated BP, protein in the urine—one reason the urine is tested at every visit, and edema (swelling.) Edema, is caused by water retention and results in excessive weight gain, which explains why your doctor gets so testy when you gain too much. He doesn't want you to have P I H.

In its initial stage toxemia is called pre-eclampsia. During this phase all efforts are geared toward preventing the advent of eclampsia. If they are unable to get the symptoms under control, the patient develops grand mal seizures and is then said to have eclampsia.

I had my first eclamptic patient during the first year following graduation. I was alone on the floor when the patient, who was on bedrest and heavily sedated, began seizuring. My heart was pounding wildly as I timed her seizure and checked her vital signs and status. Then I called her doctor to report my findings, adding that her BOW had ruptured.

When the doctor came a little later and checked her—it was kindly doctor Cannon, who never got upset or raised his voice—he looked at me and laughed. "Why, her BOW is right there before God and everyone," he chuckled. I blushed as I realized that she had just been incontinent—something that usually goes along with seizures. At least I was thinking like an OB nurse.

Whether or not her membranes had ruptured, she needed to be delivered as soon as possible. Since it is the pregnancy which has caused the problem, the ultimate solution, when all else has failed, is to terminate the pregnancy. This is never a matter of choosing the mother's welfare over the baby's as the baby is in as much danger from the condition as the mother and is always of viable age. This patient was already having contractions; so it was unnecessary to induce her. We moved her to the delivery room and gave her drip either to prevent any more convulsions and in a remarkably short time we had a brand-new baby girl.

The baby never had any discernible problems. The mother had some hallucinations—she saw snakes crawling on the walls and men looking in her third-floor window, but did not perceive these things as disturbing. Her vital signs rapidly stabilized and within a week she and the baby were both dismissed in good condition.

Over the next 20 years the treatment of toxemia remained basically constant, consisting of:

> Bedrest
>
> Sedatives
>
> Magnesium sulfate (the injectable kind, not the Epsom salts that once cost me a day off)
>
> Padded tongue blades to prevent biting the tongue during a seizure
>
> Padded side rails to prevent injury during a seizure but the occurrence of toxemia continued at a persistent rate.

I found most perplexing the cases of sudden onset with no prior warning. These proceeded directly to the eclampsia without pause. One such incident occurred shortly after I began teaching. The patient's labor and delivery had been uneventful. A student was sitting with her checking her vital signs and the head nurse and I were sitting at the nurses' station completing the paperwork when the cleaning woman ambled over and, in a deadpan voice, told us that a patient had fallen out of bed. We looked at each other and mock astonishment. OB patients don't fall out of bed. Then we both made a bee-line for the patient's room. She was indeed on the floor and in the throes of a grand mal seizure.

The student was just returning to the room with a washcloth, which the patient had requested. She reported that the patient was feeling fine and sitting on the side of the bed when she left her a few minutes earlier. Of course she never should have left with the side rails down, much less sitting on the edge of the bed. But even more distressing was the fact that in her pocket was a little notebook in which she had written down several elevated blood pressure readings that she had not reported to anyone or recorded on the charts. We would probably not have been able to avert the seizure, but we may have at least notified the doctor and gotten an order for something that would've made it less severe. I'm sure that is one nurse who now thoroughly understand the importance of keeping side rails up and will never again fail to report pathological findings promptly.

And that, ladies, is why we are always bothering you—taking those vital signs so often and checking all those body parts—just to catch that one time out of a thousand when something is going to go wrong.

It was several years later in a larger, more modern hospital when I again saw toxemia that moved that rapidly. I was still teaching but now I was working for the Community College instead of the hospital. Practical nursing students were not assigned to patients with acute, life-threatening conditions. So my responsibilities were to see that the students learned from the experience but at the same time stayed out of the way of the doctors and staff nurses.

The patient was eight months pregnant with no history of problems. She had made a routine visit to her obstetrician. He found her blood pressure so alarmingly elevated that he sent her directly to the hospital and phoned L&D with orders. Normally the admissions clerk brought the labor patients to L&D but we waited in vain for her. Then we got a call from the Emergency Department asking us to go there and pick her up.

Although I was no longer on the staff I will always be a staff nurse in my heart. So I have always pitched in when the staff needed a nurse hand and it has made for good relations between us. So that is how I happened to accompany one of the staff nurses to the ED to bring this patient to L&D.

We learned that she had had a seizure in the car on the way to the hospital. Fortunately for her, her husband was with her and was driving. We can only imagine what it cost him to maintain his composure enough to maneuver through traffic and get his wife admitted to the hospital under those circumstance. She had had another seizure in the admitting office and one more in the ED but was fairly alert and lucid on the return to L&D.

Her labor room was immediately overrun with nurses, laboratory technicians, doctors and medical students. Her husband stood in the middle of the room while personnel bumped him from all directions as they rushed back and forth. Empathizing with all this man had gone through and all that still lay ahead of him. I urged him to let me make him comfortable in the waiting room with a cup of coffee. "No" he answered resolutely. "I've been with her this far; I'm going to stay with her the rest of the way." And he did stay—as close as he could—throughout the ordeal.

Many changes in treatment had come about by then. All medications were given IV to maintain strict control. A urinary catheter was inserted for accurate monitoring of output. Plans were made to terminate the pregnancy by doing a Caesarean as soon as the patient was stabilized. When everything was set up the unit began to assume a relatively calm ambience. But there was an undercurrent of nervousness among the staff. The patient had another seizure after being admitted to the unit and all the nurses were noticeably affected. One young RN sat stiffly at her bedside, resolved to stay with her patient whatever befell.

The students noticed that the staff gave negative looks whenever they came too close. So I stationed them on the fringes listening to all the conversations. They would ask me what the doctors were going to do, but the doctors were not even sure themselves until they worked it out in the course of their discussions.

Eventually everyone dispersed to wait for the patient's condition to stabilize so they could do the Cesarean. But I was remembering my first eclamptic patient and how speedily nature had taken care of terminating that pregnancy. So every time I went in the room I placed my hand on her fundus, and each time she was having a strong contraction. Dutifully I informed the RN each time, hoping that someone would do a vaginal exam. The RN would only glare at me and eventually told me she didn't want anyone to touch the patient.

(Specifically me) It appeared that having the patient be in labor was just one more thing than she could handle. The patient stabilized and was taken to the OR without ever having to determine whether she had been dilating.

After the delivery the baby girl was taken to be an N ICU and mom went to the ICU. A week later the mother came to the OB department to pick up her baby. Both were dismissed. None of the staff nurses on post partum or in the nursery and ever seen her before and they were very matter-of-fact as they gave her the dismissal instructions for herself and the baby, while I stood there beaming—and marveling at the miraculous change that had taken place in only one short week.

Both of the women with the rapid onset eclampsia were black. The first one was of lower socioeconomic status, and the latter was upper middle class—an Air Force officer's wife.

(That might explain his remarkable composure in the face of extreme adversity.) Two or three other eclamptics I cared for were also black—a high percentage of the total number. Adding to this the black disposition to hypertension in general, I developed a theory that there was also a black predisposition to eclampsia. I discussed this with a medical student and he said, "Yes, we studied that in class. Low socioeconomic people are more apt to be toxemic." That was not what I meant. But my very limited experience does not constitute a scientific study. So I guess we will just have to wait until *THEY* get around to doing one.

Not all cases of toxemia are so dramatic. And most of them have a happy outcome. But some are not so fortunate. Many years ago I did a stint on the graveyard shift. One of my coworkers, Holly, was a pleasant, easy-going young RN, average looking, married to an OB resident and pregnant. She came to work every night, carried her share of the load and never had any complaints. When she was about seven months along she stopped coming to work. Later we heard that she had had her baby prematurely and, still later, that her baby daughter had died.

Although I had known her for only a short time I had become very fond of her and decided to pay her a condolence call. Always somewhat apprehensive when confronted with grief, my first reaction when she answered the door was amazement. This young woman was a real knockout. At first I didn't even recognize this stunning beauty.

Cheekbones and contours had replaced the previously round face. Big round eyes had replaced the slitty ones I remembered.

Unlike many grief stricken people who try to ease their pain by rebuffing sympathy and making well-wishers feel guilty, Holly graciously put me at ease and wore her grief with dignity. After we had visited for a while everything began to fall into place and make sense. Holly had had toxemia. Her face looked so different because she had had edema. Fluid had made her face puffy and changed its contour. I had not known her before; so I was unaware of the changes that occurred. But I couldn't understand how her husband, who was an OB resident, and her doctor, a noted obstetrician, had failed to pick up on the clues and put her on bed rest when the symptoms became so severe. One reason could have been because she was a nurse. And nurses, traditionally, have been kept with their noses to the grind stone through conditions that put ordinary people on bed rest. The only other reason I could come up with was denial. Since toxemia-phobia goes back well before Holly's time I can only believe they hoped it would just go away. Eventually it did. But what a price they paid!

Nurses are far from being immune to toxemia—in fact they are quite adept at developing all kinds of complications and serious conditions. And doctors have allowed or even encourage them to continue working in the face of conditions under which they would have kept a lay person on bed rest or hospitalized—probably because they themselves do not take time off for illnesses unless it is beyond their control.

The mystery of toxemia is still with us today. The latest treatment is called "left lateral recumbency." The patient is reminded to lie on her left side as much of the time as possible. Sometimes the beneficial effects are dramatic. When a pregnant woman is lying on her back the full weight of the uterus is resting on the blood vessel that carries oxygen and nutrients to the placenta and the kidneys, blocking the flow. Placing the patient on her side improves the circulation to these areas, resulting in lower blood pressure, increased urinary output and increased oxygen to the fetus. In addition there is frequent checking of the vital signs and central nervous system reactions so that we are not caught by surprise when the problem worsens. But the condition and the mystery surrounding it remain with us.

An even more mysterious facet is the occurrence of eclampsia as late as one month after delivery. Since it is the pregnancy that causes it, it is difficult to understand how it can begin so long after the pregnancy has terminated. It is rare for an OB nurse to see these patients because they are not admitted to the OB department. I had occasion to see one of these patients when I was admitted to the hospital as a patient myself. My roommate had been one of my OB patients a month earlier. She was being dismissed that day but she told me, "I had post eclampsia. (sic) That's what my doctor told me.

I got a few more details on the course of this entity a couple of years ago when I met a former student and coworker. Her daughter had delivered her eighth baby a month earlier. She had developed such a severe headache that they had taken her to the Emergency Department in the hospital where she had delivered. There they found her blood pressure elevated. Not trained to think like OB personnel, they procrastinated until she began to have seizures. Penny, the patient's mother, was an LPN who had worked in L&D for many years. She was very disgusted that the ED had failed to stay on top of the situation and allowed the seizures to develop. But the truth is that this is an extremely rare condition. Once again we can hear Frank Burns generously saying, "Anyone could have missed that." Both of these women made full recoveries.

During the early years of this century diabetes in pregnancy was not a problem. That is because juvenile onset diabetics usually did not live long enough to become pregnant. Those that did were sterile.

I had to laugh at the irony when one of my students related that her geriatric instructor had told them that diabetics couldn't have babies and all their babies had birth defects. She was an elderly woman caught in the gap between two generations. The first part of her statement was true when she was a young student. Then insulin was discovered. Diabetics began to live longer and were able to conceive. They did have a disproportionately high rate of stillbirths and birth defects. And their own health and well-being were seriously compromised.

During pregnancy a hormone produced by the placenta causes the insulin requirements of a diabetic to fluctuate a great deal and rise steeply. So the pregnant diabetic requires close and constant supervision. Modern methods for monitoring and treating diabetes have improved their outlook considerably. But it is still a touchy situation.

I have a cousin who became diabetic after the birth of her first two children. Then she conceived again. I was working in a distant city where we had a standing routine for babies of diabetic mothers. They were all placed in incubators with mist and checked frequently. I wrote her about that so she wouldn't be alarmed if that happened to her baby.

It did and she wasn't concerned. They both got along well and were dismissed on schedule. But when I returned to the city and went back to work in that hospital I learned that they were not taking those precautionary measures routinely. They had placed the baby in the incubator with mist because he was having respiratory problems. Fortunately, "all's well that ends well." Shakespeare, again. Oft times he's right.

Some women who have never had diabetes develop it during their pregnancies. This is called gestational diabetes. When the pregnancy no longer exists the diabetes disappears. These women are more predisposed to having diabetes permanently at a later point in time.

We had one patient with gestational diabetes who was hospitalized for adjustment of her insulin dosage. Every day her insulin requirement increased until, on dismissal, she was getting 200 units each morning. At that time the most concentrated insulin was 80 u / cc. So we had to give her two and a half syringefuls and stick her three times.

A few months later she delivered her baby. Then every morning her need for insulin decelerated. By the time she was dismissed she was getting only 20 units. Soon after her dismissal her doctor told us that she was completely off insulin.

I decided that my aunt had surely had gestational diabetes. It was before I was born and they probably didn't check for it at the time. Her first baby was in the normal weight range but her second weighed over twelve pounds. My aunt developed adult onset diabetes more than 20 years later. Both of these are typical of gestational diabetes.

Babies of diabetic mothers usually have the antithesis of diabetes—i.e. hypoglycemia. The high sugar content from the mother's blood enters the babies blood during pregnancy resulting in excessive body weight and the babies production of large quantities of insulin to metabolize it. After birth the baby continues to produce excessive insulin resulting in low blood sugar. Treatment involves giving the baby enough glucose to raise his blood sugar to normal without stimulating him to continue to produce large amounts of insulin.

Although they are large these babies are often premature—subjecting them to respiratory problems. Even though they are larger than average they are not mature. Often the pregnancy is deliberately terminated three or four weeks early to prevent intrauterine death which is more likely to occur at that time.

Closer control of the mothers' blood sugar with more frequent blood checking and insulin administration has resulted in fewer complications for both mother and baby. Even brighter outlooks are appearing on the horizon in such innovative treatments as beta cell transplants.

Life in L&D is never boring. Every labor is different. Although the textbook tells us that the length of the normal labor of a primigravida is twelve to eighteen hours, and the length of labor of a multipara is eight to twelve hours, in real life the variation is much greater. And often the lines of demarcation are ambiguous.

Early in my career, in the late forties, I admitted Annie, a young primigravida in labor with whom I had gone to high school. When her initial progress was slow, not unusual for a 'primip' it gave us time to visit and catch up on old times. When the day had gone by and Annie had dilated only 3-4 cm, Dr. Cannon began to consider doing a section. But then Annie dilated another centimeter. Thinking that things were about to pick up, we again played the waiting game. But once more, although the contractions continued, dilation ceased.

The next morning, with no new progress, Dr. Cannon called in an eminent specialist for consultation. Both agreed that a 'wait and see' attitude was indicated. Another day went by and Annie's contractions continued without substantial progress. But every time the obstetricians would decide the time had come to intervene Annie would dilate another centimeter.

Nobody considered that Annie's contractions might not be strong enough to dilate her cervix efficiently. Annie, not ordinarily a complainer, moaned and groaned through each one. In the absence of monitoring equipment we took her at face value. Doctors did not readily jump into surgical intervention at that time. Annie and her baby were both in good condition—their vital signs strong and within normal limits. Neither was in any danger. So medically there was no reason to be hasty.

At that time Pitocin, an oxytocic drug that stimulates contractions, was given only to induce labor. Labor patients did not routinely have IVs and most drugs, including Pitocin were given intramuscularly. No one even considered giving Annie Pitocin since her contractions seemed so painful and strong.

The pattern of Annie's labor continued in the same way until the end of the third day when she finally delivered a healthy baby girl. She had a normal vaginal delivery and neither she nor the baby suffered any ill effects. The little girl grew up to be a lawyer, but we don't blame that on the circumstances of her birth. (Just a joke. No lawsuits, please.)

But Annie had had enough and swore that she would never have another baby. And she never did. They later adopted a baby boy to complete their family.

A few years later I met Annie's mother at a social function. She introduced me to a friend with the words, "This is Carita—she was with Annie when we almost lost her." I was caught off guard—searching my mind for a time when Annie had nearly died. Then I remembered her very long labor. It had never occurred to me that her family had thought that her life was in danger. Families were kept conveniently out of sight at the time and Annie's family were not obtrusive. And I was young and naïve. I understand concern for family much better now.

Over the years I have seen many patients with sluggish labors. Despite their reaction to their contractions, they all perceive them as strong and painful, these patients have been found to be suffering from uterine inertia—a condition in which the contractions are not strong enough to dilate the cervix. The treatment is simple and generally effective. Simply add some Pitocin to a bag of IV solution and administer it in a carefully controlled drip rate. Usually the quality of the contractions increases dramatically.

As the contractions become stronger the reaction of the patient is very interesting. Up to this point she has been moaning and groaning with the milder contractions. You might expect her to lose control as they increase in intensity. But instead she settles down at the realization that at last she is getting somewhere. It is as if the poorer quality contractions were like a nagging, persistent headache that won't go away. With the improved quality of the contractions she can see that they are getting the job done and the end is in sight.

Lengthy, painful labors are quickly forgotten but babies are for a lifetime. Unfortunately, so are birth defects. Birth defects have a habit of cropping up periodically in OB casting a shadow over an otherwise utopia. Many of them are minor and many are repairable. But the ones that are major and cannot be 'fixed' are usually the most memorable.

One busy night in the L&D our labor rooms were all full and we had a new admission. It was the late fifties and the fathers' waiting room with its pot of strong coffee was still a prominent feature of the department. Since it was the only room with any kind of a 'parking' place and she was in very early labor I settled her in one of the chairs and took her history, leaving her in her street clothes until we had an available labor room. She took the makeshift arrangements with good grace and was pleasant and cooperative.

Our other patients' labors were progressing rapidly and it soon became too hectic to think of her again. One of the other nurses, freed up after her patient delivered, took over her care while I followed through on another patient. I was circulating for her delivery when I glanced out the doorway that opened into the scrub room located between the two delivery rooms. There, stretched out on the floor, were a pair of legs—the rest of the body hidden behind the wall. I went into the scrub room to investigate and found the intern lying on the floor, fully conscious. Occasionally a new intern will become faint at his/her first delivery—either from the blood or as the episiotomy scissors cut through the tissue. So I was only mildly concerned as I asked her if she was all right.

"I'm alright now," she said getting up. "It's just that the baby we had (pointing to the other delivery room) is a freak—it was awful!" She shuddered at the memory. "It made me feel like I was going to faint."

Later our two newly delivered patients spent the recovery period together in their respective gurneys in the large hall we use for recovering post delivery patients. As was the custom at that time, the babies had been whisked off to the nursery while the mothers were still anesthetized and neither mother had seen her baby. Bonding per se was as yet unheard of. Mothers were universally expected to have a maternal instinct. My patient's husband was out of town and her brother had accompanied her to the hospital. Now he stood awkwardly at his sister's side. "Hi—how ya doin'?" He asked stiffly. The other patient was the woman I had admitted in the fathers' waiting room. Her husband was bent over her gurney, holding her hand and kissing her. My patient was the one I felt sympathy for. If ever a moment was meant to be shared with one's husband, it was the birth of their baby. I felt, in my heart, that even a sad occasion shared with a soul mate was better than a happy one alone. Of course that moment is soon over and the rest of one's life is a very long time.

As busy as we had been having babies, post partum was rapidly filling up. The other RN decided that her patient should be transferred directly to a medical—surgical floor and not see her baby at all. At that time many doctors felt that defective babies should be institutionalized and the parents should just forget all about them—not become attached or, in today's terms, bonded.

Mrs. Granger's baby, Robbie, was placed in the NICU for diagnosis and treatment. Mrs. Granger was told that her baby was a freak and was transferred to another floor. I never saw her again, but later there were a lot of rumors.

Robbie's appearance was a bit startling at first. His fingers and toes were webbed and he had small, very deep set eyes. His forehead was large and dome shaped and the interior fontannel (the 'soft spot') was huge and occupied most of his forehead. Compared to many of the babies with cranio-facial deformities that appear on the talk shows today, Robbie was beautiful. In fact, as we nurses cared for him day after day, we became increasingly attached to him. And he did indeed become beautiful to us.

Robbie was a little trooper with a vigorous suck. His little eyes sparkled brightly as he grasped one of our fingers and wolfed this formula down. During this period when we were becoming increasingly convinced that he was a great little guy we began to receive reports about his mother.

Mrs. Granger was refusing to take her baby home with her—refusing to even see him. To many of the staff nurses she was the one that was a monster. I remembered what a good sport she had been when I had admitted her in the waiting room. As nervous as the expectant fathers that surrounded her, she had still been cooperative and filled with joyful anticipation. If she had become a monster that monster had been created by whatever professionals that had planted the image of a monsterous baby in her mind.

As the days passed, we watched Robbie's progress record to see what his diagnosis would be. Eventually it appeared on the chart—Cruzon's Disease or Hypertelorism, which referred to his dome shaped forehead. We could not find much additional information about the syndrome but one of the symptoms noted was mental retardation. We refused to believe that this bright little fellow was retarded.

Holley's husband was taking his OB residency at University Hospital. She happily reported that at University there was a whole ward of these kids and that many of them were very bright.

Mrs. Granger was dismissed on the fifth post partum day and the baby, soon after that since he was doing so well. From time to time in the years to come I would think about calling her and asking how they were getting along. But nurses didn't do follow-ups at that time and I was young and didn't know how receptive she would be after her unpleasant experiences in the hospital. So I never did. But I thought of them often and hoped that life had shown them some

"Tender mercies" and that they were able to overcome a bungled beginning and experience a loving bond.

"Happy little Mongol

Doesn't give a damn.

Wish I were a Mongol

My God! Maybe I am!"

The pediatrician chanted this little ditty while he examined a newborn baby. Sounds callous? Of course it does. But doctors and nurses have always used levity to relieve the stress of all degrees of horrors we see doled out all the time to perfectly nice people—and even some that aren't so nice.

In OB we don't see this dark side of life very often. There is a lot of pain, but it is only temporary. Most babies are irresistible so that, even if they were unplanned, they are made welcome. Most of the couples are young and optimistic that everything will turn out well.

So when something goes wrong in our field none of us is really prepared. In a perfect world all babies would be beautiful and brilliant and all parents, loving and wise. But our world, of course, is far from perfect.

One of the most frequent deviations from the normal to strike the newborn is the syndrome we used to call Mongolism, because one of the symptoms is slanting eyes similar to the eyes of geographic Mongolians. Technically it is known as Trisomy 21 because a part of the twenty-first chromosome breaks off and creates a forty-seventh chromosome in these individuals while 'normal' people have only forty-six. That is why most of these babies have similar symptoms, both visible and covert.

One of the symptoms is mental retardation. Because of this the full term by which these babies were formally known was "Mongolian Idiot." It is not surprising that, as we became more enlightened, the mothers of the children began to protest and the name was changed to Down's Syndrome after the man who first identified it. Early stimulation, popularly called early intervention, and concentrated education have shown that these children have a wide range of intellectual abilities and many of them are educable.

At one time I read an article citing a statistic that only fifty percent of Down's Syndrome babies have typical physical characteristics. My first reaction was, "That's ridiculous. All the ones I've seen have looked typical." I hadn't taken into consideration the fact that I just wasn't identifying the ones that were atypical. Today genetic testing can identify those babies and children that do not have overt symptoms.

But there was one unforgettable Down's baby that had momentarily slipped my mind. I was still a relatively new graduate when one of our RN's was admitted in premature labor. She was married to the son of our beloved Dr. Cannon, making their welfare doubly important to us. After a very brief labor Kathy delivered a scrawny little boy. Because he was cyanotic, we put him in an incubator with oxygen and kept him under close observation. He was definitely a strange looking baby, but there was nothing we could put our collective finger on. Later these babies would be referred to as FLK (funny looking kid.) Yes, that is really a legitimate term that doctors use as a tentative diagnosis for conditions they are having difficulty identifying.

Although baby Cannon didn't have typical Mongoloid features, we opened his fingers and examined his palms. There we found bilateral Simian lines. Simian lines are single lines that bisect the palms horizontally instead of the two lines that most people have. Simeon lines are the one characteristic of Down's syndrome. I expect that you've inspected your own palms by now. For those of you who have identified simian lines—don't panic. Many normal people have them too. Among my clinical groups one student in each group would often exhibit them usually the brightest one.

Cowards that we were we hoped that having Baby Cannon in the incubator with oxygen running would save us from the unsavory task of taking him out to see his mother. It didn't. As soon as Kathy had recovered from the anesthetic she demanded to see him. The pediatrician approved a short visit. So we had no choice. Nobody wanted the job. So it fell on me. I planned a brief encounter, keeping him tightly wrapped for warmth—sort of a quick in and out—so he could be quickly returned to his much-needed oxygen.

But Kathy was not to be put off. She opened the blanket and examined her baby carefully. Even though she was a recent graduate and inexperienced, and her baby's symptoms were not obvious, she picked up on them. "Why are his ears so low set? What's wrong with him?" She asked. Borderline panic in her voice.

"He needs his oxygen," was my evasive response. "I should get him back to the Nursery." But she persisted, opening his fingers and noting the Simeon lines.

"Is my baby a Mongoloid? I don't want my baby to be a Mongoloid!" She pleaded.

It is a helpless situation to be in when one is dedicated to serving humanity. You want to throw protective arms around them both and proclaim, "He won't be. I won't permit that to happen." But it wouldn't change the facts. She did recall that her husband had Simian lines and we both took comfort in the hope that he had inherited them and would ultimately be all right. By that time the little fellow was quite cyanotic and I took refuge in rushing him back to the nursery.

Sadly, our worst fears were realized and he was diagnosed as positive for mongolism. Dr. Cannon insisted that he be placed in an institution immediately and that the young parents never see him again. It was their first and only child at that time. I cannot fault that dear man who was the essence of kindness to one and all. He was simply a product of his time. Some doctors told their patients that in China they take these babies to the top of a mountain and leave them there.

Doctors are historically worse than nurses when it comes to situations like this. Only the strongest survive the rigors of college, medical school, internship and residency. Those survivors are accustomed to forging the events of their lives. When it comes to an event they can't control their despair runs deep. Many times they simply disappear leaving the nurses to 'face the music.'

The young Cannons survived their misfortune and went on to have four normal children. I'm sure they were all a joy and a blessing. But none would take the place of their firstborn, who would always cast a shadow of nonfulfillment on this family. Today he would have been a vital part of the family, useful and beloved.

Some twenty years after the birth of the Canon baby things still hadn't changed much for these babies. Nor had the attitudes of the 'good old doctors.' We had a forty-one-year-old mother who had just delivered an obviously Mongoloid infant. This woman had a twenty-one-year-old son and had had no pregnancies in the interval between—the classical candidate for delivering a Mongoloid baby.

The doctor strode into her room just as she was struggling to fight off the anesthetic. While she alternately opened and tried to focus first one eye and then the other, he cheerfully blurted out, "Oh say, did they tell you about the baby? He's a Mongoloid." Then he turned on his heel and strode out of the room. Flabbergasted, I followed him out, but he was quickly down the hall and out the door.

By that time the new mother was wide awake and had her signal light on. "What did he say about my baby?" I tried to comfort her but nurses were still not allowed to give out information or counsel patients.

I was furious with this doctor for dropping this bombshell while she was not fully conscious and then walking out instead of spending time with her. I called him and told him she was on the verge of hysteria and asked him if he would like to order a sedative. "What did you 'girls' do to her?" He snarled. "She was fine when I left her." Of course he didn't order anything. Nor did he return to talk to her. His hour for making rounds was 6:30 A.M. not a great time for conversation.

I think I have probably seen more than a hundred of these Down's babies. They are precious little beings. Their poor muscle tone causes them to curl up into a cuddly bundle. Of all the types of retardation, these children are the most delightful and easiest to rear. They have placid personalities and loving dispositions. Many of their parents who were heartbroken at the onset became most devoted as they bonded with these children who never grew up and left them.

At one time they rarely lived beyond the age of twelve. The picture has brightened considerably in recent years. Surgery to correct heart defects has increased the life expectancy considerably. Oral surgery makes the speech more understandable. And early intervention and special education have proven that they are trainable and often educable. Many now move into supervised adult apartments and support themselves. Institutionalization is the worst thing that can happen to them. Happily, that rarely happens anymore.

One of the most severe defects is anencephaly—the absence of a brain. These babies have a rudimentary brainstem which controls basic functions like breathing and sucking. Their heads are usually very small, having lacked the stimulation from an enlarging brain to grow.

The opposite of this condition is hydrocephalus. The head of the hydrocephalic is very large because the cerebrospinal fluid's drainage system is faulty. Unable to drain off, the fluid builds up forcing the head to enlarge to accommodate the large volume of fluid. If the condition is untreated, the head continues to grow bigger and bigger. In time the child may be unable to lift his head because of the great weight. In some cases a shunt can be surgically inserted to provide a man-made drainage system and avert the dire consequences.

One day a sixteen-year-old, unwed primigravida was admitted to OB for a Cesarean section. She was not in labor and there was no apparent indication for a Cesarean. Hospital policy required an ultrasound to be done. The Sonogram pronounced that a vaginal delivery would probably be possible. Still the attending physician insisted upon doing the Caesarean and he and the L&D Chief of Staff pow-wowed in the OR / L&D corridor for several hours. No one knew how he had managed it, but eventually the surgeon won out and the Caesarean was done.

The adoption process had already begun. A woman on the West Coast was hovering by her telephone, ready to fly in at a moment's notice to bring her new baby home.

In the operating room the appearance of the baby was a shocker. The little girl was hydrocephalic. Ultrasound was in its infancy at that time. The radiologists had much to learn about them before their interpretations would become accurate and dependable. That young mother could never have delivered that baby vaginally.

After the baby was brought to the nursery, she was examined by the pediatrician. We hear so much about the rising cost of medical treatment caused, in large part, by unbelievably expensive equipment. It is all true. But this particular problem was diagnosed with a two-dollar flashlight. The pediatrician placed the flashlight flush against the side of the baby's head and turned it on. The beam of light went through the head and came out on the other side. The normal head has an opaque brain which blocks the flow of light. But this baby, although hydrocephalic, was also anencephalic. And there was no brain to prevent the stream of light from going through.

The staff and students alike were fascinated with the procedure and it was repeated over and over again, never losing its attraction. The baby was a tragic little bit of humanity. Although tests showed that she had two small vestiges of brain tissue in addition to her brainstem, they were non-functioning. With no central nervous system to interpret sensory input she was functionally blind and deaf and profoundly retarded.

The adopting mother was notified and told not to come. The baby was no longer available for adoption. It was reported that she became hysterical and insisted on coming for "her" baby. But eventually she was convinced that her dream was ended. At least for the time being. Not only was this baby in deplorable condition but her life expectancy was estimated at two months.

Despite all this the baby girl was phenomenal. She took her formula greedily while grasping the care giver's finger. She burped, yawned and stretched just like any normal baby. It made me a little uneasy that she did all of those cute things our own babies do that lead us to say,

"See how smart he is." But she was doing them automatically—like a robot. The Head Nurse was especially enamored with her. She spent every minute she could spare feeding and holding her. She would like to have adopted her. Everyone gave her an abundance of loving until she was dismissed, but no one knew how much of it she perceived. She lived in a foster home until she died at the age of three months.

In the course of thirty or forty years an OB nurse sees a great many birth defects ranging from very serious to very minor. Only two percent of all babies born have any kind of birth defect; so the total number is relatively minimal. But to the nurses who care for them they are unforgettable. And to their parents it can mean a tremendous financial burden and years or even a lifetime of heartache.

Cleft palate and club feet are among those defects that can crop up periodically. They are correctable surgically—and those little casts they apply to the feet right after birth, are so cute. But even though they are not life threatening, they can be very upsetting to parents. Far more serious are defects like the oomphalacele, in which the abdominal contents are outside the body in the umbilical cord. Delicate handling and prompt surgery are vital. Fortunately this is a rare occurrence which I have seen only twice in forty years.

It was nearly thirty years before I saw a newborn diagnosed with Osteogenesis Imperfecta (brittle bone disease.) Or was this because methods of identifying and diagnosing this rare entity and not yet been perfected?

Spina bifida (failure of the spine to close) with Myelomeningocele (protrusion of the spinal nerves and membrane) are seen a little more frequently and often mean a lifetime of paralysis. I remember one in which the membrane had ruptured and the spine was exposed. Today, if these are diagnosed prenatally by ultrasound or amniocentesis, the baby is delivered by Cesarean to prevent rupture. But in this case the spine was exposed to infection. So I was shocked when I heard the pediatrician tell the parents that they could authorize surgery or just do nothing without telling them what the consequences might be. Doing nothing meant certain spinal infection and death. Fortunately the parents chose surgery.

Another rare defect I have seen only a couple of times is Achondroplasia. Then I was able to understand a classmate from way back in grade school. She had a full size body but was very short—much shorter then my own five foot one and a half inches, now I could see that she had been born with a normal body and short little legs. It took me back nostalgically to those kinder, gentler times when our classmates, who had never known any times except depression times and had never had fancy clothes or luxuries of any kind, none-the-less treated each other with fondness and respect. I entered that school late in the seventh grade and they made me feel welcome and encouraged me to enter in their activities. At their urging I wrote our graduation song the following year. They never chided Jodie about her lack of height. But when we played basketball and Jody made a basket they would shout. "Jody's short but she's mighty." With a world full of people like them we would not need to be so concerned with minor defects. But alas we all know that we now live in a rougher, tougher society.

Some very minor defects are polydactylism (extra fingers or toes) and tongue tie (a small membrane under the tongue which prevents it from moving freely.) Some doctors say this condition doesn't exist. Others snip it with the tip of the scissors.

One minor defect that is relatively easy to repair surgically is called hypospadias. In this condition the urethra (the tube which carries the urine from the bladder) is too short to reach the end of the penis and terminates farther up on the underside of the Glans. This is readily noticeable because nature provides for the efficient function of the organ by not covering the abnormally placed meatus (opening) with the foreskin, giving these babies the appearance of having already been circumcised.

None of this poses any physical problems and they would never need to be repaired for any functional reason. But as the child grows and matures he would have to sit down to urinate and forgo such pre-adolescent activities as contests to see whose stream can go the furthest or who can make the most bubbles in the stool. So, because of the psychological aspects, minor surgery is generally done. In a society where the phrase "penis envy" is still heard frequently the psychological implications can run very deep. I learned just how strong these feelings can be from the father of one of these babies while I was a clinical instructor.

Because I had students in all three departments—post-partum, nursery and L&D—located on two floors, I thought it would be more convenient for them to see our baby with hypospadias, just before his one o'clock feeding as we all left the floor to go to the clinical conference. When we arrived at the nursery, we found that the baby had already been taken out to his mother. "We'll try to catch him tomorrow," I told the nursery nurse.

But she had another idea. "Oh, just take the students down to his room. She won't mind. She's really nice," she gushed.

"No, I really don't like to do that," I replied. "We'll wait until tomorrow."

But she was adamant. "Really! She won't mind."

Unconvinced, I never-the-less proceeded to her room, the students following me single file like baby ducklings. Fortunately I had the presence of mind to have them wait in the hall.

When I entered the room, I found the baby all alone and the mother in the bathroom. When she came out, I asked her if she minded if the students saw the baby.

"No," she said in a little girl voice. "I don't think he would like that."

I had to chuckle at the inference. "I'm sure he wouldn't mind but if you do that's all right," I told her.

"His daddy wouldn't like it," she persisted in that thready little voice.

"That's probably true. I'm sorry to have bothered you. Are you going to stay in the room now or would you like me to take the baby back to the nursery?" It is against hospital rules—as well as unsafe—for babies to be alone in the rooms. Mothers are instructed to call the nursery if they need to leave for any reason. She indicated that they would be all right.

The students and I went to the classroom and were engrossed in another subject when we heard a knock on the door. There in the doorway loomed two Supervisors and a Patient Advocate. "Can you come out and talk to this husband," one of them asked. "He specifically asked for you." I was puzzled but went with them to the day room where they introduced me to the husband of the patient with the 'little girl' voice. He gave me a firm handshake and then immediately launched into a verbal assault that took my breath away. It was the most erudite calling down that I had ever experienced. He used flowery terms like, "I am appalled at your lack of professional decorum!" There wasn't a single obscenity in the entire tirade. He accused me of "making a mountain out of a mole hill "of his sons" minor imperfection."

Aha! Methinks the pot doth call the kettle black. Or—in psychiatric terms—he was projecting his feelings of anger and disdain of his baby's hypospadias, onto me.

He continued by asking how I dared insinuate that his wife was not "the most perfect mother in the world." It took me some time to figure out where that had come from. I finally decided that it was because I had made certain that the baby would not be left alone in the room again.

In the beginning I kept trying to reassure him that I truly viewed his son's condition as minor and that I was very sorry for the misunderstanding. But he seemed to have an urgent need to 'get it all out.' So eventually I just stood there quietly and let the outpour of words pelt me like an avalanche of stones. I felt especially bad when he said that they had really liked that hospital but that I had spoiled it for them.

I never saw any of them again as they had been dismissed by the following day. But I heard some time later that the man had told someone that he was sorry that he had overreacted. It would have been nice if he had said it to me.

Keeping newborns and their mothers hospitalized for ten days gave us an opportunity to observe the changes that may occur during that time. Jaundice due to normal, physiological processes frequently occurs around the third day of life. The umbilical cord (often referred to by lay people as the "umbiblical" cord, but there is nothing holy about it) dried up and often fell off by the time of discharge.

Because of delayed feedings and weak formulas there was generally a substantial weight loss followed by a gradual gain. If a baby was exposed to an infection, the incubation period was likely to expire while he was still in the hospital. And the infection could spread rampantly through the nursery. The nursery population was always large due to the lengthy stay. Serious infections of Streptococcus or Staphylococcus could shut down the nursery for an extended period of time. So strict visiting regulations and medical antiseptic techniques were enforced.

One condition that was poorly understood was jaundice that occurred very early in life—before the second or third day. It progressed rapidly and was called Erythroblastosis Fetalis because the babies suffering from it had a high Erythroblast (immature red blood cells) count. The babies were very sick and we transferred them to pediatrics because there were no NICU's at that time and we weren't equipped to care for very sick babies in the nursery. But we didn't know what caused it or how to cure it.

One very jaundiced baby that we had transferred to pediatrics came to visit his mother every day. "Oh, there is my little grapefruit!" She cried cheerfully on his first visit, referring to his yellow colored skin. The next day it was "my little lemon." And, as the jaundice deepened, "My little orange." We thought her quite callous or without any kind of understanding of the seriousness of his condition. But we hadn't yet learned about defense mechanisms. That was the last name she ever called him. He tragically expired before his next visit. And we could only stand helplessly by and watch.

It was many years before we learned that ninety-five percent of the severe jaundices are caused by an incompatibility between the babies blood type or Rh Factor and the mother's. The most common and usually the least severe cases are when the mother has type O blood and the baby has type A or B or AB. Type O blood contains antibodies to the other types which cross the placenta and get into the babies' blood stream and destroy his red blood cells (RBC.) The placenta is supposed to form an effective barrier between the mother's blood and that of the fetus. But in reality microscopic tears in it permits many substances to cross over. As the maternal antibodies destroy the fetus' RBC, bilirubin is produced which turned the skin a yellow color. As the bilirubin level increases it can damage vital organs like the brain and the heart and may result in retardation and / or death.

The simple treatment was discovered by some nuns working in the newborn nursery. They noticed that the babies that were located near the window (in the sunlight) got over their jaundice faster than the ones on the other side of the room. From this awareness evolved the concept of bilirubin lights. 'Bili' lights are simply a concentration of light from several fluorescent tubes placed around the baby. The baby's shirt and diaper are removed and only his eyes and genitalia are covered. When these protective coverings are removed, a striking difference can be noted between the yellow skin color under the protected areas and the pinker color of the areas that were exposed to the lights. Extra fluids are given to the babies to facilitate elimination of the bilirubin which was removed from the skin to prevent it from damaging the vital organs. None of this alleviates anemia caused by the red cell destruction. A transfusion may be given but this is rarely necessary in an ABO incompatibility.

The most severe incompatibility, which is what our little grapefruit / lemon / orange baby had is the Rh incompatibility. This can occur if the mother is Rh negative and the baby is Rh positive. Since only about fifteen percent of the population has Rh negative blood and we would expect half of them to be men, it is fortunately not a frequent problem. When the baby is also Rh negative there, will not be a problem. Often even an Rh positive baby will not have a problem.

Unlike type O women, the Rh negative mother does not have antibodies in her blood, but manufacturers them after she has been exposed to Rh positive blood. It may take one or two pregnancies before she has produced enough antibodies to cause a problem. But if she has received a transfusion of Rh positive blood she will already have manufactured enough antibodies to destroy any Rh positive baby she will ever conceive.

The trend toward smaller families has averted a large number of these incompatibilities from cropping up, but during the years when many people were having large families, it became the scourge of some unfortunate families. Once a woman has manufactured these antibodies they remain with her for the rest of her life.

Do you remember the patient who had the post-partum psychosis because of infidelity? She had four children with Rh incompatibilities. She had the advantage of having her babies after the time when we had started using exchange transfusions in the treatment of these babies. All of her children had survived because of them.

After their advent exchange transfusions were often done in the delivery room right after the birth of the baby. It removed the fetal blood with the antibodies, bilirubin and the broken down red blood cells which would produce more bilirubin and replace it with fresh Rh negative blood which could not be damaged by any antibodies left behind. If the exchange could have been done like an oil change on your car, the problem would have been resolved. Unfortunately, so would the baby. So it had to be done ten or fifteen cc's at a time—infusing a little fresh blood alternately with withdrawing an equal amount of fetal blood. By the time the exchange was completed the old and the new blood had become mixed together. So many times it was necessary to repeat the procedure one or more times.

As the years passed they were able to begin treatment during pregnancy and save babies that would otherwise have been stillborn. Now the doctors could run a titer on the blood of the pregnant woman to check for the presence of antibodies. If the titer count rose, he could do an amniocentesis to check on the status of the fetus. If the amniocentesis showed that there was excessive bilirubin the fetus could be transfused in utero. Before that procedure was available in the United States many women had to pack up their families—they usually had two children already—and travel to Canada or Mexico, perhaps two or three times, to receive their intrauterine transfusions. This procedure simply provided enough red blood cells to tide the fetus over until he was mature enough to be delivered. They did not remove any antibodies or bilirubin. Eventually intrauterine transfusions were approved and could be done in this country.

These innovative treatments saved thousands of lives but they were invasive, expensive, time-consuming and psychologically devastating. Then in the late sixties a simple solution was found to the whole Rh problem. It is called Rho Gam. Rho Gam is obtained from, gamma globulin taken from the blood of Rh negative individuals who have been sensitized to Rh positive blood and so carried the antibodies. In the beginning it was obtained from Rh negative women who had borne Rh positive babies. Later they began to use convicts who volunteered for the work. They were sensitized by receiving injections of clinical doses of Rh positive blood. In that way they became contributors to society. It looked good on the records and was a positive factor at their parole hearings.

When Rho Gam is injected into the mother within seventy-two hours after delivery it prevents her from manufacturing antibodies, since the greatest exposure she has to the fetal blood is after delivery when the blood from the placenta (which is the fetal blood) backs up into her bloodstream. The antibodies in the Rho Gam play the same role in eliminating the antibodies from her blood, but they differ from the ones she would manufacture in that they are passive and are eliminated from her body rather than remaining behind to damage the fetus in her next pregnancy, as her own antibodies would. For that reason it must be given after the termination of every pregnancy—even abortions and miscarriages.

After several years of using Rho Gam after delivery, they began to give small amounts of it during pregnancy to 'clean up' any a stray positive cells that have found their way into the maternal bloodstream. But women who had already become sensitized before the advent of

Rho Gam or through a blood transfusion could not be helped by Rho Gam. Since it has now been more than twenty-five years since Rho Gam came on the scene, most of these women have passed out of the childbearing years.

It has been many years since I have assisted with an exchange transfusion. Intrauterine transfusions are also no longer necessary. Most of the younger nurses have never seen these procedures or any manifestation of this problem. But until science has found a way to make all blood types compatible, Rho Gam must remain on the scene and be used faithfully.

I know this is a complicated entity and, because this isn't a textbook, I have made this an abbreviated version. But to me it represents the most important and exciting discovery for saving lives of newborns and is representative of the dedication and progress of our ever seeking scientists.

CHAPTER 15

DEATH AND DYING

*W*e become nurses to prolong and improve life. Yet we are often faced with the antithesis of life—that bittersweet release, sometimes welcome but often begrudged, called death.

As a teenaged student I don't recall being terribly distressed by the passing of some ancient cronies I scarcely knew. We students would prepare the bodies for the morgue together and chat about unrelated things. One of the men from the mortuary who came to pick up the bodies was a Clark Gable look-alike and we had more pleasant conversations as we helped them move the body to the stretcher. We had to take our social interactions where we could as our opportunities were few.

It was just a little different the first time I lost a patient of my own—while I was caring for her. She was an isolation patient and had been unresponsive since I had known her. So there wasn't any particular bond between us.

Although she was comatose she would swallow when she felt the pressure of the spoon on the back of her tongue. So I was standing at her bedside feeding her a liquid diet. We always stood in the patients' rooms. It was many years later when they decided that a standing figure looming over the prostrate patient could be perceived as menacing by the patient. After that it became preferable to sit so that we were at eye level with the patient. But because of the rigidity of the early training I still have to remind myself to sit down when it is appropriate.

So I was standing there spooning sips of liquid into her mouth and thinking of all the chores I still had to accomplish before the day had ended. She had been swallowing quietly and then she began to gargle it. But she still swallowed it eventually. So I kept on feeding her. Then she stopped gargling and stopped swallowing and began to turn blue. We didn't call codes at the time. There were no CPR and no telephones in the room. Because of the isolation, I couldn't leave the room easily. So I put on our signal light so that the Head Nurse would come and inject some adrenaline into her vein and perhaps restore her life for an hour or two. But, in the long run, it wouldn't make any difference. She had died of advanced tuberculosis and nothing would change that.

While I waited for help to come, I stood there in the middle of the isolation room that had been her milieu for such a long time. Isolation is an apt term for what happens to the patient who is imprisoned within its confines. Visitors could not come in and the patient could not go out. The nurse or doctor entering the room had to don, mask, gowns and gloves. So the only thing the patient saw was the care giver's eyes. Even the nurses did not go in and out of isolation freely. Getting into all that garb was time-consuming, and getting out of it without contaminating ourselves required care, skill and a lot of valuable time.

But all I was thinking about at that time was how there had been a life in that room one moment and then—a split second later—without fanfare, as if someone had just blown out a match, that life was no longer there. There was no perceptible change in the room—just the cessation of that eerie gargling sound. You had to put a stethoscope over her heart to determine that life no longer existed in that body. It was just an empty shell now.

In the years ahead I would see new life enter the world with the same swiftness. But it would be different because there had been a baby there all along inside the mother's uterus. The real miracle occurred at conception and there was no fanfare then either. Life just seems to slip in and out almost unnoticed.

I didn't really know this woman who had been comatose since she had become my patient. She was only in her forties—not old as the others had been. I wasn't thinking about her having died so young or even that it was a blessing that she had been released from such a sick body—I was really thinking that I had been feeding her just as I had every day and that she had used her last breath to gargle her soup.

Rachel Rosen was the first patient for whom I felt a personal loss after her death. Everyone on the floor did. Although she was terminal from the time of her admission, and she knew it, she never displayed any anger. Neither did she complain nor make any demands. She was interested in each of us and spent her time with us finding out about our lives, hopes and dreams. She made it so pleasant to be with her that we all spent as much time in her room as we could even when she wasn't our assigned patient.

Although everyone loved her, she was especially dear to me because she was Jewish and portrayed a good example of our people. She didn't incite people to say things like, "You Jews are all bossy, complaining, demanding or whatever." Of course they didn't say, "You are all appreciative, kind, patient etc. like Rachel," either. But that is how stereotypes work—if someone doesn't fit the stereotype they say that person is an exception.

When Mrs. Rosen died we went in the kitchen and cried behind the carts of dirty dishes. It was unthinkable at that time to show any emotion on duty or to share our own grief with the family.

A few years later when I was an OB staff nurse Mrs. Rosen's daughter-in-law came in and delivered a baby girl. True to Jewish tradition she named her daughter after her deceased mother-in-law. She had never had the good fortune to know Rachel and I wanted to tell her what a wonderful woman she had been. Before I could begin, she launched into her own feelings. "I hate that name!" She told me. "I say it real fast with her middle name—Rachellyn—so it doesn't sound so bad."

I could hardly speak for the lump in my throat. I am all for modernizing names. Hadn't I refused to name my own son 'Morris?' As long as the Hebrew name is the same, the English name is not important. Customarily, most people retain the first initial and modernize the rest of the name. We have no wish to be set apart from our contemporaries. But in Rachel's case I thought her name should be savored and not "said real fast."

One of the most unforgettable people I have ever met, I met not as a nurse but as the mother of the patient. My six-year-old son had been hit by a speeding car and I had rushed from the hospital where I was employed to the one where he had been taken. Because I was still wearing my nursery scrubs, they knew that I was a nurse and left me in charge of transferring him from the ER to the pediatric ward—one trembling hand holding the bottle of infusing blood while the other pushed the cart. After I had settled him in bed, I became engrossed in taking his vital signs, adjusting his oxygen and traction, and watching for a sign that he was emerging from this coma. I was existing in my own little vacuum, not conspicuously aware of the blustering noise and activity that swirled around me.

Finally, after visiting hours had ended, preparations for bedtime had been made and the last cries for "one more drink" and "one more bedtime story" had died down, quiet descended on the large, double room ward. Now only one sound pierced the silent darkness—the labored breathing of an infant in the other room. A lovely young woman dozed in a chair by the baby's crib. She roused periodically to suction the baby's throat whenever she coughed or became blocked with mucus. Still in her twenties and looking more like a coed than a wife and mother, in time this slender wisp of a girl revealed herself to be a most remarkable young woman.

She was called "Jolene" but her real name has long since escaped my memory. The little tomboy of her childhood had acquired the name "Joe" as being more suitable to her personality and temperament than her own name. Later, as she matured, it was feminized by adding the last syllable.

For almost a month Jolene and I kept our lonely night vigil together. We became acquainted when she insisted that I exchange chairs with her. Hers was a rare gem with armrests while mine was just a straight back. She assured me that by now she was conditioned to sleeping on anything. Then, in a burst of sympathy, she added, "I feel so sorry for you!" She told me that her baby had cystic fibrosis. Little was known about CF at that time except that it was always fatal and the life expectancy was very short. The lump in my throat kept me from responding. "I know my baby is going to get well," she insisted, seeing the doubt in my eyes.

Through those long nights Jolene and I comforted each other as best we could and shared our life's stories. I learned that Jolene had married when she was only fifteen. The child of an unhappy home with a stern and rigid mother, she had eloped with a man many years older than herself. They proceeded to defy all odds and all doubting Thomases by building a strong marriage and maintaining a deep love and mutual respect.

In the early years of their marriage they were blessed with a fine sturdy son and a lovely, healthy daughter who were, at that time, ten and twelve-year's old. After that they lost several babies through miscarriages and in infancy. Eventually they learned that the monster that was stealing their children away was called cystic fibrosis. It was 1955 and even the doctors knew little about this mysterious malady. So they joined together with other desperate parents in a frantic effort to obtain any available information. They became a chapter in a national organization. Although they learned that somehow parents were passing the CF onto their babies, Jolene had insisted upon trying one more time and bore this baby against despairing odds. She seemed healthy at birth and was the last hope for the large family they both longed for. Then, slowly and insidiously, the old familiar symptoms had appeared and tragically worsened until hospitalization had become necessary.

Both her respiratory and digestive systems were severely affected. She was receiving oxygen with Alevaire, the new wonder drug that dissolved thick mucus. Dietary adjustments brought occasional temporary remissions from the diarrhea. At seven months of age she weighed only seven pounds—her drawn and wizened and face intent only on the rugged business of drawing the next breath that would sustain her tragic life a little longer.

Nights were her worst time. So Jolene chose to keep her vigil during that time when the nursing staff was minimal. She was always cheerful and sensitive to the needs of others. At bedtime she would tuck the other little patients in, giving them drinks of water and listening to their little problems with earnest interest. When I would doze, she would listen for signs of restlessness from my still comatose son and often woke me to report excitedly, "He called 'Mama,' I'm sure he did."

But beneath the placid exterior serious problems were plaguing Jolene. Her beloved husband had suffered a severe heart attack and was warned that the next one would probably be fatal. Instead of the quiet life that had been prescribed for him, he was staggering under the financial burdens imposed by the many illnesses and the impending death of his youngest child.

Jolene's mother, who was now a widow, was living with them. Her demands and criticisms were an added burden and disturbing to Jolene's older children. She had wanted their childhood to be warmer and happier than her own had been.

After three and weeks my own son began to emerge from the depths of the darkness in which he had been imprisoned and was taken off the critical list. At last I was able to go home for a real night's sleep. When I returned in the morning, I learned that Jolene's baby had died during the night. Jolene had taken her belongings home but I could still see her sweet smile and hear her uttering those heart felt words, "I know my baby is going to get well."

When she returned to the hospital later, she was quiet and composed without any hint of self-pity. "I'm glad she doesn't have to suffer anymore," she confided. "It was too hard on her." She had drawn out all the money in the baby's savings account—twenty-five dollars—and divided it into envelopes for the nurses. "She would want you to have it," she told them. "We just couldn't use it." To me she beamed and earnestly told me, "I'm happy for you."

The next day my husband and I went to the funeral home to pay our last respects to that tiny, brief spark of life. She was surrounded in death, as she had been in life, with all the love and material manifestation that Jolene could muster. The room was bright and banked with flowers. The sweet strain of organ music filled the air. The little casket was ornate and dear beyond their means. Inside, the little body, at peace at last but still bearing traces of pain on her wizened face, was dressed in a lovely white lawn dress flounced with lace and rested on white satin.

Jolene just couldn't bear for her final moments on earth to be drab and dreary.

I threw my arms around this valiant young woman who had been my constant companion, my confidant and my solace. I didn't have words to express my feelings, which were a mixture of sympathy and admiration for the way she conquered life's problems by giving of herself and her vast love. "I'm going to stay active in CF work," she promised. "It's all that I can do for her now."

Caring for a brain-injured child in a body cast kept me constantly occupied for some time and we moved away from that city soon afterward. So I never saw Jolene again. But whenever I hear of a new breakthrough in the fight against CF I can see again her shining face and feel her vibrant spirit reaching out so that others might be spared the heartbreak that was hers.

Donna was in the class behind me in nursing school. After graduation we found ourselves working together in OB. We also found that we had a lot of other things in common as well. We had both gotten married at the same time. And both of us found that we had married charming, ne'er do well boys who used us and gave back nothing in return. We also both had domineering, demanding in-laws. Two months after our weddings we were both pregnant. With all we had in common, and because we liked each other, we became good friends.

During the first trimester of our pregnancies we took some comfort in comparing morning sickness. Then, in the second trimester, my nausea subsided but Donna's persisted. We urge her to tell Dr. Cannon how much she was vomiting but she always shrugged it off. People began to ask me why I was so much bigger than Donna. It wasn't very flattering and put me on the defensive. But the real problem was, why wasn't Donna keeping pace with me? The answer, of course, was that she wasn't retaining any of her food.

In spite of her problems Donna came to work every day and carried her full load. We were still working six days a week, but on her one day off, Donna would go clean her mother-in-law's house as well as her own because it was "too hard on" her mother-in-law to do it herself.

Things went along in this vein until we were in our fifth month. Then one morning as I was walking through the Gyn floor on my way to OB I glanced in one of the rooms. There was Donna, in bed, wearing a patient's gown. I stepped into the room. "What are you doing here?" I asked.

"I had surgery last night. I finally had to call Dr. Cannon. It turns out I had a bowel obstruction." She seemed cheerful and pleased with the outcome.

I sighed in relief. Now Donna would be all right. And finally there were people taking care of Donna instead of the other way around. Everyone on staff was happy for her and she seemed to be making a rapid recovery as she laughed and visited with all who stopped in.

Two days later Donna was dead. Swiftly and brutally an embolism had claimed her. What a shock! Sweet, generous Donna—snatched from us just as her problems seemed to be coming under control.

The funeral home was crammed with all the nurses that could get off duty for Donna's funeral. The line which filed up to view the body was very long and the first ones were returning as the rest of us inched forward. "She looks beautiful," some reported.

"She looks so natural—like she's still alive and will wake up," commented others.

Someone who had been to her wedding told us, "she's wearing her wedding dress."

I had never seen a dead body other than our patients who had died. The few funerals I had attended had closed coffins. So I was unprepared for what I saw when I finally reached Donna's casket. I didn't think she looked alive at all. That wry little smile didn't look anything like Donna's exuberant grin to me. I hadn't been to her wedding: so when they said she was in her wedding dress I had pictured a white gown. But Donna had gotten married in a green dress just as I had. One more thing we had done alike. But Donna had died and taken her unborn baby with her, while mine was kicking furiously in my belly. It was all too much for me, as I choked back a sob and ran out to the parking lot to have a good cry behind a parked car. A hospital employee saw me and, to my chagrin because I never cried in front of anyone, came over to comfort me. I was even more embarrassed when I later learned that she was Donna's cousin.

One year later George, Donna's 'bereaved' widowed husband, appeared in the OB department. His second wife was in labor with their child. George hadn't wasted much time on grief.

Katherine Sand was a head nurse on the third floor when I was a student. Because we didn't have clinical instructors, the older students and the head nurses had to provide what guidance we were given on the hospital floors. Mrs. Sand was always gentle and easy-going. I was still a Probie when, one morning, I found my patient having a difficult time breathing. I ran to the nurses' station looking for someone to correct the situation. "Mrs. Sand," I cried. "Mr. Gambol can hardly breathe!"

"Okay," she replied calmly pulling out his chart. "We're going to chart that—'7:30 AM . . . very d-y-s-p-n-e-i-c.'" I saw a newly learned word reinforced. She had called me down without ridiculing me. Mr. Gambol made it through the day as he had for some days before.

Mrs. Danby, the assistant head nurse on that floor, had none of Mrs. Sands charm. She was the same one who, as head nurse on that floor two years later, would take away my day off on my twenty-first birthday. One day all of the students on the floor had to go to class at the same time, leaving Mrs. Sand and Mrs. Danby alone on the floor for two hours. When we returned from class, Mrs. Sand had a big smile on her face. "You should've seen Mrs. Danby and me running. We've been answering lights ever since you left." Mrs. Danby just sat slumped in her chair with a big scowl on her face.

A few years later Mrs. Sand came to join us on the OB staff. Now we all called her Katie and she was every bit as delightful as I had remembered her. She entertained us with tales of her husband and twelve-year-old son, who obviously adored her as much as we did.

Katie wore thick prescription glasses and when contact-lenses came on the market she decided to get rid of those pesky glasses. She had a great deal of trouble adjusting to the contacts and made repeated visits to the ophthalmologist. About the time she began to get the hang of the contacts she started experiencing numbness in both hands. Her cheerful nature and normal good humor were being sorely challenged. The head nurse commented that she thought that when we got Katie's "Eyeballs" straightened out that she should be her old self. But that was not to be. Katie's latest problem was finally diagnosed as a herniated cervical disc and she was scheduled for a laminectomy.

On the day of Katie's surgery I was home with a bad case of flu. One of my coworkers called to tell me that Katie had died in the operating room. Everything had gone well and they were beginning to close when a sudden gush of spinal fluid and blood had erupted. In the wink of an eye Katie was taken from us. My head was spinning from the news and the flu and I could barely respond. Does anyone ever come to understand the miracle of life and it's certain, and sometimes abrupt, reversal?

That night I dreamed that I was lying in my bed and a gurney was wheeled up next to me. On the gurney, covered to her chin with a white sheet, was Katie. All I could say was to repeat, "Oh Katie, Oh Katie" over and over.

And Katie just repeated, "Oh, Brownie. Oh Brownie."

And then my clock radio woke me up with the news that Charles Starkweather had just received another stay of execution. Charles Starkweather was the young punk who had gone on a killing spree in the Heartlands with his girlfriend, Carol Fugate, resulting in ten deaths. It was not a good way to start that day in 1959 when a murderer received a stay, but for Katie there was no reprieve.

I have always wanted to believe that my experience was more than a mere dream—but that Katie had really come to say goodbye to me.

Bye, Katie.

Rhonda Seldon was also an RN. But she wasn't a colleague. She was one of our Gyn patients. At that time our students spent six weeks in their OB rotation. At the end of the year there was one extra week which they spent in whatever rotation they happen to be in. I elected to assign my students to Gyn patients since they had fulfilled their State Board requirements for maternity nursing and had no other opportunity to be in the Gyn area.

Ronnie had been diagnosed with breast cancer sometime earlier. Despite bilateral mastectomies and a total hysterectomy and salpingo-oopherectomy, the cancer had metastasized and Ronnie was now on oxygen and terminal. In morning report they told us that Ronnie would die within the week.

When I stopped in her room on rounds, I was startled to see her bed empty. An attractive young woman in her thirties in a nightgown was sitting in a chair shaving her legs. I felt strangely disoriented. There wasn't supposed to be another patient in that room. Who was this woman? And where was Ronnie? The patient smiled and said, "Good morning, how are you?"

"Good morning," I stammered, still at a loss. She finished shaving, ran a comb through her short hair, picked up some magazines and embroidery work and walked around the bed slipping on her oxygen cannula as she slid into bed.

Now I was really startled. This young woman was the picture of health and vibrant life. I could see no way that she could die that week. That was my introduction to Ronnie. And the few days that she was our patient I learned to respect and admire her abundantly. She was a model of how to die with dignity. She planed and controlled every step of her death. Even though she left the actual event to her God.

Ronnie was also a nursing instructor. She had taught B.S.N. students. While these programs do not place much emphasis on bedside nursing care, Ronnie made sure that the students assigned to her care gave their best. She was determined that her body would remain a temple as long as she was in charge of it. She insisted that the students give her a complete bed bath, soaking her hands and feet in the bath basin as they had been taught, and then massage lotion all over her skin.

She was especially proud of a method of shampooing a bed patient's hair that she had contrived using an upended (new) bedpan. She taught it anew to each student and her hair was always clean and bouncy. Each day when I stopped by on rounds, she would tell me how her student had done that morning.

Knowing that her funeral would be difficult for her husband, she made all of the arrangements herself. Her in-laws had come from out of town to spend her last week with them. Because her mother-in-law was a diabetic, Ronnie made an appointment for her with her own doctor. She also made plans for the care of their two young children. Every afternoon she would have a conference with her husband and his parents to fill them in on the latest plans. She made sure that she did not receive any pain medication before these sessions so that she would be alert and lucid. Yet she was always calm and void of self-pity.

Each morning when I visited Ronnie she would give me a progress report on the advancement of her cancer. "I saw my x-rays and I have three new nodes on my liver," she would announce, then looked at me expectantly as if she were expecting me to say I thought that was very exciting. Instead it made me feel uneasy and I would just nod tacitly.

One day I could no longer hold back my real feelings and responded, "do you really think it's wise to watch it so closely?"

She gazed at me steadily and replied, "That's how I handle it." At last I understood. She had detached herself emotionally from all the bad things that were happening to her and, from a safe, distant place, was following her case as she would any other patient. And she was making sure that the patient was well cared for. To the end of her life she carried out all her responsibilities from her chosen professions—those of wife, mother, nursing instructor and good daughter-in-law.

Ronnie remained lucid and in charge of her life all the time that we cared for her. On Thursday while the students were attending their final classes at the college she slipped into a coma. On Friday, at about the time the students were walking down the aisle to receive their diploma's Ronnie, her work completed, left this world. She'd left behind a beautiful legacy.

Just as Jolene had shown us how to handle the death of a loved one with dignity, so had Ronnie taught us how to live those last moments and lose your own life with dignity.

I have always considered myself a dedicated nurse. I have gone to work with fevers, colds, aches, pains and emotional stress. There are many such dedicated nurses. But there are also many at the other end of the spectrum—like the assistant house supervisor who had "walking pneumonia" on Christmas Day and, no doubt due to the miracles of the Christmas season, was fully recovered the next day and able to return to work.

Then there was the LPN who worked part-time on the 3-11 shift. One day she called in and asked if we were busy. She had been considering staying home that day although she was scheduled to work. I told her that we were very busy and that she had better come on in. "Oh no," she replied. "I don't feel like working. I'd come if you weren't busy."

One day the 3-11 house supervisor called in and said she was too tired to come to work. When I heard about it, I thought, "Not that again!" Why hadn't she jazzed up her excuse a little? Unlike the dramatic "walking pneumonia, "tired sounded pretty lame.

We never saw or heard from her again. Three days later they broke into her apartment and found her body. She was midway in the process of crawling back into bed—perhaps right after the phone call to the hospital. Her last act on earth had been the responsible act of notifying her employer of her inability to cover her shift.

She really was tired—really tired.

One of my med—surg stints was done at a VA hospital. Yano was admitted to our ward with inoperable esophageal cancer. Because his esophagus was becoming increasingly obstructed, he was to have a Gastrostomy to provide a new route for feedings. Far from being a down and outer as many of our VA patients were, Yano was upper-middle-class, good-looking and only fifty-five years' old.

Dylan Thomas must have had just such a man as Yano in mind when he wrote, "Do not go gentle into that good night." Yano had exhausted his reserve funds in private hospitals and trips to Mexico for Laetrile treatments. Now he had run out of hope along with his money. No longer able to deny his imminent death, Yano seemed to be perpetually locked into the anger stage and persisted in taking it out on the students and me and probably everyone else who got into his path. If we didn't do something fast enough he would tell us to get out and send someone in who knew what they were doing. If we asked which side he wanted to turn on for his hypo he would rage, "YOU DUMMY. DON'T YOU KNOW YOUR LEFT FROM YOUR RIGHT?" We never seemed to be able to make Yano feel better.

The students took turns being Yano's primary care giver for a week at a time. When he was transferred to D Wing, we knew that he had reached the last turn in the road. Our rapport with Yano remained at a low level. We were, of necessity, the perpetrators of much of his pain by insisting on turning him and getting him up in a chair. He continued to vent his anger by demeaning us. In a strange way this was acceptable as one of the few things we could do for him. As he became increasingly resistant to the enforced activity, we began to wonder what difference it really made. But we had to carry out the doctor's orders.

Yano had the most rapport with a member of the VA's Operations Support who came daily, listened to his fears and frustrations, and helped him work through his family and marital problems. I learned that she had 'contracts' with him. E.g., he would promise to comply with specific activities in exchange for a visit from his grandchildren. Armed with this information we began to use these contracts in expediting our treatments. While they didn't bring about instant cooperation, they did provide us with a bargaining tool which helps to some extent. What is more important, they gave Yano some measure of control in a situation where a loss of control loomed menacingly.

We timed as many activities as possible to coincide with his favorite son's visits, when he wanted to appear at his best. At those times he would even joke a little. One day he asked us if we thought it was safe to let his bearded son shaved him when he hadn't used a razor in years.

Still, the students dreaded being assigned to Yano although they willingly helped the student who was. We centered many conferences around the feelings that Yano evoked in all of us, but they were never completely resolved.

Gina was the student who seems to get along with him the best. Because of her thick black hair and olive skin I jumped to the conclusion that she, like Yano was Italian and that this bond might help him through an especially bad period of depression and withdrawal. Reluctant to give up on Yano I assigned Gina to a second week with him. I soon learned that my stereotyping Gina did not make her Italian and that, far from having a bond with Yano, she was having a particularly difficult time coping with the conflicts he evoked with his sarcasm and degrading remarks.

When I saw how upset she was I offered to change the assignment, but Gina decided she would use the opportunity to try to resolve these conflicts herself. She had never seen, much less been the object of, such vehemently displaced anger. During that second week she began to understand and build up a tolerance for it.

Although the Gastrostomy feedings were keeping him nourished and the IVs were keeping him hydrated, Yano's body was showing the ravages of his disease. His skin had become deeply jaundiced and his body was swollen to twice its normal size. Although his features were still handsome, this loss of body image must have been devastating to him. All the chemotherapy seemed to accomplish was to make him extremely nauseated.

As his resistance to infection waned he was placed in protective isolation. Now he saw only our eyes surrounded by the caps, masks, gowns and gloves that covered our bodies so that we would not bring any microorganisms into his room that we might have picked up on the outside. One day while I was holding Yano on his side so Gina could provide his treatment, I squeezed his hand on an impulse. To my surprise he squeezed my hand back. It was then that I fully realized that all the ranting and blustering were not really directed at us at all but at the circumstances that had brought him to this fate of pain and impending death.

Although Yano was not much older than I was at that time, I had managed to confuse him with the authority figures in my life, when he was really just a frightened man reaching out for something to pull him through his final challenge. My biggest regret was that I had waited until my hands were covered with rubber gloves to squeeze Yano's hand. On the other hand that may have been the only way that Yano could have accepted it. It wasn't a turning point. Yano still fought to maintain the authority and control he had always had. He remained angry for the rest of his life. He died alone early one morning while we were in report. At first we were sad that nobody had been with him during his final moments. Then we noticed the filled emesis basin placed neatly on the bedside stand and we knew that he could have called us if he had wanted us to be there. Instead he had chosen to die alone just as he had long battled his cancer alone.

We were glad that Yano's ordeal was over and glad that the resident had been persuaded not to code him so that he wouldn't have to endure death twice. Tenderly and reverently the students prepared Yano's body for the morgue and gathered up his personal effects for his wife. This was the last thing we could do for him and it helped somewhat to finalize it in our minds. We would never forget Yano and, in that respect his wish to continue to live was granted.

Coding is a late twentieth century phenomenon that replaced the IV adrenaline used to save or prolong lives during the earlier part of the century. Coding saves more lives but it can also be brutal. And sometimes it is used to save the doomed over and over so that they are forced to endure the process of dying many times rather than only once.

While we in the health field are dedicated to saving lives, the reasons we code people are not always so altruistic. In teaching hospitals where medical students abound, codes give them much needed experience. These hospitals are often County and VA hospitals and are gratuitous, so that the patients are not encouraged to be involved in decisions concerning their treatments. They are often elderly and isolated from others who could help them make educated decisions.

One day I accompanied a resident when he went to convince one such patient to consent to having a diagnostic procedure for which there was no apparent indication. I could see that the patient was becoming increasingly puzzled as he listened to an explanation aimed way over his head. The resident was called to the telephone and, while he was out of the room, I hasten to assure the man that he didn't have to consent to the procedure if he didn't feel comfortable about it. Appearing relieved, he told the resident when he returned, that he was refusing the procedure. The resident replied, "that's okay, I have something else I have to do anyway."

When I first went to that hospital, I didn't know that they had a rule that the nurses were not to assist the residents when they were working with the patients. One day I saw that they were having a problem with a highly agitated patient who kept thrashing about, making it difficult for them to get his IV started. I help them by holding his shoulder down while they inserted his IV. When I removed my hand from his shoulder I was horrified to see that the skin where I had held him had turned a dark purple and was peeling. After that I endeavored to make sure that I didn't ever again become the perpetrator of additional trauma.

I began to notice that they did a lot of codes in that hospital and that they often coded the same people repeatedly. One man seemed to be on a continual circuitous route between our floor and the ICU. Every time they would send him back to the floor he would code and be returned to the ICU. It began to seem more like a curse than a blessing.

One day I had the satisfaction of watching them working frantically on this man. But on that day he was very obviously well beyond their reach. I've often imagined him floating near the ceiling and looking down at them and laughing and chanting, "Nya, Nya, ya can't catch me."

I can't honestly fault the resident for seeking learning experiences. As a nursing instructor I have spent a lot of time and effort to do the same for my students. It must remain the responsibility of the health care recipient to make sure that he is well informed of his options, makes an intelligent, informed decision, and make sure that decision is known to the health care providers and his significant others. Each individual must decide for himself whether the quality of his life is worth having heroic measures applied. When you are admitted to a hospital, you need to communicate whether or not you want to be coded if your heart stops and if you want to be maintained on life-support equipment when you are no longer able to sustain life on your own.

When these decisions are made by your next-of-kin, they are often made for emotional reasons rather than practical ones. One of our patients remained on life-support in a comatose state for a year and a half. Her family had signed a consent form for her to have gall bladder surgery against her wishes. She was a psychiatric patient and not legally responsible of making that choice. She suffered a cardiac arrest in surgery and sustained irreversible brain damage. Because of deep-seated guilt feelings, her family couldn't bring themselves to permit her life-support to be discontinued.

Because she had a tracheostomy, several groups of students became adapt at deep suctioning tracheostomies by frequently practicing on her. So there was some purpose and meaning to her state of suspended animation.

At the other end of the spectrum are relatives who are anxious to be rid of a troublesome kin or to get their hands on their possessions or money before it is used up.

It is your inherent right to make these decisions for yourself so that they are consistent with your own principles. Most states now recognize living wills in which an individual specifically addresses these issues. We can retain control of what happens to our bodies as well as our assets. On admission to a hospital these decisions should be discussed frankly and noted on your legal documents. Your family should also be aware of how you feel about these matters. There is never a question of euthanasia, which is illegal.

You should also make known to these same people how you feel about having an autopsy and donating organs after death, or donating your body to science. These should be informed decisions, made when you are mentally competent and completely aware of all that is involved in each of these situations.

While death rarely comes to the OB department, when it does it is especially tragic. Few experiences transcend the joy of bringing a live, healthy baby into the world. That happiness is so beautiful that it overshadows other incidental tragedies. Two of our patients hemorraged so intractably after delivery that they had to have hysterectomies. They never expressed any regret about losing a part of their body or the ultimate consequence—that there would be no more babies in their future. In fact their whole outlook was joyful and bubbly. I have no doubts that reality eventually settled in some time after their dismissal from the hospital. But the experience of the creation of a new life is too elating to allow sadness to spoil it.

By the same token the death of the progeny is often the most calamitous thing that can occur. Many people are totally devastated when they have a miscarriage, even when they barely knew they were pregnant. When a full term or near-term fetus dies it is perceived as same as a death after birth.

One of our patients came in for an induction because she had gone past her due date. Ultrasound revealed the presence of twins—both with beating hearts. This was her first inkling that there was more than one baby. The induction was canceled and a Caesarean delivery was scheduled for the following morning. By morning one of the heartbeats had stopped. She delivered one live baby boy and one stillborn son. Although she had one baby, which was all that she had expected less than twenty-four hours earlier, she continued to mourn the loss of his twin. And it cast a pall over her happiness over her new baby. When anyone would go into her room and admire her little baby she would always tell them, "I had two babies, you know. My other little boy died."

The loss of a baby is always poorly accepted. It goes against the natural order of things for children to die before their parents. Nurses feel that too. One day we sent an LPN to the morgue with a stillborn baby. She returned to the floor still carrying the baby. "Couldn't you get into the morgue?" We asked her.

She began to sob. "I opened the refrigerator door and saw an amputated leg in there. I wasn't about to leave him in the fridge with that leg!" Everyone understood.

I've learned that it's best not to look for the silver lining. Nobody wants to hear, "You'll have more babies." Or "God knows what's best."

One of our mothers who lost her baby had a one-year-old at home. "At least you won't have to go home with empty arms," I told her, hoping it would offer some consolation. Instead it seemed to evoke all her grief and anger.

"How does one baby take the place of another?" She snapped back at me. I hadn't meant to imply that. But I learned that the less you say the better. A simple, "I'm sorry," and a hug are best.

Not all patients project their grief. One day one of my students came looking for me. Her patient had just learned that her newborn baby had died. "You have to come," insisted the student. "I don't know what to do." Going down that long hallway was one of the longest walks of my life. And yet it was not long enough. I wasn't sure I knew much more than my student what to do. When I reached her room, I found her all alone. I asked her if I could call her husband. She said he was on his way. The room seemed chilly and I offered to get her a blanket. She said she was fine. I said I would bring her a cup of coffee. She declined. I offered to stay with her until her husband came. She said it wasn't necessary. She thanked me warmly. She knew that I shared her pain and it was enough.

I have never seen a mother die from childbirth although it still does happen occasionally. Good medical and nursing care combined with good luck have spared me from witnessing this calamity. One of our post partum mothers did die while still with us. She was too ill to be dismissed with her baby and died from advanced alcoholism. Her death was tragic and probably hastened by, but not caused by, her pregnancy. Technically, any maternal death that occurs within thirty days after delivery is considered statistically a maternal death. So if a new mother leaves the hospital and gets fatally hit by a car she becomes a maternal mortality. But happily, death rarely visits the OB department.

CHAPTER 16

GERIATRICS

$\mathcal{I}$n the forties we had never heard of nursing homes. We had many old people who lived the last several years of their lives in the hospital. I never heard of the science of geriatrics. We specialized in bedside nursing care and that is what we gave to all of our patients.

Although we didn't have clinical instructors when I was a student nurse, for my first catheterization, three instructors from the School of Nursing emerged to supervise me. I was startled to find that the patient had been my eighth grade school teacher. I don't know which of us was more embarrassed, but I was definitely more nervous as the three instructors loomed menacingly over me.

With trembling hands I picked the catheter up with the forceps as I had been instructed and attempted to aim it toward an unseen meatus. Predictably I missed the target. The instructors hastened to assure me that it was a difficult one and that they would take care of it. Humiliated, I slunk out of the room, vowing that I would never again fail to successfully complete a catheterization. Thankfully, I never have. In fact I came to consider myself something of an expert at catheterizing and often volunteered to do them when others were having problems with them. Some years later, on a quiet night in L&D, we were sitting over our coffee break discussing how we always called on one particular nurse if we wanted confirmation of our rectal exam. From there we went on to discuss how each of us had one area of expertise in which we were one-step above the others. We proceeded to point out what each of us excelled in. When my turn came I was certain they were going to say that it was catheterization. Instead they said that it was bedside nursing care. I couldn't have been more pleased.

A couple of years later when I found myself, for a variety of reasons, working in a nursing home, bedside nursing was the one thing I really liked about it.

I have been managing my husband's electrical contracting office the previous four years and had been absent from nursing. Then it became necessary to increase our income and I found myself working two jobs—in addition to homemaking. The nursing home where I worked was only a few blocks from where we lived and had the shop. And it was a less scary way to re-enter nursing than going to a hospital, where four years of progress had passed me by. A social worker who had been working with my son told me that I was needed there. So I applied for the job.

It was 1965 and district regulations which now govern the operation of nursing homes were still in the future. The aides had managed to retain control through a series of power struggles which sent previous licensed personnel who had been employed there scurrying. The head aide was carrying on an affair with the administrator and consequently he closed his eyes to all the 'monkey business' that transpired. In return they closed their eyes to the fact that he did his 'grocery shopping' in the home's kitchen.

After I arrived on the scene they immediately set about attempting to get rid of me as fast as possible. My orientation consisted of the administrator taking me to the nurses' station and saying, "This is

Mrs. Sommer. Show her where to hang her coat." It wasn't necessary to introduce her to me. She wore a large pin proclaiming that she was:

Lynn Baden

Nurse in Charge

It took me a week to learn that there was no bathroom for the staff. We had to share one with the residents. Some of them were none too clean. Fortunately I lived close and could usually wait until I got home.

The two aides who were in charge of the day shift and 11-7 a.m. shift combined forces to accomplish their goal of disillusioning me and forcing me to resign. Lynn would get there at 4:00 a.m. and they would give all the residents laxatives so they would have diarrhea all day. I found that they had been "sterilizing" equipment by holding it under hot, running tap water. There was an autoclave sitting in the treatment room and the engineer promised to put it in working order on the following Monday morning. When I got there that morning the autoclave had mysteriously disappeared and no one knew what had happened to it. It was eventually found and I spent many happy hours sterilizing everything. It was a shallow victory after I found Lynn running her bare fingers through the sterile boat looking for just the right syringe—although they were all alike and sterile pickup forceps had been made available. Disposable syringes had long been on the market but the administrator refused to purchase them until the old ones were "used up." There was no way of "using them up" short of dropping them all on the floor and breaking them.

Until I got there the medicine for the residents in the hospital wing had been passed by Oley, the day assistant to the administrator. His wife, who was epileptic, retarded and prone to temper tantrums did the laundry for the home and his mother-in-law "specialed" one of the residents in the residential wing. Talk about nepotism! Oley was an administrator's 'yes man.' What else could he be with so many jobs depending on his agreeableness?

Most of the residents on the hospital wing were ambulatory at the time that I started. As they became bedridden I would ask each of the aides if they knew how to give a bed bath. When they seemed hesitant I would take them in to the patient's room, one at a time, and demonstrate the technique by bathing patient and changing the linens myself. Later I learned that they were snickering at me behind my back because all of those aids had given bed baths. I didn't care because I knew that I had shown them the correct way. And I knew that the patients had received the best care that I could give them. And I had enjoyed it. I will always see the role of the nurse as being one of providing hands on nursing care, despite the fact that today's nurse is often called upon to be more of a mechanic to all of the equipment at the bedside.

Everyday I hung in there and refused to let them drive me away. As it turned out, it was only Lynn and Smitty, the night aide, who wanted me out. The other aides soon became my friends and allies. They were the ones who made sure that I knew about the affair between Lynn and the administrator. To ensure that I believed them, they took me to the whirlpool room in the basement and had me listen to them outside of the locked door. It was not evidence that would have been admissible in court, but something was definitely going on.

An interesting epilogue to this story occurred a few years later when I was working in a hospital. A nurse from another floor came to OB to tell me that one of her patients had asked to see me. I didn't recognize her name but went upstairs and peaked into her door. I didn't recognize the patient, so I assumed she had made a mistake and left without going in. The next day I saw that nurse again and she was very insistent that the patient knew me and I must go visit her. So I returned to the room and this time I went all the way in and introduced myself.

At that close vantage point I finally recognized her. She had lost well over hundred pounds but now I could see that it was Smitty, the night aide from the nursing home. She didn't speak to me at all. I wasn't sure whether she was aphasic from her stroke or just couldn't put into words what she wanted to say. But she gripped my hand tightly the whole time I sat with her.

When I had worked in the nursing home she and Lynn had ridiculed me for being nice to the patients and complained that the patients would consequently expect the same treatment from them. I hardly thought that the patients were likely to expect more from them than they had ever gotten. But now I wondered if this woman was finally realizing what it was like from the patient's viewpoint. Did she want to tell me that she had been wrong but couldn't bring herself to admit it? I never found out and she died unexpectedly a few days later.

A couple of months after I started working in the nursing home the State paid me a surprise visit. I had never received any orientation and was still feeling my way around. The inspector went right to the medicine cabinet and began pulling out all the medicines. "Show me your orders for these," she demanded as each patient's medicines were pulled out in rapid succession. I was frantically searching through the doctors' orders sheets, mostly in vain. She stood over me while I flushed down the toilet every medication for which I couldn't produce a current order. Hundreds of dollars worth of medicine went down the drain that day. I learned later that as the patients' charts got too thick they had simply thrown away the oldest part. Some of the medicines the patients were getting had been ordered long, long before.

In order to reinstate the patients on their medications I wrote to each one's doctor and explained that, to comply with State Board regulations, I would need a current set of orders for all medications that they were to receive. To simplify matters for the doctors, I enclosed an order sheet with their medicines and treatments listed. If they wished the patient to continue as before they needed only to sign the sheet and return it in the self-addressed, stamped envelope I had provided. I also enclosed a blank order sheet in the event that they wanted to change the orders. I am still amazed all these years later that almost all of them didn't bother to return the order sheets, failed to return my phone calls and were rude when I did manage to reach them.

Some of the patients were in self-care areas and took their own medications, which they kept in their rooms. I found that one patient had three different prescriptions for phenobarbital, a dangerous and addictive drug when misused. She asked me for help in understanding the instructions on the bottles. I truly feared that she was getting an overdose. And State Board had been adamant that these people were not to be allowed to take their own medicines. But the doctors were even worse, if that was possible, about giving me orders for them. They were just as adamant that the patients could manage their own medications.

The only doctor who came to the home on a regular basis—once a week—came to visit his mother, who was a patient. They all seemed unhappy to be there and anxious to leave. I think they must have felt out of control to handle these people's problems. They were in the business of saving lives and these people's lives were not to be saved. Even worse, it was a reflection of something few of us want to face up to—our own mortality.

There were numerous other problems in addition to the apathy of the doctors. The aides were even more poorly paid than I was and often bickered over whose turn it was to clean up a mess or to take care of a difficult patient. They would often leave an incontinent patient on a commode for an extended period of time and when I asked them to put her to bed they would counter with, "She's still going."

Lynn would engage in power struggles with the patients as well as myself. If she was miffed with a patient she would take away her privilege of going to the dining room in a wheelchair and tell her that she had to walk. When I told the administrator I didn't want Lynn taking the patients' privileges away, he said, "That's therapy."

"From now on I'll determine their therapy," I responded

"the doctors should order the therapy," was his comeback.

"Fine," I agree. "Just tell Lynn not to do that to the patients anymore."

Actually the doctors didn't care what I did with the patients as long as I didn't bother them. The one time they would back me up was when I told them I hadn't been able to reach them in an emergency and had acted independently.

While working conditions in the nursing home were far from desirable, there were many unforgettable patients that I felt privileged to know. One of them had been my neighbor when I was a little girl. She and her husband, who was deceased by that time, had owned and operated the neighborhood grocery store on our block. One of her sons had continued to manage the store and the other had become a doctor and was then living and practicing in California. They were all gentle people and a devoted family.

Mrs. Golden was a diabetic and quite elderly by that time. Although she was mentally alert the quality of her life was poor. She was on bed rest and could go to the bathroom only with the help of a walker and a nurse. Her days were spent waiting for one of us to stop in and provide a little care and conversation. And she was always so grateful. "Dear girl," she would murmur.

"How did you know I needed you?"

Soon after I began working there she developed gangrene in her foot. The doctor and her son decided that she could never survive the surgery. To save her from the necessity of suffering the trauma of surgery they decided to simply allow her to die from the gangrene. Her doctor son in California concurred.

Weeks passed and Mrs. Golden clung to life. The gangrene worsened and spread up her leg. Finally they had no choice but to amputate her leg. Her son came from California and the surgery was done. Mrs. Golden survived the amputation and the first post operative week. And then she died.

One of my all-time favorite patients was Sam. Sam was only sixty-one but his Parkinson's was so advanced that he was completely paralyzed—literally frozen into a fetal position. His only movement was an involuntary one—a palsy in his left hand. Sometimes the tremor was so forceful that he would inch his hand to his nose and let the tremor scratch it. He had no adipose tissue—only skin stretched tightly over his bones—and no hair. His whole being was encompassed in two enormous brown eyes which gazed earnestly out of his skeletal face.

Even his voice was gone and he could speak only in a whisper. Yet he had been placed in a room at the far end of the hall and was given a roommate with angry, uncontrolled behavior. Fred would bluster around, swinging his cane at poor Sam, who couldn't lift hand to defend himself or even call out for help. Many times Fred had come dangerously close to injuring him. Often I would be working in a nearby room and become aware of a rustling noise that had been going on for a time. As I stopped to listen I would realize that it was my name whispered over and over—caricaricaricaricaricari. I would rush to Sam's room and whisk Fred away from him. Then Sam would fix those big brown eyes on me and whisper, "What's wrong with him? He's too young to be senile." I had no answer for him. It was many years before we learned about Alzheimer's disease. That would undoubtedly have been Fred's diagnosis today.

I learned Sam's story from his sister one day when she came to visit. He had been twenty-seven years old and engaged to be married when he began experiencing problems with his eyes. When he was diagnosed with Parkinson's he broke off his engagement without any explanation to his fiancée. Heartbroken, she left the state. A few years later she married an abusive man and bore him four children. How much better off she would have been if she had married Sam and enjoyed the good years that were left. But Sam's decision, although emanating from love and selflessness, deprived them both of the love and comfort they could have been sharing.

Sam had many complications but he never complained—not even of the callous treatment he sometimes received. And strangely he never wished for death to release him from the prison of his paralyzed body and restore some control to his destiny. We discussed it one time and he assured me that, for him, life was too precious to lose. I had been gone from the nursing home for several years when I saw Sam's obituary in the newspaper. I knew that it was a blessing and was sure that Sam was now happy to be rid of that cumbersome body. But it was also sad to contemplate the world without him as yet another lovely flame had been extinguished.

Of course deaths are inevitable in nursing homes. That is acceptable because it is consistent with the natural order of life. While there are some younger patients, most of them are elderly and have experienced a long, full life. Often when someone is admitted to a nursing home he sees that as the next inevitable step and it becomes a self-fulfilling prophecy. But it is not always possible to predict who will die and who will linger on—perhaps for many years.

The Coltons were a very devoted couple. Mrs. Colton was mentally alert and physically active. Deprived of her kitchen to cook family meals and her home to care for, she turned her time and attention to caring for her husband. Mr. Colton was mild-mannered and easy-going—and completely disoriented. His wife doted on him, fussing over him constantly and making sure that all his needs were met.

When Mrs. Colton died unexpectedly we were certain that her husband would wither from neglect and die soon after. But to our surprise he seemed not to even notice her absence. He continued his aimless rambling in his usual blissful state for several more years.

As patients' conditions deteriorated and they became dyspneic, cyanotic or comatose, I would call their doctors and remind them, since they were unaccustomed to having licensed personnel there, that I could start an IV or administer oxygen. The answer was always the same—

"Why do you want to hang on to her? Let her go." In each instance I would explain that I didn't want to hang on. I just wanted to make her comfortable. Their response was to reiterate, "let her go."

Working in the nursing home had a profound affect on my outlook. I reached that big 4-0 birthday soon after I began working there and began to understand that I, too, was mortal. But far worse than mortality was the realization that I was also approaching old age. Even though there was a whole generation between most of the residents and myself—most of the 'children' who came to visit them were old enough to be my parents—it was still a discomfiting feeling to be surrounded by elderly people with such a startling variety of infirmities.

Statistics tell us that only a very small percentage of the elderly live in institutions. Of course these statistics include 'young' people in their sixties. As the age increases so too the odds of becoming institutionalized. And, from the perspective of the nursing home, the statistics are one hundred percent.

While I had a good relationship with most of the aides, working conditions never improved, and I missed the professionalism of the hospital environment and my happy OB patients. And most of all, I missed the babies.

The patients weren't always on my side either. They were childlike in their need for attention and, at the same time, demanding of obedience to their authority. One diabetic was running a 4 + glucose in her urine. I inquired about her diet and she insisted that the serving women wouldn't let her have the right foods and she had to fill up on bread. When I accompanied her to the dining room and saw that she was given the correct diet—limiting her bread until her glucosuria came down—she reported me to the administrator and told him I was trying to kill her. He thought that was hilarious and couldn't wait to share it with me. Another patient insisted that I call the doctor about her foot but kept both of her hands wrapped around it so I couldn't see what was wrong with it. One little lady I had chosen to be my surrogate grandmother constantly insisted that I give her aspirin. I really became concerned for my own professionalism one day when she refused to leave the nursing office while I was trying to concentrate on setting up the medications without any errors and she kept imploring in my ear, "Be a good girl. Give me aspirin." In desperation I began to push the chair in which she was sitting out of the office. She grabbed hold of the doorknob and it turned into a scene from a Marx Brothers comedy.

The doctors remained noticeably inaccessible. One day a patient became so unmanageable that I gave him some Demerol which was in his medicine stall but for which the order had been thrown away. When I was finally able to reach him I was certain he would be angry. But he was delighted. They would accept anything as long as I didn't bother them. I suspected that they felt safe from aging and dying as long as they didn't have to face it head on.

But I didn't leave the nursing home for any of those reasons. I stayed on because I thought the patients needed me. Then an incident occurred which made it impossible for me to remain.

One of our patients, Mr. Stein, had been hospitalized with a duodenal ulcer. He had returned to the home with explicit dietary instructions. I tried to explain to the kitchen aides what kind of food he needed and how to prepare it. There was no dietitian there. When I saw that they were getting agitated I even offered to prepare it myself. I think they interpreted this as a criticism of their cooking. I don't think that they had ever been called upon to prepare a special diet before.

So they reported me to the administrator. Part of the milieu there was the immature behavior of employees who ran to the father figure at the slightest provocation. The administrator, acting in the capacity of a father settling this children's disputes, actually fanned the flames more than any resolution of the problems. He called a meeting of all the employees. He made a farcical speech designed to embarrass me, but never addressed the issue of Mr. Stein's diet except basically to tell me to "mind my own business." I became so frustrated that I went home early, but told him that I would return in the morning.

When I returned the next day I found that Mr. Stein had had a gastric hemorrhage during the night and died. At last I was defeated. I knew that it would probably have happened even if he had received the proper diet. But it was apparent that, if I could not be allowed to provide quality nursing care, there was no point in my remaining there. I submitted my two week notice on the spot. There was another RN working there at the time. She was a kind and decent person but timid and an alcoholic. She was undoubtedly no match for these people, but then who was? I had been there a year and eight months. It seemed like an eternity.

Later I wrote up a detailed report describing the activities and practices that took place there and presented it to one of the doctors on the board. He never responded and there were no immediate changes. They were kind enough to let the administrator continue for a few more years until he could retire. Gradually things began to improve there and today it is on a par with the best of them. I have no doubt that tightening of regulations by the State Board of Nursing was largely responsible for the improvements. I hoped that I had played a small part.

The aides told me they wanted to give me a going away party but it had to be at my home. We had a grand time. They gave me a lovely gown and négligée fit for a bride and brought lots of liquor. My successor got drunk and passed out and had to spend the night. My daughter was at camp. So we put her in that room. In the middle of the night she sat on my daughter's music stand looking for the bathroom. The stand did not survive. I hope Helen fared better.

The weekend after I turned in my resignation I checked the Sunday want ads. They were loaded with opportune nursing positions. Previously I had always just gone to the nearest hospital. But now I had finally learned to drive and no longer lived on a bus line. So the world was my oyster. One of the ads was for an obstetrical nursing instructor. It had always been in the back of my mind that I would eventually go into teaching when my back problems became too severe to lift patients anymore.

I made an appointment for an interview. The Director of Nursing at the hospital was impressed with my qualifications and offered me the job on the spot—and twenty-five dollars a month more than I had been making at the nursing home.

That was my lucky day. You could say it was "the first day of the rest of my life." For the next twenty years my employer change twice and I changed hospitals several times. But I kept that job until I retired.

CHAPTER 17

BACK TO THE FUTURE: EDUCATION

*T*he Director of Nursing was anxious for me to start my new job as soon as possible, but she recognized the ethical necessity of giving adequate notice. Since there was another RN at the home already I felt that two weeks were sufficient. I scheduled my first day at the hospital to fall on the first Monday after my resignation became effective. That meant I worked New Year's Day, which fell on Sunday, at the Home and the legal holiday, which was observed on Monday, at the hospital. It was worth it. The Administrator was spreading rumors that I had obtained the new job before giving notice and that was the real reason I was leaving. I suppose he had to do that to save face.

When I arrived at the hospital at 6:30 a.m. that first morning I found that the students were on their holiday break. I hadn't considered that as we had always worked holidays as students. I used the time to get oriented to the hospital and the department and to go over the materials left in the classroom by the former clinical instructor. How good it felt to be back in the hospital again and working with professionals! I felt like I had come home at last.

The hospital was old and small—much like the one where I had taken my training. Only we didn't call it "training" anymore. We called it "education." The classroom with large with a folding table and chairs on one side and two hospital beds on the other side where the residents could sleep.

The nursing students returned from their break the following Monday. They had been under the direction of the staff nurses since the instructor left. I gathered that the staff had not been very patient in their dealings with them. The students were frightened and wary of them. There had been only one delivery during my week there and I didn't feel very well oriented. So I made them a proposition. "I'll teach you everything I know about OB and you can teach me all you learned about this hospital's routine," I said. We made a great team. We all helped each other and we all benefitted. Today such a statement could well be lethal. One or more of the students would probably run to the Director of the nursing program and tell her that I didn't know what I was doing. Some would be uncooperative or defiant and try to take advantage of my lack of experience. But it was 1967 and the students of all ages still demonstrated respect for their elders and people in positions of authority. That attitude worked to their advantage. They learned a lot and when they graduated a few months later they were ready to assume the responsible positions and function maturely.

It was a small OB department. They had only thirteen or fourteen deliveries a month. There were usually only two staff nurses on duty besides myself for all three areas. The staff loved to have the students and me take over and do everything. In that way the students got to participate in everything that happened on the floor including Gyn patients and other clean cases that were taken to fill in the gap left by the low OB census. There were opportunities they would not be exposed to in their other rotations and I appreciated them along with the students.

I was employed and paid by the hospital. So on the day the students went to classes at one of the many storefront buildings the Public

School System retained for their adult education programs, I stayed at the hospital working as a staff nurse. I worked every other weekend and each of the students was required to work one weekend of her six-week rotation. That meant that there would be students working on my weekend off and also the weekdays I was off for working the weekend. On those days the staff was responsible for the students and I, in turn, had all the responsibilities of a staff nurse. It wasn't too far removed from twenty years earlier when I had graduated. I found it ultimately satisfying.

The education and training of practical nurses and legislation for their own licensure had begun in 1952 and was still in it in its infancy in 1967. There was a vast need for LPN's to ease the shortage of RN's. The School of Practical Nursing accepted 100 entrants twice a year. By the time they were ready to begin their hospital experience four weeks later they had generally shrunk to seventy-five, and by graduation a few more had been lost. There were three OB clinical instructors, each working in a different hospital, two pediatric clinical instructors, two geriatric CI's and three medical—surgical CI's all working in various hospitals.

Four years after I began working there the Director of the School of Practical Nursing asked all of the instructors who are employed by the hospitals to resign and become employed directly by the Public School System. They were already paying the hospitals stipend for our services. Now they would be paying our whole salary. She told us that they had enough funding for two years. For a long time I envisioned myself as jobless at the end of that time. It never happened.

From that time on I was no longer a staff nurse. It was a sad loss for me. I always saw myself as a team worker and a bedside nurse and understood teaching to be an incidental role of all nurses. I didn't see myself as a teacher per se. Case in point: One day a little boy approached me in the parking lot of my apartment building and asked, "Weren't you our fifth grade substitute teacher one day?"

I pulled myself up to my full five feet one and a half inches and pointed to my white shoes and hose. "Did your teacher were these?" I asked him.

"Oh, you're a nurse, aren't you?"

"That's right," was my proud reply.

But I enjoyed teaching students at the bedside and conducting the clinical conferences about the clinical specialty I've spent many happy years pursuing. The next twenty years were varied and interesting and often hectic. Our students ranged in age from seventeen to seventy-two, from single "girls" to married (and unmarried) women with children. Some of our students already had Bachelors and even Masters degrees. Several had been teachers and were looking for a change. Several were beauticians. One year was not a big chunk out of anyone's life and a wide variety of people were willing to give it a try. Many of them went on to become RN's with an Associate or a Bachelor's degree. Continuing education has become a lifelong pursuit for those who want to be successful and keep abreast of the times.

The younger students began to reflect changing attitudes in child-rearing and educational practices. Respect for authority became rare and much of the interest centered on being dismissed early. When a procedure became available for them to enrich their experience the less mature ones would often say, "Let someone else do it." Especially if it were getting near the end of the shift.

One senior told me she didn't need to do a catheterization because she had already done one. I recalled my own first experience and a number of experiences it took to master the sterile technique and the mechanics of inserting the catheter correctly. The student would be graduating in two weeks and would then be held responsible for having mastered this procedure. This was not her assigned patient but the staff was kind enough to offer experiences like this to my students as they became available.

Guiding a student through a "cath" was not one of my favorite things. Their sense of sterility is not developed and they are clumsy and reluctant to invade this very private area of the body. Memories of my first cath made me sympathetic. But it was a necessary part of their education and therefore a necessary function of my job.

So I responded to the student, "in that case you should be able to breeze right through this without any assistance from me." It was no surprise that she needed a great deal of assistance and direction from me and still inserted the catheter into the vagina instead of the meatus. I was fuming as I waited by the "tube" system for another sterile catheter to be sent to the floor. "I'll just put this one in myself," I muttered half aloud.

A young RN, not long out of nursing school herself, pleaded the student's cause. "Oh, let her do it. I'm sure she'll do it right this time."

By that time the catheter had arrived I had regained my composure. So I gave the student another chance. I wish that I could report the happy ending that we all love so well. Perhaps the student was as flustered as I had been. Once again she inserted the catheter into the vagina. By that time the orderly from the OR had been cooling his heels outside her door for some time as he waited with a gurney to take her to surgery. Now he needed to get her there stat. There was no time to obtain another sterile catheter. I had no choice but to clean this one off with the antiseptic solution on the tray and insert it into the bladder where it belonged. It bothered me that her bad attitude and sloppy technique and forced me to use less than optimal standards.

This is not to say that all students are now bad. Quite the opposite. By far the majority of our students continue to be dedicated to their patients and learning experiences. My years of association with them has kept me young and abreast of the times. They have been an endless source of delight and humor. Like the teenager who was "constantly amazed at how well (her) parents got around." It turned out they were thirty-nine and forty years old. But the immoral majority are the most outspoken and muddy the waters for the others.

Now that I was working for the school system I spent the students' class day at the storefront building that served as the school. I taught Community Health and Vocational Adjustments in the beginning. Later I taught Psychiatric Aspects of Nursing and, I was assigned to teach several other courses that required me to spend all my off-duty time studying to refresh my memory and update me on forty years away from the subjects. I taught just about everything but my old archenemy, pharmacology.

Reading the students' written work was an eye-opener and paralleled changes in teaching methods used by the school system. During the period after phonics had been abandoned and look—see was thought, the papers were almost illiterate. Sentences were fragmented, punctuation was almost nonexistent and grammar was unrecognizable. Spelling? Don't ask. While I knew the six students in each of my hospital groups, most of the fifty or more students in those theory classes were unknown to me. As I read their papers I would envision lower-class, illiterate slum dwellers. I was frequently surprised to meet the students face to face and find them to be bright, polished young women. What a sad commentary to the educational practices of the time.

In time the written work improved dramatically. It was evident that phonics and teaching better writing skills had been re-introduced into the public school system. Since charting is such an important part of nursing practice, especially in these times of increasing malpractice suits, a basic knowledge of the written language is essential. Even with an adequate background, charting is a difficult skill for many students to master.

One interesting change that has taken place in all levels of nursing has been the number of males that have entered the field. In the fifties male nurses were rare and often had effeminate personalities. I remember overhearing a conversation between two male private duty nurses. They were complaining about their patients' rooms being cluttered and untidy and lamenting the fact that they had to clean up the rooms before they could begin to give nursing care. Today male students are as masculine as any segment of the population and their conversation frequently centers around sports and current events, topics many of the women are interested in as well. Many of them, both men and women, are in military or National Guard programs.

When I first had male students in OB I was more than a little nervous. Caring for OB patients requires constant invasions of very private parts of women's bodies. I could envision women being embarrassed and their husbands becoming enraged by the presence of male students.

In the beginning, the hospital where we were working was sedating their labor patients heavily. So I solved my problem by starting each male student in the labor room with a female student as a buffer. The patient was unaware of their presence and her husband was in the waiting room. After my first male students had seen his first delivery I breathed a sigh of relief. The deed had been accomplished. To my surprise and delight he looked up his patient on the post-partum floor the next day to congratulate her and check on her progress. That was a class act. I was duly impressed and it was one of many valuable lessons I've learned from my students over the years.

But because I was now sold on male nursing students didn't mean that the rest of the world was. In that hospital they had a rule that permission had to be obtained from post-partum patients before assigning them to male students. It was a large Catholic hospital with a very impressive OB patient census. So it should not have been too much of a problem. Every afternoon at three o'clock when the students had gone home, I would visit the patients seeking those that wouldn't object to having a male student care for them the next day. It was a traumatic experience—for me. I think most of them would have been accepting of the situation if an issue had not been made of it. But when given the choice it seemed safer to just say no.

To complicate matters even more, there were always visitors at that hour. One patient told me to come back if I couldn't find anyone else. When I returned later she told me that she really didn't mind but hadn't wanted to say so with her mother-in-law sitting there.

One day I was sure I could complete my mission quickly and soon be on my way home. The patient had just come from the Recovery Room and her stertorous breathing told me that she was still under the effects of the anesthetic. I planed to ask my question and accept her grunt as assent. To my surprise she opened her eyes wide, looked me right in the eyes, and said, "No. No, I don't want a male student." Then she returned to her semicomatose state. In time the hospital began having the admitting nurse ask the patients about this and then all I had to do was check the kardex.

Most of the male students were delightful, demonstrating that men can be masculine and still have a softer, nurturing side. Of course there is always the exception. I always accompanied the men when they checked their patients and did the more personal procedures myself. When Jeff came to the rotation I had begun putting the men on postpartum first to get that part over with. Jeff seemed to especially enjoy it when we checked breasts and got that lecherous gleam in his eyes. Perhaps it was only for my benefit but I made a mental note to transfer him to the nursery as soon as he had completed the minimal postpartum requirements. When that anxiously awaited day came I learned that Jeff had broken his ankle and wouldn't be coming. He never returned to nursing. Probably a wise decision on his part.

Having black male students, on OB was a special concern. It needn't have been. I guess I had watched too many TV programs depicting racial conflict. Most Americans are not the bigots we are portrayed as being. My black male students were an especially outstanding group. Most of them were in the military, often officers, accustomed to assuming responsibility and they eagerly sought nursing experiences. One of them called me in Labor and Delivery to tell me he had completed his patient load and wanted to give post recovery care to the patient we were going to bring up to the floor. He greeted us in the hall, helped us get her in bed, took report and proceeded to take excellent care of her.

The only patient who ever rejected one of them was a young black teenager. She told the student that was reassigned to her that she was afraid her boyfriend would be jealous.

"When I woke up and saw him standing over my bed," she said. "He was so good looking I thought I had died and gone to heaven!"

In 1967 and for several more years, the LPN program was a one-year course with two weeks vacation in the summer and a two week break between Christmas and New Year's. There were pre-and post-conferences in which we would spend a good part of the day discussing the cares we were going to provide and then evaluating the effectiveness of those cares. The emphasis was On The Job Training. It was the way I had learned and I have always thought it was effective. Who ever coined the phrase, "Experience is the best teacher" must have thought so too.

Even the best students often find it difficult to correlate theory learned in the classroom with actual experiences in the clinical areas.

One afternoon we had just discussed a situation in pre-conference when we encountered that very situation on the floor. The student who was assigned to that patient was above average in both theory and practice. But she was stymied by the situation and couldn't tell me how she could go about resolving it. "Don't you remember?" I asked her. "We just talked about that in pre-conference today."

"Yes, but I didn't think that applied here," was her answer. Still, the trend toward classroom learning experiences, led and supported by the American Nurses Association (ANA) has moved toward the goal of having all levels of learning take place in educational institutions rather than under apprenticeship conditions.

In 1974 the Community College was organized in our city. They assimilated all of the storefront buildings and included the School of Practical Nursing among their programs. It took some time for us to absorb the fact that we were no longer a school of nursing. A college is a school and therefore does not contain schools within itself. We had become a practical nursing program.

For the first few years we were the mainstay of the college. Our capping ceremonies, which took place twice a year, were very impressive. The public loved to watch the instructors in their white uniforms and caps pinning the newly earned caps on the kneeling figures of the students in their gray and white uniforms. They loved it even more when the sixty something graduating seniors walked across the stage clad in their brand-new white uniforms to accept their diplomas. When the college decreed that the nursing students must graduate with the rest of the college rather than having their own ceremony at the completion of the program year, our students comprised the majority of the graduating class.

Conditions began to change. The multitude of storefront buildings were replaced with three college campuses—two of them built from scratch and one located in remodeled buildings on a former army fort. The College was not happy about the dominance of its nursing program. They decreed that its graduates must wear caps and gowns like all the other graduates, as they did in other colleges and universities. Often the graduation date did not coincide with their completion date. They might graduate and then have to return for another month to fulfill their State Board requirements. They didn't like it but they learned to live with it.

The College was a boon for the facility. Many of us were in our forties and had accumulated many years of working experience. This experience was reflected in our new salaries. Prior to this, at each new hospital where I began to work, I always started at their beginning base salary. I have never before received a salary adjustment that recognized length of experience.

Previously it was considered unethical for nurses to bargain for wages. Most of the time I didn't even know what my salary was to be until I received my first paycheck. Now that we were affiliated with educators rather than staff nurses, we had our own bargaining agent. The facility voted to have the National Education Association (NEA) become our bargaining agent. Every two years the members of the negotiating committee went to the bargaining table to negotiate contracts for the next two years. We never failed to get a reasonable salary increase and often increased benefits as well. After living on less than poverty level wages for so many years this was really heaven. I was able to buy a house and a car and take several exotic vacations, as well as being generous with my children. I've never understood why teachers complain so bitterly about their wages.

The college focus, like the ANA's was on classroom theory rather than hands on experience. The one-year course was extended to five quarters—the first quarter consisting of prerequisites, all in the classroom. Clinical hours were cut. This was a boon to the many students who have families and full-time jobs. Hopefully that will result in fewer divorces, which have always occurred at a high rate among our students.

The cost of the education required to become an LPN, which was three hundred dollars in 1967, increased to over two thousand dollars. But most of the students are on scholarships, grants, loans and G.I. benefits.

RN's have been graduating for many years with their heads full of theory but unable to fulfill the practical responsibilities required of them. Many hospitals set up apprenticeship programs designed for them to acquire the experience needed to function in their chosen roles. LPN's generally must struggle to gain this experience in their day to day work. Their largest field of employment has been in nursing homes where the pace is somewhat slower and the emphasis is on bedside nursing care.

If I had to choose one quality about the practical nursing student that I find the most admirable it would have to be their ability to come back from failure and try, try again until they eventually succeed. I had always felt that if I had failed at something I would have had to crawl off with my "tail between my legs." But I learned to have the utmost admiration for these students, some of whom have failed four or five times at a particular course, and returned each time until they were able to conquer it. I find that infinitely more heroic than the mere talent to master things the first time around.

Because of the many schools and universities in this area graduating RN's at two-year, three year, and four year levels, and the large classes graduated twice a year from our practical nursing program, this city has finally overturned the nursing shortage. And there is now a shortage of nursing opportunities in this area. The practical nursing program now takes only one class of 30 students a year. The facility, which used to boast of twelve instructors, now has only two full-time instructors and an occasional part-timer. But in my opinion there will always be a need for the LPN.

CHAPTER 18

NURSING AND MOTHERHOOD

I don't know of any group of women more prolific than nurses. One fourth of the girls that graduated from nursing school with me were pregnant. And that was in the shadow of the Victorian era. Marriage was not permitted during the training period, but apparently pregnancy was too powerful a force to resist, although birth control was readily available.

In the years before the Women's Movement opened up the job market to the majority of women, nurses comprised, by far, the largest female working force. A dependable, dedicated group, nurses would often work until the day their babies were delivered. It was not unusual to say good night to a coworker at 11:30 P.M. and return in the morning to find her a postpartum patient. Generally she would have been returned to the hospital in labor at midnight and delivered before morning. Four to six weeks later she would be back at work—and not because her job would not be held for her. There were always more nursing positions than there were nurses to fill them. Because of a bad back and nerve compression my record wasn't that good. But I did spend the day after my first delivery answering the phone and charting medicines for the staff on an especially hectic day.

Finding suitable babysitters was the major problem of working. Nurses who had a loving relative who could babysit were the luckiest. The country was not yet acclimated to working mothers. I was always the only working mother in my neighborhood, but my neighbors didn't baby sit because they weren't working mothers.

Over the years I ran the gamut in seeking conscientious, reliable sitters for my children. Qualified care was always my first priority and that expense came off the top of the budget. Sometimes people were perfectly nice as acquaintances and neighborhood teenagers, but would turn into monsters as babysitters—much as some people do when they get behind the wheel of a car or sit down to a game of bridge.

One summer I hired a teenaged neighbor to watch my children during summer vacation. She had played with them every day after school all year and they loved her. I anticipated a worry free summer. Instead my children complained every day. When I would confront her, the conversation would go something like this:

"Lisa said you woke her early in the morning, made her get up, and stuffed a whole hard-boiled egg, in her mouth."

"Yes. I did."

"Why on earth would you do that?"

"Mark was going to do it. So I did it first before he could."

By the time we got all the problems straightened out the summer was over.

During the years I worked 3-11 p.m. I spent a great deal of time pacing back and forth looking out the window for sitters that were late or just didn't bother to come. The neighbors would report that my children would be outside all day without their coats. One peaked in my window and found the sitter doing laundry (hers) or studying, even though she couldn't do so much as wash the dishes they had dirtied because she "was there only to look after the children." That explained the mystery of why my dryer was always turned on the low setting even though I invariably left it on high.

When I questioned her about this she told me that she had spilled something on her hose and had to wash and dry them. When I asked about the huge bundles she brought every day she said she had to drop them off at the dry cleaner on the way home.

One day one of the private duty nurses gave me a ride from the bus stop to the hospital. I learned that she also ran an agency that placed private duty nurses and babysitters. I told her that I desperately needed a reliable sitter. She sent me an easy-going grandmother. She arrived early every day and never voiced any complaints.

Mrs. Kramer was with me for two years. I could afford her only by working from 3-11p.m. while she worked from 2:30 to 6:30 when my husband took over. He wasn't as good but he was cheap and it gave the youngsters some time to be with their father before bedtime. By working forty hours a week I was able to share my check equally with Mrs. Kramer, who worked only about sixteen hours since she didn't come when I worked on the weekends. She was well worth it. And she didn't keep her whole check either. Every week for two years she would go to the agency and pay them their commission, until they finally told her it was no longer necessary.

Then Mark was hit by a car and I had to resign from my job to take care of him. I didn't blame Mrs. Kramer—it could have happened to anybody. But I could no longer afford to pay her. When I eventually returned to work it was only on weekends when my husband was home.

Two long-distance moves later I was back in my hometown. After the usual problems with sitters I decided to try one who would watch them in her own home. That would solve the problem of the sitter not showing. She would always be there—especially at 6:30 A.M. as I was now working days. I found one who lived two blocks from the hospital where I was working. Since I didn't yet drive at that time I would get them up very early in the morning and take them on the bus with me, drop them off at the sitter's house and walk the rest of the way to the hospital.

The sitter made a big production of how religious they were. That was before people were "born again." In those days people just "got religion." That is what she reported had happened to them. "But now we serve God." I had high hopes.

But before long the "sitter monster" once again reared its ugly head. The children were happy for a while and then they began to complain again. The sitter and her children would have hamburgers for lunch while mine would get only a bowl of canned vegetable soup. They were used to a balanced diet and plenty of food.

My kids were not able to eat breakfast at home that early in the morning. So I would send over eggs, milk, cereal and bread so she would have something to feed them. She began to give them the cereal for breakfast every day and the eggs for lunch—even though lunch was supposed to have been included for the fee I paid her.

There were numerous other complaints and soon the children begin to come to the hospital every afternoon and call me from the lobby. In no time at all we were looking for a new sitter—a task complicated by the fact that Mark was hyperactive with attention deficit disorder. These conditions were not yet being diagnosed at that time. So he was never treated. I was always told that I was too lenient—or too strict—or too something else. Otherwise my child would be perfect. It was the old "tabula rosa" theory, universally accepted as fact—a child is a blank slate, reacting to his environmental stimuli. So his behavior had to be a reaction to his mothering.

When Mark was in the first grade and went to school all day and Lisa was pre-school age I finally found the ideal surrogate care.

I enrolled Lisa in a day care center located in the YMCA. Mark went to his grandmother's house until it was time to go to school. I bought him a YMCA membership so he could go to the Y after school and play games. It was only two blacks from his school. Lisa had to be dropped off at 6:30 A.M. so I could get to work by 7:00. The day care center didn't open until seven o'clock but the cook was there at 6:30 and offered to watch her until the teachers arrived. She was as quiet as Mark was raucous: so it was an ideal situation.

I don't know how widespread these problems were. But one nurse I knew, whose husband was in jail, solved the childcare dilemma by working nights and leaving her apartment door open so her landlady could hear the baby if she cried. I've always hoped that landlady was a light sleeper.

I don't know if nurses in general have a higher rate of complications with their pregnancies and labors than the general population or if it just seems that way. But there was at least one instance in which being a nurse was an occupational hazard. There was one particular group that we were sure was having a disproportionately high rate of birth defects and stillbirths. They were the OR nurses. We would often speculate on why the statistics should be so skewed against them. We were sure it must be something in the OR environment. We conjectured that it may have been exposure to anesthetics. What else could it have been? Although Lamaze was just entering the scene at that time, we OB nurses all had our share of exposure to anesthetics. Many of us had administered drip ether and inhaled both its fresh and secondhand fumes as well as those of the nitrous oxide administered by the anesthetists. But our statistics were overwhelmingly low compared to those of the OR nurses. We made our observations when they came to the OB department to deliver. It was some time before our mystery was solved.

A new, innovative antibiotic skin cleanser was being used in the hospital. We bathed the newborns with it and no longer had to fear the dreaded staph infections which had forced newborn nurseries to close down in past years. When used as a pre-op scrub it prevented surgical and obstetrical patients from becoming infected from a pin prick in the rubber glove or a wet scrub gown. We happily slathered on our new miracle soap—the more the better, we thought.

Then one day when we had reported on duty we found that all the Phiso-Hex had disappeared from the nursery shelves. Studies had shown that this product was absorbed through the skin and could cause brain damage in newborns. What a horrible blow! Once again we saw that for every yin there is a yang. The loss of the miracle soap was eventually compensated by the advent of early discharge. Babies were no longer in the hospital long enough for the incubation period to expire. If a baby becomes infected he doesn't exhibit symptoms until after his discharge. So it is not spread to other babies and an epidemic in the nursery is averted.

They continued to use the Phiso-Hex as a surgical scrub in the OR. It was much later when a new study showed that Phiso-Hex was also absorbed through the skin of pregnant women and damaged the developing fetuses, resulting in miscarriages, stillbirths and the birth defects. The mystery was finally solved. Phiso-Hex was removed from the shelves and became available only by prescription.

CHAPTER 19

BACK TO THE FUTURE:
A STUDENT AGAIN

*A*fter I graduated from nursing school and settled into my new job I was glad to be finished with studying. We worked six days a week and, while we were paid for an eight hour day, they often stretched to nine or ten hours long. My time seemed full enough. And off duty I was finally free to enjoy a social life.

One day as I was going home from work I met a former schoolmate getting off the bus from a nearby metropolis. "Where have you been?" I greeted her.

"Oh, I'm just coming back from the University," she informed me. "Working on that B.S.N."

"That's great!" I said out loud. But to myself I was thinking, "Some people never get enough." At that time I had never heard the word "burn-out," but I was experiencing something akin to it. It had been a hard three years.

In the years ahead I thought of her many times. How wise she had been. At that time it was possible to attain a B.S.N. in just two additional years. I soon married and had two children. My husband was frequently unemployed and I worked extra days, vacations and double shifts a lot. I remained much too busy working, raising the children, preparing tasty, nutritious meals and trying to keep our home as spotless as those of the stay-at-home mothers to worry about higher education. There were no convenience products and most men did not help with the housework or children in those times when motherhood and homemaking were the only acceptable career choices for women. There was no time or money for college and I tucked the idea of a B.S.N. away as a dream for the future.

A couple of decades later I was divorced and my youngest child had left home to go to college. Finally I had no one to worry about but myself. I decided it was my turn. I enrolled in our local state university. I was still working full time. And teaching involved after-hours duties and responsibilities. So I took only one three-hour credit course a semester.

Although it was the same University my long ago school mate had attended, the rules had changed in the intervening years. I would not be given any credit for my three years of nursing school. I would have to repeat difficult courses like chemistry and microbiology. Eventually I would have to take a leave of absence from my job to meet clinical requirements—i.e. I would have to prove my proficiency in every field of nursing, including the one I was teaching.

I had to go through the university's student nurse program to register for each course that I took. Yet the advisor was never there at registration time. She pointedly informed me that she was not on vacation than as I had assumed—she simply was not paid to work at that time. By coincidence I happened to know her secretary, whose salary covered her to work all year round. So I would figure out what course I would take and have the secretary initial it on my registration card. In that way I was able to avoid the dreaded science courses.

But as the years passed I began to realize that attaining a B.S.N. was more of a fantasy than reality. So I switched to a General Studies Program. This program was set up "with the adult student in mind." I began taking courses that were of special interest to me. Since I felt I would probably be going to school for the rest of my life, I decided that I might as well enjoy it. Maybe someday I would accumulate enough credits for a BS in general studies.

I took mostly English and Psychology courses because I was especially interested in those fields. I found two courses in Eastern Psychology especially enlightening and I was very impressed with the practicing Buddhists in the class. They were all American-born and observing traditional religions, but found additional meaning in Buddhism. The optional reading that I pursued while taking that class brought me to new ways of viewing life and the universe that remain with me today. I had just signed up for a course in paranormal psychology that I was very excited about when I saw a newspaper advertisement telling about an analog only college which was bringing in a degree program designed specifically for RN's and other health care professionals.

The college promised to grant full credit for two or three years of nursing school and two years experience. All that would be required would be an additional thirty-two hours from the college. All of their courses were four credit hour courses. So eight courses were all that would be needed.

I decided it was too good to be true. I would stick with my previous plans. Then I learned that most of the nurses on our faculty who did not yet have their degree were enrolling. Reluctantly I withdrew from the University course and enrolled in the Illinois college.

I had been attending the University for six years and had not accumulated enough credits for the Associate Degree. By taking an educational sabbatical leave, to which I was entitled with full pay because of longevity with the community college, I was able to complete the program and less than three years and realize a B.S. degree. While it wasn't a B.S.N.—it was a Bachelor of Science in Health Arts—I thought it was wonderful. I was finally a college graduate. I was fifty-five years old.

If a young woman today were to ask my advice in pursuing a career in nursing, I would strongly advise her to enroll in a college program rather than a hospital school. I still believe the hospital programs turned out excellent nurses. But with the emphasis on degrees the nurse protects her own interests by going the educational institution route. A one-year practical nursing graduate can usually link into an associate degree program and become an RN with an associate degree in one additional year. The A.S.N. graduate can then link into a B.S.N. program and graduate in two additional years, avoiding the stress I experienced.

CHAPTER 20

NURSING AND THE LEGAL SYSTEM

*D*uring the first half of my nursing career we were not concerned with legal considerations. Doctors were rarely sued for malpractice and nurses, not at all. Nurses wages during this period were below the poverty level and, as the saying goes, you can't get blood out of a turnip. But the principal reason was that people were just not conditioned to think "lawsuit" in response to every adversity. We were all doing the best we could and the public understood that.

Today we teach student nurses to document every chart as if it will appear in court some day. And there is a reasonably good chance that it will. In the forties we were taught to chart neatly and thoroughly. No particular reason was given. Any information that we wanted to convey to the doctors was done directly. We respected and obeyed the authority figures that issued the orders and did as directed. All nurses' notes were neatly printed. Any literate person could pick up a chart and read the notations without difficulty. Today nurses write their comments as the doctors do in hastily scrawled, and sometimes unreadable, cursive.

Many hospitals had a committee, that spot checks the charts and writes expensive reports on any discrepancies it finds. This report is printed up and sent to every floor. Nurses do not like to see their charting publicly criticized—even though their name is not included—and go to great pains to chart according to hospital policy.

There is an old adage that says, "if it wasn't charted it wasn't done." Literally that doesn't make any sense because anyone could give a treatment and inadvertently forget to charge it. The treatment was still done. But in a court of law the adage is acceptable. How does charting something prove that it was actually done? That is a scary thought in these devious times. Records can be falsified. One such case is portrayed in the movie "The Verdict" which I used to show to my OB students to point out pre-anesthesia precautions and legal aspects. I may not have gotten James Brolin but I did have Paul Newman. In the movie he portrays an attorney who painstakingly uncovers evidence that a chart was falsified to cover up a doctor's error. Until he was able to do this the case was essentially lost. Even though the cantankerous judge refused to allow the new evidence, the jury had seen the light and found overwhelmingly for the plaintiff.

Yes, I remember that I mentioned that in ancient times we were taught to sometimes chart false information. In these literal times it is difficult to explain convincingly that it was moral and ethical for those times. Most of our doctors were elderly—octogenarians. The training was scanty and outdated—obtained in the nineteenth century—and they hadn't kept up with the times. The only orders we failed to follow were the ones we knew to be dangerous. The doctor might have ordered a cc of Pitocin to be given to a labor patient stat. Following such an order would undoubtedly have resulted in a ruptured uterus, a dead baby and perhaps a dead mother. At that time it would have been unthinkable to tell a doctor that we were refusing to follow his orders. So we just gave the patient a safe dose—which was one minim (one drop) or one sixteenth of the dose which he had ordered. Charting it as one cc kept the doctor happy and the patient had received safe care.

What would have happened if that chart had appeared in court? In a word, they would have murdered us. But at that time only doctors read the charts. And we would have been amazed if anyone had suggested that we might be called upon to appear in court.

As the younger doctors returned home from the war things began to change. With the changing times it eventually became permissible to tell authority figures that their order is unacceptable, either because it was unsafe or because you are not qualified to do it. Of course that is not to say you might not lose your job. But you will retain your self-respect. And your license to practice nursing.

Today only honest, truthful charting is acceptable. Any deviation from those standards is generally cought up with somewhere along the line. Tales about the nursery nurse who charted rectal temperatures on a baby who was soon found to have an imperforate anus. And the night nurse who repeatedly charted a patient as "resting comfortably" on rounds who was found to have expired long before.

One of the instructors on our faculty lost her job due to teaching a student to make up vital signs for the times that she didn't get them taken. She was my age and I knew that she had learned that as a student. If vital signs were ordered to be taking every fifteen minutes and, for some reason, they were obtained only three times an hour, it seemed harmless to interpolate some numbers that reflected the factual ones on either side. It was presumed that the reason for the omission was one of priorities and not of malingering.

But the instructor had failed to adapt to changing times. I have found it wise not to ever teach shortcuts to students. They make their own soon enough. And if they don't need to be making shortcuts on the shortcuts. It is better for them learn to do their very best in every situation. If there is an honest reason why something didn't get done it is better to be honest about it. After all, nobody can't be in two places at one time.

Theoretically, the best way to avoid lawsuits is to always give acceptable, quality care. As nurses, our job is to follow orders. But we are legally required to assess these orders and determine that they are safe and acceptable and that they are meeting all the needs of the patient. We must not do anything that is not within the scope of our educational preparation and covered by our license to practice nursing. And we must refuse to carry out any orders that do not meet these guidelines.

If a doctor is not providing acceptable care for a patient, it is our responsibility to make subtle suggestions. If he refuses to acknowledge our suggestions, we are obligated to report this to the proper authority. That would be our immediate superior, who would relay the information to the doctor who is the current chief of the department.

In practice this will not necessarily deter a lawsuit nor will it necessarily determine the outcome of the suit if one is filed, but it may have some bearing. A plaintiff may just be looking for revenge for an act of fate that was nobody's fault. Or he may be just plain greedy. A jury of twelve peers does not always follow logical reasoning. They bring into the court room with them all of their own frustrations with the medical profession. Every hour that they had to wait in a doctor's reception room and every call light that went unanswered for a seemingly long time can now be avenged vicariously. The outcome of a malpractice case may have little to do with the case at hand.

Another theoretical deterrent to lawsuits is to be so nice to the patients that they wouldn't dream of suing. I love the true story of the patient who had surgery on her hand. The hand remained painful and dysfunctional post-operatively. Repeated office visits failed to determine the source of the problem. So she went to see another surgeon. He operated and found the cause of the problem. Dr. Jones, the original surgeon, had sutured the severed nerves to the severed tendons instead of reconnecting the nerves and tendons to themselves. In the second surgery the error was corrected and the problem was resolved.

When the doctor reported his findings to the patient, she pleaded, "Oh, please don't tell that nice Dr. Jones. He would feel so bad." This incident occurred many years ago. Would it still hold true today? Perhaps—in rare instances. But the crowded court dockets prove that greed, avarice and vengefulness are the trend of the times.

Thankfully, I have never been sued. I have made depositions as an expert witness in two malpractice cases and testified at one trial. If I had needed convincing that I would not like being the defendant, that would have done it.

My first experience with the legal system began when an in law, in a distant city, called to ask my advice on a malpractice case her husband was handling. (They were both attorneys) I told her that I am no expert to use in any area of nursing other than obstetrics. She assured me that it was an OB case and that the baby was retarded.

I was dubious about the validity of an OB malpractice action. I presume that the parents, in their grief, wanted to blame someone for their baby's affliction. I was accustomed to the majority of OB patients being happy and had rarely heard of any lawsuits. My niece assured me, and I later validated it from several sources, that by far the greatest number of malpractice cases are OB related. Even knowing this I have a difficult time imagining what specific sets of circumstances could lead to all these lawsuits.

I was hesitant to pass judgment on fellow nurses but agreed to review the transcript and give her my opinion on them. The transcripts, when they arrived, were a real eye-opener. This was not one of those nebulous cases I had anticipated. Altruistically, I wanted to believe that all nurses are nurturing and compassionate. Of course I knew from personal experience that wasn't strictly true. Still, I wasn't prepared for the nurses that were revealed by these records—nurses who were completely uncaring and callous and failed to carry out their responsibilities, resulting in total disaster.

The patient was a twenty-eight-year-old primigravida—Polish immigrant who spoke very little English. She was undoubtedly reacting to the unexpected pain and enormity of an unusually rapidly progressing first labor. Her response was not unlike the response of women of other cultures in the same circumstances. But she brought with her elements of her own culture which were different.

An elderly neighbor had accompanied her to the hospital. Her husband would come only after the birth was completed. Her mentor did speak English but maintained a tacit, stoical demeanor with the nurses. To the patient she reinforced in Polish the Polish custom of stay out of bed until the delivery was imminent. This the patient did, much to the consternation of the nurses who, according to their brief nurses' notes, instructed her in English to go to bed.

I have known nurses who were not particularly kind to their patients, but the apparent behavior of these nurses was shocking. There did not appear to be any physical contact—like a hug or holding her hand. They would stand in the doorway, bark and order—in English—and turn around and leave without waiting for a response. I have no doubt that, had they established a rapport with the patient and her support person, the latter would have been more open and cooperative with them and a compromise could have been reached and catastrophe averted.

Instead, the patient took refuge in the bathroom, sitting down on the cold floor. Her neighbor took a bath blanket in and placed it on the floor for her. The doctor came, looked in from the doorway, told her she should be in bed, and left. Apparently he had also neglected to establish a rapport with her—a pity, as most women have a special feeling for their obstetricians and want to please them.

Finally, sensing that the delivery was imminent, the patient attempted to walk back to the bed. But she was too late. The baby delivery headfirst onto the floor with such force that the cord was torn away from the placenta. Small wonder that the child was retarded.

An intern reported walking by the room and seeing the baby sliding across the floor to the other side of the room. Stunned, he ran to get an isolette. If the nurses felt any reaction to all of the excitement and trauma, it was not conveyed in either their nurses' notes or the depositions.

Still I have no doubt that they related their feelings about the patient to the nurses in post-partum and the nursery. Their comments on the chart were laden with observations about the patient's lack of understanding about baby care. They called in the social service department although she was probably as competent as the average first-time mother. None of this had any bearing on the case, but I felt it pointed out the general attitude of the nurses toward this patient—that her inability to speak English meant that she was ignorant.

I sent Dan my analysis of the situation. Sometime later I received a letter from another lawyer, also named Dan, asking me to make a deposition about the case. I contacted Dan # 1, and learned that he had turned the case over to a larger firm. He urged me to consider making the deposition. So I consented.

When Dan # 2 asked me where I would like to do the deposition I jokingly responded,

"At my home." He took me up on it-not in my house but in the city where I lived. He flew into town and rented a car and a hotel room—as did the attorneys for the doctor and the hospital. Not a horrendous amount of money to spend—compared to the national debt, but to hear my lowly opinion!!!

I couldn't believe that anyone would think that I had anything that important to say—certainly not my students or my children.

Dan—a citizen of the world—knew of a public building with a court reporter only 10 min. from my house and had everything set up. On the appointed day I went home after work to feed my dog and let him out. Dan met me there and impressed me with his charm and good looks. My only instruction was, "Just tell the truth." He told me that they would ask me how much I was being paid and suggested a figure I could ask for. I had assumed the position of self employed paralegal. I don't remember what the hourly fee was but it was far more than I had ever earned at my job. I was so embarrassed at how high it was that I reported only about half the number of hours that I had actually spent poring over the charts and depositions.

Dan drove me to the designated place and I soon learned what a Discovery Deposition was. Unlike in the movies, real-life lawyers do not like to go into the courtroom and be surprised with unexpected evidence. Armed with a list of prospective witnesses, they take depositions in advance to discover what they will say in court.

Making the deposition was not difficult. It's like being cross-examined without having first been questioned by your own attorney. That was how I was beginning to feel—as if Dan were my attorney and the plaintiff's case were "our side" although I should have just remained neutral.

The defense attorneys made an issue of the fact that I was being paid for my time (as were they) but for the most part I found them to be quite bland. But Dan thought otherwise and interrupted several times to remind them to be more respectful of me. Having dealt with numerous cantankerous doctors, I felt as though they were handling me with kid gloves, but I didn't mind at all having a white knight protecting my honor.

After the deposition was completed, Dan drove me home. I wanted to invite him to dinner but he told me it was customary to have dinner with the other lawyers—just like in the movies. He told me that he had had reservations, himself, about why I was doing this. But while he was listening to my testimony he had thought, "Why, she's just a nice person." That was a nice warm fuzzy to bring out to warm myself on a cold night.

When the case went to trial my employer refused to give me release time to go and testify. I can't say that I was upset. I didn't relish the idea of testifying. I thought they could use my deposition in court and it what amount to the same thing. If I had known that was not possible I would have tried harder to get the time off. But the outcome would probably have been the same. Dan wrote me a letter and said that they had been awarded seven million dollars. He said that whenever he had been discouraged I had inspired him to push on. (That Mrs. Dan is some lucky lady.)

An appeals court reduced the amount of the award to one hundred six thousand dollars—a large sum of money, but hardly enough to compensate that child for what was taken from him. But then neither would seven million dollars—or any other amount.

I thought the malpractice case was so interesting that I wrote an article about it which was published in RN magazine. It was read by an RN who worked for a law firm in another Midwestern state. She called me and asked if I would be a consultant on an OB case they were representing. I was getting concrete evidence that obstetrical cases constitute the largest percentage of malpractice suits.

Diane mailed me the transcripts and once again I was astonished at the low standards practiced by the nurses. Again there was a bias involved—this time it was obesity. The client, Brianne, was not grossly obese. She was just a large, solid woman, which made it difficult for them to be obtain FHT and contraction readings on the monitor.

Breanna had severe toxemia with a BP of 160/110 and could have become eclamptic at any time. The nursing staff seemed completely unimpressed by the solemnity of the situation. They checked the patient very infrequently and failed to keep the doctor apprised of the unrelenting blood pressure. When Brianne's Bow ruptured, they failed to keep her on bed rest—a universal practice to prevent prolapse of the cord. Bedrest is maintained unless there is a specific order by the doctor for the patient to be up—preferably a written order.

But most alarming of all was the fact that they had increased the rate of the Pitocin drip above the maximum rate, that was ordered and beyond the acceptable rate that is considered safe practice. And that was despite the fact that her contractions were charted as occurring every two to three minutes and lasting forty to sixty seconds. Pitocin can be a dangerous drug if not carefully monitored. And in this case they were not getting FHT and had no way of determining the effect of the Pitocin on the fetus.

The nurses' depositions were astonishing. In their efforts to minimize the consequences of their actions they came off looking uncaring and unknowledgeable. I couldn't help but wince at such statements as, "I gave her an enema and took her to the bathroom and said, 'Don't ask me why there's no toilet paper. That's just the way it is.'" I still haven't figured that one out.

They sailed blindly through the course of her labor—with no knowledge of the quality or rate of the FHT or even whether they existed, and no accurate indicator of the quality or frequency or length of her contractions yet they could have asked for internal monitors after the Bow ruptured and they would then have had access to accurate monitoring of both of these.

The baby was eventually delivered with a large, ugly welt across her forehead. The plaintiff was alleging that the excessive amount of Pitocin had caused a band to form across the uterus which pressed against the baby's head and resulted in the welt and retardation.

This time I wasn't asked where I would like to make the deposition. But by then I was retired and could travel at will. So I made arrangements for the care of my cat and dog and soon found myself aboard the first of two small propeller commuter planes which were the only means of transportation between the two metropolises. I was a little uneasy when the attendant asked a slender little woman to change seats so the plane would be balanced and again when the attendant left and we were all alone with the pilot for several hundred miles. After two such experiences I arrived at the city where the deposition was to be made. My airfare, luxury hotel suite and meals were all paid for. But it was all business—there was no time for sightseeing or shopping.

This time I did find the lawyers rude and condescending. They tried to make it appear that I was doing this solely for the money. They also attempted to get me to "admit" that patients are responsible for their own care. While I do believe that the better informed you are about your health, your medications, your treatments, your condition and what you should be able to expect from your health care professionals, the better off you will be, I certainly don't feel that this is the patient's responsibility rather than that of the health care professionals'.

When the trial began there was nothing to prevent my going to testify. So back I went on the two little "prop" planes that were the only available transportation from point A to point B—back to the luxury suite. Diane met my plane and we had dinner together—two veteran RN's who had been around the block a couple of times and believed in quality nursing care. We hit it off right from the start and agreed on all the major issues.

As with Dan, I was given no instructions on what to say in court. The attorney for the plaintiff told me that he would ask me a series of questions which would result in bringing out all the details which Diane and I had discussed.

When I arrived at the court room the next day there was a doctor on the stand testifying at great length. It certainly wasn't Perry Mason quality. Instead it was rather dull. I couldn't help but notice the nurse sitting at the defendants' table giggling and making faces. While I realized that these were probably defense mechanisms they did nothing to create an image of a caring nurse.

When it was my turn to testify I swore to tell the truth and took the stand. The plaintiff's attorney asked me a few lead-in questions and then abruptly said he was finished with me. It was very frustrating. I felt that I hadn't gotten in any of the details I had planned on giving. Once again I was feeling that loyalty to "our side" and wanted to give my best. But even more strongly I felt that I wanted to be a "patient's advocate" for this young woman who had found herself helpless in a hospital situation. I decided that "our" attorney must have been having an off day.

During the cross-examination I tried to compensate for this by cramming in all the information I could with each question. No one was admonishing me to "just answer yes or no" as they do in the movies.

The defense attorney didn't seem as menacing as he had at the deposition. He did make an issue of the fact that this was not my first malpractice testimony, insinuating that I did it on a regular basis and found it lucrative. He also made a point of the fact that, because I'm a 'hunt and peck' typist and therefore slow, I had sent my hand written notes to the attorney at Diane's suggestion for his typist to transcribe as time was catching up with us. The defense attorney alleged that I was quoting not my own opinions but those of the attorneys. I don't think he thought I was capable of expressing myself in words of more than one syllable.

Then he began asking questions about the nurses' notes on the chart—skipping from place to place—presumably to confuse me. When he came to the place where the Pitocin had been increased well above forty-five drops a minute, which was the maximum ordered by the doctor, and the maximum that is considered safe, he tried to get me to admit that the patient was not having contractions at the time. Now he was playing right into my hands. What the chart actually said was that they were unable to monitor the contractions. I pointed out that they had given her several doses of Demerol during that same period." Couldn't they have been giving her Demerol for something else? "He responded." Like a headache? "He immediately realized his mistake and cut me off before I could answer or add any information of my own. I was told that he was finished with me and to step down. My day in court was over.

I had watched Diane's and the attorneys faces while I was testifying to get their reactions and feedback on what I had been saying. They were inscrutable—almost glum. I didn't think that they were pleased. But Diane told me that my testimony was excellent. They had trained themselves not to give away their reactions by their facial expressions. Although I was booked at the hotel for one more night and the room was already paid for, Diane called the airport and changed my flight reservation so that I could go home that evening. She told me to send her a bill. I told her I would leave it in her hands and she promised to send me a check when the trial had ended.

A month later I still had not heard from her and thought that we might have gotten her signals crossed. So I wrote her a letter asking how they all were and how the trial had turned out, enclosing a bill. Diane called me right back and told me that the trial was still in progress and that was why I hadn't heard from them. I was really surprised to hear that the trial was still going on, when I had been rushed through so fast. I had been the only RN to testify for the plaintiff and therefore the best qualified to outline what standard of care could reasonably be expected from the nursing staff.

I received a check right away and never heard the outcome of the trial. Since Diane had promised to let me know, I thought she might have been miffed that I had jumped the gun and sent the bill. Or perhaps the outcome had not been favorable. At any rate I retired from my legal 'career' lest I become known as a professional witness.

I found these two cases so interesting that I almost wished I were young enough to pursue a new career combining nursing and the law. This is not to say that I favor the thousands of contrived malpractice suits that are clogging the arteries of the courts. Greedy people trying to get something for nothing are not a pretty sight and are a primary factor in driving healthcare costs up to the dizzying heights it has reached. But on the other hand there must be some recourse for the ones who have been sacrificed to the system. And there must be some measure of accountability for everyone in the system to prevent further carelessness, negligence and apathy from thundering in.

For her own protection every nurse should carry her own malpractice insurance. If she works for a hospital she will be covered under the hospital's blanket policy but it may not be enough. Malpractice policies for nurses are relatively inexpensive—only around a hundred dollars a year and well worth the peace of mind, alone, that they bring.

Lawsuits can spring up from anything. Our nursery head nurse, with the best of intentions, place a hot water bottle in an isolette with a baby because he wasn't warming up fast enough. The water was too hot and made a blister on the skin of the tiny little premie. The hospital admitted their mistake and very generously told the young couple there would be no bill. Since it was a Cesarean delivery and the baby received additional care because she was a preemie we all thought that would be the end of the matter. But the parents of the baby were not about to lose their one big opportunity and took the case to court. When I read in the newspaper that they had been awarded over a hundred thousand dollars I was astounded.

"How could they have collected all that money for a little blister?" I asked one of the staff nurses.

"She rubbed dirt in it and it got infected," was the sarcastic reply.

She could have been right.

CHAPTER 21

THE WAY I SEE IT

*A*BORTION is not a dirty word. It is simply the medical term for the termination of a pregnancy before the age of viability—viability being the age at which a fetus can survive outside of the uterus. This age varies legally from state to state but most states consider twenty weeks as the viable age. Babies born at this gestational age have been known to live for short periods. With modern technology these babies are surviving earlier and living longer all the time. But to return to the subject at hand, the word abortion is simply the medical term for miscarriage.

There are several types of abortions. There is the spontaneous abortion—the one that lay people, we think of as a miscarriage. A missed abortion occurs when the fetus or embryo dies but remains in the uterus. In an incomplete abortion that fetus or embryo is expelled but the placenta or some part of the pregnancy remains in the uterus. An induced abortion can be done for therapeutic reasons—usually to save the mother's life. Before the 1970s most other types of induced abortions were considered criminal abortions, although they were occasionally done for psychiatric reasons or for conceptions that were the result of rape or incest. Since the legalization of abortion, induced abortions are now classified as elective abortions.

Even before the sexual revolution, problem pregnancies always existed. Until very recently pregnancy in an unmarried woman was considered to be socially unacceptable. Those unfortunate girls were commonly sent away—to a home for unwed mothers or an aunt in a distant city if the pregnancy was allowed to continue to term. But throughout history women have sought abortions for unwanted pregnancies. Surprisingly, the largest number of abortions were obtained by married women.

The number of personal reasons for wanting an abortion is roughly equal to the number of women seeking them. The one thing that they have in common is the depth of the desperation that is driving them to commit frantic acts to rid themselves of problem pregnancies which are inconvenient, humiliating or impossible for a variety of reasons.

Lacking other resources some women will jump off of tall buildings, fall down flights of stairs, swallow potent potions, crash their cars and poke pencils and knitting needles through their cervices to dislodge the stigma that is causing their distress. Before abortions were legalized they were sought from back alley butchers and granny practitioners. Lack of medical training and fear of apprehension on their part resulted in massive numbers of hemorrhage, infection and sterility.

True to my generation, I was shocked when the sexual revolution roared in and again when abortion was made legal. I could see our great country going down the drain just like the holy Roman empire. Now, some twenty years later, life goes on as usual. Which is not to say that all is well. But other forces seem to be tearing our world apart much more efficiently.

In the course of those twenty years, a number of things have occurred to cause me to modify my feelings about abortion. In the first incident, a student wrote in her Community Health notebook, "I believe that if a baby is aborted its soul will float around heaven until it gets another opportunity to be born in another fetus." I responded that I admired her viewpoint and wished that I could share it. Later, while taking an Eastern psychology course at the University, I began to internalize some of this philosophy. Some of the readings I did while researching this field regarded subjects who were hypnotized and regressed to the period before their birth. Almost all of them related that their soul did not enter the fetal body until the end of the sixth month or later. And even then it periodically entered and exited the body until the moment of birth. There seemed to be some choice of fetuses that each soul, with limitations, could enter. This all made abortion seem a little less tragic. The absorption of Eastern beliefs inevitably leads to belief in reincarnation. In this concept the sole has infinite opportunities to be reborn.

Another thing which has been highly instrumental in weakening my anti-abortion feelings has been the fanaticism of some of the pro-life advocates. I find their public demonstrations to be an embarrassment as well as a nuisance. And to take a human life in the name of a belief in the pro-life movement is, to me, the ultimate in oxymorons.

One day I ran into a former student who had graduated. She was a sweet, attractive, all-American, girl next door type. She told me that she was working in the office of Dr. Cross, an OB/GYN specialist. Outwardly I smiled and remained composed, but inwardly I was shocked. It was a very short time after abortions had been legalized and Dr. Cross and his partner were doing all the abortions in that city. I wondered how this lovely young woman could work for an abortionist.

Some years later I had several opportunities to work with Dr. Cross. The first time I met him his young partner, Dr. Waring, had a patient in with severe eclampsia. She had had several seizures and he was working frantically to stabilize her so he could terminate the pregnancy with a Cesarean section. Dr. Cross remained unobtrusively involved, offering support and suggestions. Later in the evening he reached across the patient's bed and laid his hand over his partner's hand. "I have to leave now," he said softly. "But I know she's going to be all right now. You're doing a fine job." I had never seen a doctor display such compassion and warmth.

In the ensuing years I saw Dr. Cross repeatedly dedicated to delivering live, healthy babies. I have seen him biding his time and patiently waiting long hours in the hospital so that a baby could be delivered vaginally in situations where most doctors would have jumped in and done a Caesarean or at least have pulled the baby out with forceps to get it over with so they could get home to their families. I came to realize that he was one of the most skilled and dedicated obstetricians I had ever known.

I came to the conclusion that a man like this would not be doing abortions for the money or to "kill" little babies. Doing abortions had to be an extension of his dedication to his patients. As devoted as he was to delivering healthy babies to women who wanted them, so did he also strive to give the others what they wanted and were determined to have—no matter what they had to do to get it.

I can only guess at the inner turmoil he had to work through to arrive at the courage of his convictions. The human spirit has the capacity to rationalize its way through a maze of concerns to arrive at a foregone conclusion. Dr. Waring eventually left the practice and joined another OB/GYN team of doctors because he didn't want his name to be associated with abortions. But Dr. Cross has stood behind his convictions for more than twenty years.

More than twenty years later he is still plagued by disasters. Demonstrations and sit-ins take place outside his clinic daily. They trespass on this property, block his entrances and harass his patients. Later they began harassing the members of the church that he and his family attend. They mailed out picture postcards of aborted fetuses to each member's home, unconcerned that children and other innocents may have been removing them from the mailboxes. One day some of them chained themselves to some tar filled barrels on the clinic grounds so that they couldn't be removed by the police. Understandably angry, Dr. Cross turned a hose on them. Then he tied a rope around the barrels and headed for his truck. They inferred that he was going to attach the rope to his truck and drag them away. Consequently they took him to court. He was eventually acquitted but he continues to pay high price for standing up for his convictions. This is a large part of the reason I have come to feel that, although abortion would not be my choice, I concede it to be a choice every woman must be allowed to make for herself.

Before elective abortions were legalized, I helped care for a patient who had a therapeutic abortion. She was in her forties and had two grown children—and a one-year-old baby whom she had nearly died delivering. We had all been with her at that time and knew, first hand the seriousness of the situation. She had a severe cardiac condition and would probably not survive another pregnancy and delivery. We all agreed that a therapeutic abortion was definitely indicated.

My involvement was minor. I administered her pre-op medication and prepped her for surgery. After the D&C I gave her post-op care. Yet I felt lousy about the whole thing. So did the patient. For the most part we reassured each other that it was a very sad but more important that she be around to care for her one-year-old baby.

All this has led me to the conclusion that I would never consider working in an abortion clinic. I suspect that the majority of these women feel as bad about their abortions as our cardiac patient did. And that their reasons were just as urgent to them as hers was to her. I refuse to believe that anyone could ever feel good about having an abortion. Yet there are nurses who elect to care for abortion patients and, treat them cruelly—telling them things like, "they threw your baby in the garbage can and it cried all night." I have no idea what a nurse like that is doing in an abortion ward. In my mind it makes her worse than the patient because she is doing something that she perceives to be wrong, while the patient may sincerely believe that it is not.

Abortion patients no longer stay in the hospital overnight so a lot of this problem has been eliminated. But opportunities still abound for harassing abortion seekers.

My heart goes out to the judge who quit his job because it required him to give his consent for an underage girl to have an abortion. I don't believe anyone should have to abandon his religious or moral principles for a controversial law. That duty could have been delegated to someone whose principles were not compromised by it. But this particular judge had such high moral standards that he refused to function in a job unless he could live up to the letter of its legal requirements. He made no criticism of the law but made a clear-cut distinction between his own beliefs and that of the law.

While most abortion seekers have traditionally been motivated by desperation, easy access has laid the foundation for a new mentality about the process. One day I was telling my students that, although it was now possible to determine the sex of the baby by amniocentesis, no one would use that to determine whether they should have an abortion. As soon as the words left my mouth I got an uneasy feeling that made me wish I hadn't said it. The next day Dr. Waring told us that three of his patients had had amniocentesis to determine the sex of their babies. "Fortunately," he reported.

"They were all the right sex. So it wasn't necessary to abort any of them." While it would be tremendously sad to abort a baby for being the wrong sex, it would be even sadder to punish a child for a lifetime for that reason.

In an overcrowded world where homelessness, hunger and child abuse are increasingly prevalent, some of us can view abortion as an acceptable substitute. We can be grateful that we do not live in a country like China, where that choice is made for its citizens. Nor has adoption proven to be a suitable alternative. Human nature is rarely altruistic. The modern day tendency to take back babies that were given up for adoption shows the widespread attitude of, "If I can't have it nobody else can either."

The best solution that I can see is for each of us to live within the confines of that which is comfortable for us. The time is rapidly approaching when the question of assisted suicide, perhaps followed by its nemesis, will overshadow the abortion issue

ILLEGITIMACY is one of the leading problems in our country today. There are those who insist that there was always as much extra-marital sex as there is today. I think that is highly unlikely, but it is true that it has always been with us to some extent. We just didn't hear about it hawked and flaunted at us every day and night. But one thing is certain. There was far less illegitimacy in earlier times.

Of the four pregnant women in my nursing graduation class, three married the fathers of their babies before delivering. The fourth, a reputed nymphomaniac, met a man on a bus, married him the next day and delivered a baby girl the day after that. I had never wanted to believe the rumors about her nymphomania. She was a small town girl, neat and maternal. Her obesity was a convenient cover up for her pregnancy. I doubt that the Johnny-come-lately bridegroom knew what was about to hit him. I think it likely that he had been drunk. Twila's mother, thinking he was responsible for Twila's condition, threw him out of the house. I don't know if they ever got back together again. But Twila had what she needed most in this world—a name for her baby.

I finally learned the truth about Twila when we took our psychiatric rotation and were roommates. Twila would go out with anyone who rang our doorbell looking for a date. She had a deep-seated yearning for love. She might have just finished putting her hair up in fifty pin curls, but if the prospect of a date emerged she would comb them all out. That was where her baby was conceived. Despite all that promiscuity, Twila's baby was legitimate according to the law.

In those post Victorian, pre-Lamaze times most women in labor screamed and thrashed about. Not so the unmarried ones. They bore their pain (and humiliation) in silence and asked for nothing. Most of the nurses were not judgmental although there were some that were. Most of us respected and even admired the way they accepted responsibility for their actions and bore the consequences unflinchingly without blaming their parents.

Before the sexual revolution, unwed mothers rarely kept their babies. They were not entitled to welfare and were forced to assume responsibility for their own survival.

Mothers who gave their babies up had no rights. They were not allowed to see their baby or even know the gender. The hospital records were marked "No Information" or "Do Not Report." No notice appeared in the newspaper. The baby was kept behind a screen or in a room not visible to the public. If a visitor or caller inquired, they were told that there was no available information.

"No Information" meant everyone. The delivering mother left the hospital without ever having seen her baby. I never knew one to make a fuss. The baby stayed in the hospital nursery until the adoptive parents came for it if it was a private adoption. It was not too difficult to adopt a baby at that time. A woman might just tell her doctor that she wanted the next baby that became available. A lawyer then drew up the necessary papers. This was called the "Gray Market." But it was perfectly legal and quite inexpensive. The adopting parents assumed the medical expenses and the legal fee, both of which were modest.

The proper way of going through an adoption agency was a bit more difficult. The prospective parents had to live up to the agencies requirements of age, financial status, home conditions, race and religion. Babies who were already born were matched to new parents with similar eye, hair and skin color. Usually the babies were well past the newborn stage by the time they were ensconced in their new homes.

I never heard of a birth mother—a new term which was not in use at the time as she was not considered a mother after giving her baby up—wanting to take her baby back. The only thing the new parents feared was that the judge would find them unworthy when they appeared in court six months or a year later.

When a baby remained in the nursery after his birth mother was dismissed he was called a boarder. There is no need to feel sorry for the little guys. Nursery nurses are nothing if not nurturing. And we all love newborns. Those babies received around-the-clock loving. That was probably not appreciated by the new parents, who couldn't be expected to relish being "on duty" around-the-clock. But most of them were so elated with their new babies that they didn't mind.

The first boarder baby that we had after I graduated was with us for an especially long time because he had been born prematurely. I nicknamed him "Bambi" and became very bonded to him. One beautiful spring day I decided that Bambi needed some fresh air and sunshine. So I took him outside on my lunch break. I still have a snapshot of the event—a slim young nurse with curly black hair holding a tiny wisp of a baby with skinny arms and legs. Eventually Bambi's medical and legal problems were resolved and, with the fatty tissue we had managed to implant on his body and the love that we had instilled in his heart he was dismissed to his new family. Today Bambi would be more than forty-five years old—possibly a father himself—maybe even a grandfather. He probably has a fine name like John or James. I hope that he's had a good life and that somewhere deep inside of his heart lingers a little of the love we gave to our Bambi.

One of the rare young mothers who kept her out-of-wedlock baby was so pleased that she sent out birth announcements. She was retarded and her widowed father seemed to be a lonely man. They were both so happy about the baby that it would have been difficult not to be happy for them. They were used to being a non-traditional family; so this would not seem as strange to them as one might think. People didn't talk about sexual harassment and abuse then or of taking advantage of the mentally incompetent. We never knew how Sally had gotten pregnant or who the "father" was. Surely the end did not justify the means, but these two lonely people would now have someone who would always love them—and there would now be someone to take care of his daughter after the father was gone.

It was many years before society began to accept illegitimacy. It was a necessary outcome of the sexual revolution. At the same time children were no longer held responsible for their behavior. That responsibility became the burden of the parents. With this societal attitude the demeanor of unwed mothers in labor changed. They became very demanding—as if we had to make it up to them because they were having pain. They were often angry and uncooperative, and frequently there was friction with their parents.

Today the scenario is so varied that there is no description that would depict a generalized picture. The Lamaze coach may be a boyfriend (who may or may not be the father of the baby) a girlfriend, the pregnant woman's mother or father, or a neighbor. It is no longer possible to walk into a room and assign traditional roles to the visitors. There are unlimited racial and generational mixes. For the most part, the parents, especially the mother, are accepting of what ever the situation is. They probably have little choice if they want to maintain contact with their daughter and grandchild. Aid to Dependent Families gives the young mother a measure of independence.

Several years ago I attended a workshop presented by a group known as Primiparas

(pronounced preema-PAIRAS.) Primipara (pronounced prime-IP-era) means "a woman who has delivered one viable baby." Presumably, these women, who were all unwed mothers, made only one 'mistake.'

There were three presenters scheduled but only two came. Their presentations were a revelation to me. They showed me a new way of looking at the situation that had never occurred to me before. I had always supposed that pregnancy would be, at best, unpleasant, if the end result were relinquishment of the baby. To my surprise both women said that they had enjoyed their pregnancies.

They were proud of the new life they were creating and intrigued with the changes that were taking place in their bodies and feeling the baby move.

They had both seen their babies after the birth and cherished the memory. One carried a picture of her baby in her billfold. She proudly showed it to us. It was dog-eared from taking it out and looking at it so much. Her sorrow, though tacit, was evident. The other one told us that she carried in her heart the certainty that she would one day be reunited with her child. When asked if she would ever try to contact the child she replied emphatically that she would never do that. It was just a fantasy that made her loss bearable. Today, some twenty years later, it has become commonplace for adopted children to seek their biological parents. It is quite possible that her dream has been realized. That particular child would be assured of learning that he had been given up out of love.

Today almost every unmarried mother that doesn't have an abortion keeps her baby. There is no stigma attached to being a single parent. Even divorced mothers call themselves single parents, as do men who rear their children alone. It is just considered one of a number of alternative life styles.

In many states Aid to Dependent Families (ADF) begins when pregnancy begins to ensure that prenatal care will be obtained and the fetus will be nourished and cared for. In Nebraska in 1992 the governor wanted to save four million dollars a year by delaying ADF until the third trimester. There was a public outcry against the idea. The taxpayers don't want their tax dollars spent for abortion counseling, but they will spend four million dollars for ADF for the first six months of pregnancy, even though many of the women will spend it on drugs, alcohol and cigarettes.

Women that give up their babies today can just about write their own ticket. Adopting families are willing to allow them visiting privileges and send periodic pictures and letters updating them on the baby's progress. In the hospital they can see and hold their baby whenever they wish. Some even breast-feed. It is their baby until they have signed the final papers and left the hospital—theoretically abandoning the child so that they cannot later claim that they never really meant to give their baby up.

One thing that today's unwed mothers insist upon is that we called them "women" rather than "girls" even when they are as young as thirteen. Since I still think of my sixty-something friends as girls it is hard for me to relate to teenagers as women. One day when we were still calling our patients Miss and Mrs., a student who was taking care of a sixteen-year-old unwed mother complained, "I just can't call that little girl Miss Dodson."

"That's all right," I replied. "Just call her Angie." Today that is not a distinction. All of the patients are called by their first name. So are we. The whole world seems to be on a first name basis, from the bank teller to the telephone salesman who calls out of the blue.

I will leave the staggering statistics to the experts who compile such things. I will only comment that illegitimacy is growing year by year. If it continues to grow at the same rapid rate it will soon be the norm and married families will be in the minority.

EPILOGUE

*A*ll good things must come to an end. When I first began teaching in my forties, the students were unable to keep up with me as we raced through the hospital corridors from room to room. By the time I was sixty I was having difficulty keeping up with them.

At the Golden age of sixty I had surgery on my back. It resolved the acute condition but left me with ever increasing chronic pain. When a staff nurse asked me to help her lift a patient I had to refuse. Her dubious look made me feel even worse.

I was also being required to spend more and more time teaching in the classroom and working in unfamiliar clinical areas and less and less in my beloved OB.

My aunt used to tell me to always leave a party while you're still having a good time. So when I turned sixty-two and became eligible for Social Security benefits I retired. In the six years since retiring I have kept my license to practice nursing active and worked from one to three months every year.

But at the end of this year my license will not be renewed and, for the first time in forty-eight years, I will not legally be an RN. I'm sure I will mourn it like the loss of a dear friend or a beloved old car. But in my heart and my memories I will always be that same young nurse who transcended the ages. And if I ever find it necessary to justify my existence I will say,

"I was a nurse. I was a gal in a proud profession."

GLOSSARY

Amniocentesis—Removal of a sample of amniotic fluid via a stick through the abdominal wall to determine the presence of bilirubin or genetic disorders, gender of the baby etc.

Amniotomy—Manual rupture of the amniotic sac (bag of waters) through the vaginal vault.

Anaphylactic reaction—An intense, often fatal reaction to an allergy producing substance.

Anencephalic—Absence of all or part of the brain.

Aphasia—Aphasic—Unable to express oneself by speech.

Autoclave—A sterilizer which uses steam under pressure.

Braxton—Hicks contractions—painless, rhythmic contractions felt during the last trimester of pregnancy.

BOW—bag of waters—the amniotic sac and fluid surrounding the fetus.

BP—Blood pressure—expressed in terms of the systolic number, the pressure during a contraction of the heart, over the diastolic reading, the heart at rest.

B.S.N.—A Bachelor of Science degree in nursing.

Baruch Atau Adonai—Beginning of a Hebrew prayer.

Translation—Blessed art thou, O Lord.

Camisole—A straitjacket. It slips on the patient like a backward jacket. The arms are crossed over the chest and the elongated sleeves are tied in the back.

Catheter—a slim, flexible tube which can be inserted into the bladder to drain out the urine.

Cervix—The neck like mouth of the uterus. In labor it effaces (thins out) and dilates (stretches) to allow room for the expulsion of the fetus.

Cervical disc—Platelike structure between vertebrae in the neck.

Code—A life-saving procedure used when a patient is in respiratory or cardiac arrest.

Crowning—Appearance of the fetal head on the perineum. The vulva forms a "crown" around it.

Cyanotic—Blue discoloration of the skin caused by lack of sufficient oxygen. cm—centimeter—a metrical measurement used to determine the amount of dilation of the cervix. 2 ½ cm = 1 inch.

CPR—Cardio-pulmonary resuscitation—see Code.

CI—Clinical instructor. One who teaches students in the hospital.

Catgut—Suture made from sheep intestines. Used to close tissues that have been cut or torn.

Decubitus—pl. decubiti—Ulceration of the skin caused by pressure or rubbing on that linens. Bedsores.

Dilate—dilation—Stretching and widening of the cervix.

D&C—Dilation and curettage. Surgery in which the cervix is dilated and the uterus scraped—e.g. after an incomplete abortion.

Dyspnea—Labored breathing.

E.C.T.—Electroconvulsive therapy. Induction of a convulsion by use of an electric shock.

Embolism—A foreign body in the bloodstream, as a clot or air, which can obstruct the blood vessel.

Epidural—Space between the membranes surrounding the spine where an epidural anesthetic is given.

Episiotomy—Incision made during childbirth to prevent stretching or tearing of the perineum.

Erythroblastosis fetalis—Condition in which the red blood cells of the fetus are being destroyed faster than they can be manufactured resulting in the appearance of immature red blood cells (erythroblasts) in the blood.

Esophagus—The canal extending from the throat to the stomach.

Esophageal—Pertaining to the esophagus.

Etiology—Cause.

Extrovert—One with an outgoing personality—enjoys being with people.

Fallopian tubes—Also called oviducts. Tubes leading from the uterus to the ovaries. They carry the ovi (eggs) from the ovaries to the uterus.

Fetus—The unborn baby from the third month to term. It is a zygote for the first ten days and an embryo until the third month

Fundus—The upper rounded part of the uterus which contracts the hardest during labor and postpartum.

FHT—Fetal heart tones. The heartbeat of the fetus.

Gastrostomy—An opening made into the stomach through the abdominal wall for the purpose of feeding—usually because of an obstruction in the esophagus.

Gestation—The length of pregnancy.

Glans or glans penis—The penis.

Grand mal seizures—Violent contractions alternating with relaxation of the musculature of the body during an epileptic like seizure.

Grand multi-para—A woman who has delivered four or more viable babies.

Gravida—A pregnant woman or the number of pregnancies.

Gurney—A hospital cart or stretcher.

Gyn—Gynecology. The science of diseases of women.

G.P.—General Practitioner.—A doctor who treats the whole family and does not specialize in any one field.

Hemostat—A clamp like surgical instrument. Also called a Kelley.

Herniated disk—Condition in which the pad between two vertebrae slips out and protrudes.

H. S.—Hour of sleep. Bedtime.

Hypoglycemia—Low blood sugar—the opposite of diabetes. Often the forerunner of diabetes.

Incontinent—Involuntary passing of urine or stool.

Introspective—Looking within oneself and analyzing thoughts and behaviors.

Introvert—Someone who would rather be alone than with other people much of the time.

IV—Intravenous.

I CU—The Intensive Care Unit.

L&D—Labor and Delivery.

Laceration—Tear.

Manic depressive—A psychotic condition which manifests itself with periods of extreme depression with periods of extreme agitation or frenetic activity. Also called bipolar disease.

Med-surg—Medical and surgical.

Metastasis—Spread of malignant (cancerous) cells from one part of the body to another.

Multi-para—A woman who has delivered more than one viable baby.

Meatus—The opening to the urethra.

Nosocomial infection—An infection acquired in the hospital.

NG tube—Naso gastric tube. A tube inserted through the nose into the stomach for feeding and / or suctioning.

NICU—Newborn Intensive Care Unit.

OB—Obstetrics. Maternity.

Octogenarian—Someone who is in his / her eighties.

Oopherectomy—Surgical removal of the ovaries.

Operant Conditioning—Producing a response to an artificial stimulus as well as the stimulus which elicits it. E.g. Pavlov's dogs were conditioned to salivate to a bell which was rung whenever food was produced. Eventually they salivated to the sound of the bell alone.

Ophthalmologist—An M.D. who specializes in diseases of the eye.

OR—Operating Room.

Palpate—Diagnostic touching.

Pathologist—An M.D. who specializes in the causes of disease.

Perineum—The anatomical area between the anus and the vulva (the lips) slang—peri

Pitocin—An oxytocic or drug which induces uterine contractions.

Placebo—An inert substance given to a patient instead of the legitimate medication. E.g. sugar pills.

Placenta—An organ developed in pregnancy to receive oxygen and nutrients from the mother and deliver them to the baby through the umbilical cord. The afterbirth.

P.O.—Per ora. By mouth. Also post operatively.

Post partum—The six week period following delivery. Also the floor where post-partum patients recover.

Premie—A premature baby born before thirty-eight weeks gestation.

Primigravida—A woman pregnant for the first time.

Primipara—A woman who has delivered, or is about to deliver her first viable baby.

Private duty—Nursing only to one patient. Popular before the advent of the ICU.

Probie—Probationer. The first nine months, of a three-year nursing course was considered probationary. At its successful completion the student was awarded her cap.

PP—Post Partum.

Projection—A psychological behavior mechanism in which one accuses, or projects onto, another his own traits. E.g. suspiciousness or paranoia.

Psychotropic drugs—Mind altering drugs such as tranquilizers and mood elevators.

RN—Registered Nurse.

Salpingo-oopherectomy—Surgical removal of the Fallopian tubes and the ovaries.

Scalpel—Knifelike instruments used to make surgical incisions.

Schizophrenia—A type of psychosis in which the patient loses touch with reality and usually has delusions and hallucinations.

Sclera—The white part of the eyes.

Spinal (anesthetic)—Injection of anesthetic into the spinal canal causing numbness and loss of feeling in the lower portion of the body.

Sponges—Folded gauze squares used in surgery and childbirth.

Stat—Technically means "One time only" but generally interpreted to mean "immediately."

S.T.D.—Sexually Transmitted Diseases.

Stertorous breathing—Raspy, snoring respirations.

Suture—Surgical material used to sew up an incision or tear.

Suture lines—The lines which divide the cranium into the four parts of the fetus and newborn baby.

Trimester—A period of three months; one of three equal divisions of pregnancy.

Umbilical cord.—The structure with two arteries and one vein which carries oxygen and nutrients to the fetus from the placenta and waste products from the fetus to the placenta.

Urethra—The tube which carries urine from the bladder to the outside.

Vertigo—Dizziness.

Viable—Capable of living independently outside of the uterus.

V.D.—Venereal Disease. Same as S.T.D.

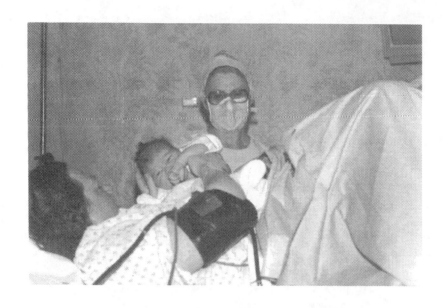